Beyond S

Scottish Cultural Review
of Language and Literature

Volume 2

Series Editors
John Corbett
University of Glasgow

Sarah Dunnigan
University of Edinburgh

James McGonigal
University of Glasgow

Production Editor
Gavin Miller
University of Edinburgh

SCROLL

The Scottish Cultural Review of Language and Literature publishes new work in Scottish Studies, with a focus on analysis and reinterpretation of the literature and languages of Scotland, and the cultural contexts that have shaped them.

Further information on our editorial and production procedures can be found at www.rodopi.nl

Beyond Scotland
New Contexts for Twentieth-Century Scottish Literature

Edited by
Gerard Carruthers
David Goldie & Alastair Renfrew

Amsterdam - New York, NY 2004

Cover design: Gavin Miller

The paper on which this book is printed meets the requirements of "ISO
9706: 1994, Information and documentation - Paper for documents -
Requirements for permanence".

ISBN: 90-420-1883-6
©Editions Rodopi B.V., Amsterdam - New York, NY 2004
Printed in The Netherlands

Contents

Contributors

Gerard Carruthers is Lecturer in Scottish Literature at the University of Glasgow. He has published many articles on eighteenth- and twentieth-century Scottish Literature and he is co-editor of *English Romanticism and the Celtic World* (CUP, 2003).

Cairns Craig is Professor of Scottish and Modern Literature at the University of Edinburgh, where he is also Director of the Centre for the History of Ideas in Scotland. He is the author of *Out of History* (Polygon, 1996) and *The Modern Scottish Novel* (EUP, 1999).

Sarah M. Dunnigan is Lecturer in English Literature at University of Edinburgh where she was also British Academy Postdoctoral Fellow. She has published articles on medieval and renaissance Scottish literature and twentieth-century Scottish women's writing. She is author of *Eros and Poetry at the Courts of Mary Queen of Scots and James VI* (Palgrave, 2002), and co-editor of *Scottish Literature* (EUP, 2002) and *A Flame in the Mearns. Lewis Grassic Gibbon: A Centenary Celebration* (ASLS, 2003).

Douglas Gifford is Professor of Scottish Literature at the University of Glasgow and Honorary Librarian of Walter Scott's library at Abbotsford. His books include studies of James Hogg, Neil Gunn and Lewis Grassic Gibbon, as well as edited histories of nineteenth-century Scottish literature and Scottish women's writing. His latest book (with Sarah Dunnigan and Alan MacGillivray) is an extensive study guide, *Scottish Literature in English and Scots* (EUP, 2002).

David Goldie is Senior Lecturer in English Studies at the University of Strathclyde. He has published several articles on Scottish twentieth-century literature and popular culture and is the author of *A Critical Difference: T.S. Eliot and John Middleton Murry in English Literary Criticism, 1919–1928* (OUP, 1998)

Edna Longley is Emeritus Professor in the School of English, Queen's University Belfast. She is the author of *Poetry & Posterity* (2000), editor of *The Bloodaxe Book of 20th Century Poetry in Britain and Ireland* (2000), and co-editor of *Ireland (Ulster) Scotland: Concepts, Contexts, Comparisons* (QUB, 2003).

Alexander Mackay is Research Fellow in the Comparative Literature program at the University of California at Los Angeles, and teaches British and American Literature at Orange County College. His main current research interest is the politics of Modernism, and he is editor of a forthcoming collection of essays entitled *Between the Lines: Poetry on Trial in Inter-War Europe*.

David Miller is Adjunct Professor of Literature, John Cabot University, Rome and was previously Director of Studies for the Philosophy, Religion and Culture section of the Centre for Continuing Adult Education, University of Edinburgh. His most recent articles and conference papers include "The Prosaic Sublime: Wordsworth and Kant", "Symbol and Image in Bakhtin and Cassirer" and "Hegel, Adorno and 'Aesthetic' History". His primary interest is the relation between philosophy, art and ideology. He has a forthcoming book with Duke University Press on the legacy of Frankfurt School "aesthetics".

Edwin Morgan is Professor Emeritus in English Literature at the University of Glasgow and is Poet Laureate of the City of Glasgow. In 2004 he was appointed to the position of national poet for Scotland, "The Scots Makar", by the Scottish Executive. His *Collected Poems* was published by Carcanet in 1990; his most recent collection is *Love and a Life: 50 Poems* (Mariscat, 2003).

Richard Price is a Curator of Modern British Collections at the British Library, London. His study of the novelist Neil M. Gunn was published by Edinburgh University Press in 1991. His co-edited works include an anthology of César Vallejo translations (Southfields / Au Quai, 1998, with Stephen Watts), *La Nouvelle Alliance: influences francophone sur la littérature écossaise moderne* (Université Stendhal, 2000, with David Kinloch), and *The Star You Steer By: Basil Bunting and British Modernism* (Rodopi, 2000, with James McGonigal). His elliptical novel, *A Boy in Summer*, was published by 11:9 in 2002; his latest full-length poetry collection, *Frosted, Melted* was published by Diehard in the same year.

Alastair Renfrew is Lecturer in Russian at the University of Exeter. He is author of *Towards a New Material Aesthetics* (Legenda) and *Mikhail Bakhtin* (Routledge), both forthcoming in 2005.

Randall Stevenson is Reader in English Literature and Deputy Head of Department in the University of Edinburgh. His books include *Modernist Fiction* (Harvester Wheatsheaf, 1998); the *Oxford English Literary History Vol. 12 1960–2000* (forthcoming, 2004), and *The Scottish Novel Since the Seventies* (1993), edited with Gavin Wallace.

Acknowledgements

The editors are grateful to the Universities of Strathclyde and Glasgow for funding the "Beyond Scotland" seminar series from which this book has come. They acknowledge also the invaluable help of Rhona Brown in preparing the index.

Introduction

Gerard Carruthers, David Goldie and Alastair Renfrew

The relationship between Scottish political and cultural history, which had been defined by varying degrees of discontinuity since the "Unionist" moments of 1603 and 1707, entered a new phase in the less hallowed year of 1919. As the Treaty of Versailles gave birth to the modern "Europe of Nations" in which Scotland would play no autonomous role, G. Gregory Smith's seminal *Scottish Literature: Character and Influence* effectively gave birth to "Scottish Literature" as a discrete area for academic study and critical attention. The work of Gregory Smith, and of his contemporaries who promoted the teaching of Scottish history and literature in the nation's schools and universities, would ensure that while Scotland might have no autonomous political status, it would at least be assured of its own authenticated culture.

This effective declaration of literary independence was, however, more contested and complicated than it seemed. For Gregory Smith, the defining characteristic of Scottish writing was its bipolarity – its tendency to swing, sometimes manically, between realism and fantasy. The category of Scottish literature thus defined was one in which the single most important identifying feature was doubleness – the "two moods" or "polar twins" that Gregory Smith memorably encapsulated in the image of "a gargoyle's grinning at the elbow of a kneeling saint". While this conception has, when used discriminatingly, been a productive conceptual tool, it has also constrained Scottish criticism in its insistence on the idea of a tradition defined by its internal oppositions. Scottishness, in this light, has too often come to be regarded as a state of internalised contradiction. In a magnificent, if not hubristic, gesture of personal and national ambition, Hugh MacDiarmid not only embraced the self-contradiction of the "Caledonian Antisyzygy", but sought to make it the basis of a revived national art. In his desire to "aye be whaur extremes meet", MacDiarmid did not anticipate that the place of intersection might be as likely to occur on the periphery as at the centre. When forced to confront the spectre of cultural marginalisation, MacDiarmid sought a consoling explanation: just as the modern worker had become alienated from his labour by the processes of capital, so the Scottish artist, sundered from his Celtic roots, had become a practitioner in an inauthentic culture. To avoid the danger of becoming "cosmopolitan scum", as MacDiarmid would later call Alexander Trocchi, the Scots artist must reach inwards to his self-contradictions, and backwards to the authentic culture of the past.

Edwin Muir, MacDiarmid's only serious rival for the office of Coptic Pope of Scottish Letters, also grounded his notion of Scottish literature in internal division. For Muir, there was a fatal "split" in Scottish culture that originated in the Calvinist schism of the Reformation and which had denied Scottish culture the organic coherence and continuous "Humanist" development of the larger European cultures of England, France, and Germany. Muir's crypto-Catholicism idealised the Medieval period as a time of essential psychological, spiritual and linguistic coherence, in comparison to which the twentieth century, embodied in the physical terrain of industrial lowland Scotland, was a cultural wasteland.

Scottish criticism has been diverted ever since by the drama of determining who was right, or at least more consistent, in their cultural mapping of the distance between the Glasgow slum and a pre-industrial Eden. And this largely personal drama has obscured the fact that the ostensibly "opposed" views of MacDiarmid and Muir have a common heritage, and are, like Gregory Smith's book itself, heavily dependent on wider British and European contexts. As a member of the academic staff of Queen's University in Belfast, Gregory Smith was writing out of a situation in which the Scottish tradition was not only more contested, but in which it mattered in crucially different ways. In addition, Gregory Smith's conceptual model of "Scottishness" was – like the national ideals articulated by contemporaries as diverse as W.B. Yeats and Rudyard Kipling – largely a development of the attempts of Matthew Arnold to carve out an "English" literary and racial identity from "Celtic" and "Roman" elements. The strength of this influence was such that it had even persuaded the late-Victorian and Edwardian Scottish critical establishment, secure in the fastnesses of its douce lowland manses, to allow "Celticism", previously a deeply suspect Highland phenomenon, as the key constituent of a revived indigenous "Scottish" literature. The formulation for "native" Scottish literature, then, was derived from a convoluted set of "British" cultural concerns.

Muir's subsequent analysis of dissociated Scottish culture was similarly the product of a wider European expression of historical disaffection. His argument was modelled, as he acknowledged, on the idea of a historic "dissociation of sensibility" that the Anglo-American T.S. Eliot had identified with England in the time of its Civil War. Eliot's analysis had drawn significant elements from French critics Remy de Gourmont and Charles Maurras, and was part of a wider dissociationist argument after the First World War, which argued for various types of return to a lost originary cultural moment and which included thinkers as diverse as John Dover Wilson and D.H. Lawrence, Virginia Woolf and F.R. Leavis. That MacDiarmid shared with Muir in this argument, unwittingly or otherwise, implies their typicality not as Scots, but as Britons and indeed Europeans. It also implies that the terms in which their argument has been "developed" – indigenous versus imported, nationalism versus internationalism, essentialism versus cosmopolitanism – are little more than a series of false oppositions, produced by the initial premise from which they are consciously or unconsciously derived. The terms in which the twentieth-century debate on Scottish literature has been conducted occupy the two sides of an increasingly devalued coin. Or, in appropriation of Gregory Smith's terms, these are the new – and more destructive – "polar twins" of contemporary Scottish culture.

The currency of an independent Scottish literature has at times been bolstered by foreign as well as domestic investment. It was a French critic, Denis Saurat, who named the new literary and cultural activity he witnessed in Scotland in the 1920s "The Scottish Renaissance", and it was a German, Kurt Wittig – whose 1958 book *The Scottish Tradition in Literature* became, after Gregory Smith's *Character and Influence*, perhaps the most influential volume in the history of Scottish criticism – who established Celticism as the *technical*, as well as historical, focus of Scottish literature. Yet these continental "confirmations" of the historical accuracy of MacDiarmid's broad approach are not just a function of that component of Modernism which longs for the recovery of a pre-lapsarian "dear green place", they are also a direct echo of the primitivist reflex which had earlier led Romantic Europe to idealise the Scottish (Highland) wilderness. Saurat's label "The Scottish Renaissance" in fact colluded with and aggrandised the persistent notion of the late arrival in Scotland of the Renaissance "proper", and had the paradoxical effect of entrenching the idea of Scottish literature in the twentieth century as a self-contained "republic of letters". The more this republic insisted on its self-containment, however, the more it revealed the complex entanglements of its heterogeneous backgrounds. From the point of view of criticism, the idea of an integral Scottish literature became, like MacDiarmid's Synthetic Scots, a chimera – a fantastic organism that bore the marks of its disparate origins and which dissolved into its constituent elements the moment an attempt was made to catch it and grasp it whole.

It has only been in recent times, as the need to disaggregate political from cultural nationalism has become apparent, that an end to the critical impasse has come into view, and we can discern more clearly the damage wrought by an over-determined, self-defeating essentialism fostered by Scottish criticism's overweening desire for cultural self-determination. It is significant in this respect that Scottish literature in the twentieth century has been much less inhibited by such considerations than Scottish criticism, much less beguiled by the apparent need to untangle a single-stranded Scottishness, and has found its "proper ground" in heterogeneity and *inter*-dependence. Sorley Maclean, for example, remade "authentic" Gaelic poetry with his lament for the effects of fascism in "The Cry of Europe", while Edwin Morgan, George Campbell Hay, Ian Hamilton, Iain Crichton Smith and Muriel Spark have all found in ostensibly foreign cultures the elements necessary for the various cross-fertilisations on which their art depended.

What these and other writers have shown is that throughout Scotland's long experience of the vagaries of European and global religious contention, war, trade, emigration and immigration, Scots themselves have shown a greater gift for interdependence than independence – a value that eludes and obviates the kinds of false opposition created out of a yearning for wholeness that we have located at the heart of Scotland's critical self-consciousness. Interdependence is not the opposite of independence, but in fact reveals the folly of recourse to the latter term in the cultural domain. Independence is little more than an illusion or an aspiration that has been projected onto the cultural sphere through its persistent lack in the political sphere. The philosophy of "ourselves alone", rather than entrenching a coherent sense of national identity, is more likely to deform the very idea of Scottishness itself – to mistake a complex, forward-looking, heterogeneous identity for one that is narrow and reductive in its nativism. This book arose from a conviction that Scottish culture was and is emerging from its long subservience to its darker "polar twins". It aims to explore and reaffirm the centrality of international contexts to the Scottish literary experience in the twentieth century, to highlight the continuing dialogue – in its successes and its failures – between writers in Scotland and other countries, and to show just how important that dialogue has been for the development of a sophisticated modern Scottish literature.

Re-mapping Renaissance in Modern Scottish Literature

Douglas Gifford

The time period of the "Scottish Renaissance" is far more complex than normally admitted. In poetry, fiction and drama there is a sceptical and realist strain which counterpoints the regenerative ideology of the "Renaissance". Furthermore, the myth of "rebirth" proceeds from the unfounded belief that Scottish culture was moribund.
Keywords: Alasdair Gray, Eric Linklater, Hugh MacDiarmid, William Soutar, Scottish Renaissance, Scottish culture.

This essay is essentially an attempt to complement this volume's engagement with modern Scottish literature by questioning some orthodoxies of literary history with regard to "The Scottish Renaissance" of the years between the First and Second World Wars. It is also an attempt to chart the significance of the emergence and subsequent revaluation of those orthodoxies for contemporary Scottish literature and criticism; to assess, in other words, the impact certain misprisions of the cultural dynamics of the "Renaissance" have had on the cultural dynamics of contemporary Scotland.

As such, the essay offers two main propositions: firstly, it argues that recent attempts to widen our conception of the movement called "The Scottish Renaissance" in the inter-war years need to be continued and extended. The aim is not just to reclaim neglected writers of the period and create a more inclusive "Renaissance" than that described by Hugh MacDiarmid and his followers, but also to question the appropriateness of the term itself. "Renaissance" implies the rebirth, regeneration and celebration of Scottish language, history, literature, and culture generally, as well as a renewed confidence in national identity and destiny; yet Scottish literature of the period was just as concerned with ideas of social and cultural decline as it was with ideas of revival. There is a paradox at the heart of the period, exemplified by major writers such as Lewis Grassic Gibbon, Neil Gunn, and Eric Linklater, whose fiction more often laments the passing and mocks the confusions surrounding ideas of Scottish identity and culture than it celebrates them.

My second argument is somewhat simpler, and acts as a kind of counterbalance to certain potentially overdetermined effects of the first: since Edwin Muir's *Scott and Scotland* (Muir 1936), too many views of Scottish literature have tended to start from the assumption of Scottish underachievement in comparison with other major cultures, forgetting Scotland's proportionately small size. And too often theories such as Muir's Scottish version of T.S. Eliot's theory of English cultural "dissociation of sensibility", or the negative fall-out from Gregory Smith's and MacDiarmid's concept of "Caledonian antisyzygy" (Smith 1919), or the later ideas of critics like David Daiches (Daiches 1964) and Kenneth Simpson (Simpson 1988) as to the recurrent crises of creative identity in many Scottish writers from Ramsay, Fergusson and Burns through Boswell, Scott, Hogg and Stevenson, to Davidson, Munro, and Gibbon – and even MacDiarmid – seem to me to imply unique Scottish failure. Instead we should recognise how confrontation and articulation of what Muir called "the predicament of the Scottish writer" can result in innovative and effective creativity.

Scotland is a small country; but arguably it is not its cultural achievement which is to be criticised, but its own and others' sustained failure to recognise Scottish achievement and confidently to represent it through our educational curricula in schools and universities. As the twig is bent, the tree grows; Scotland is a country where the majority of Scots do not know very much about the important historical facts and cultural achievements of their own country, let alone the achievements of Scottish literature in the late nineteenth and early twentieth centuries.

1.

My first contention, then, is that we must continue to review, widen, and perhaps even re-name our assessment of the achievement of Scottish literature in what is often termed the "Scottish Renaissance" of the inter-war years. What are generally considered to be the core features of the major writers of the period? Most critics would agree that they include a return to roots in terms of language and respect for tradition; in terms of folk belief, legend and mythology, a search for an

essentialism of racial inheritance; and a resurrection of national consciousness and a – single – Scottish identity. The major writers of this
"renaissance" rescued, adapted and pressed into service Scottish traditional folklore, a task perhaps made easier due to the fact that folk
tradition had survived more extensively in the various regions of
Scotland compared with its more rapid decline in English and other
European cultures. The Scottish writers combined these with their
own and non-English versions of Modernism. This was most obvious
in MacDiarmid's fusion of traditional ballad, caustic comment, lyric
intensity and cosmic significance in his early poetry, followed by his
development of what he termed a "poetry of facts". In fiction, it was
found in Lewis Grassic Gibbon's adaptation of Joycean "stream of
consciousness" of the individual to that of an entire community, as in
Sunset Song (1932); or Neil Gunn's innovative use of prolepsis and
analepsis in *Highland River* (1937). And widening the Renaissance
net has more recently included major re-assessments of writers like
Willa Muir, Nan Shepherd and Nancy Brysson Morrison – all of
whom appear far more original and innovative than critics of
MacDiarmid's period allowed. Much of this literature, and particularly
fiction, foregrounds mythic protagonists and supra-rational epiphanies, with the Jungian concept of the "collective unconscious" producing in its protagonists co-existing moments of ancient time with
time present. It foregrounds also an underlying use of Modernist
Wasteland ideology, with Corn Kings and Spring Queens emerging
either as re-incarnations of mythic heroes as in Gunn's *The Silver
Darlings* (1941) and *The Green Isle of the Great Deep* (1944), or as
sacrificial scapegoats for the process of regeneration of the land.[1] In
this Scottish version of Joyce and Eliot's Wasteland mythology, the
kings (or queens) who die or sacrifice themselves for the people are
exemplified in figures such as Long Rob of the Mill or Chae Strachan

---

[1] Such epiphanies, moments of time past informing time present, are exemplified in
Sunset Song in Chris Guthrie's childhood perception of the prehistoric man who cries
of the coming of "the Ships of Pytheas", and in Chae Strachan's on-leave encounter
beside standing stones with the warrior from the army of Calgacus on the eve of the
battle of Mons Graupius (and shortly before Chae's own death in France in the First
World War); and in Gunn's *Highland River*, when the boy Kenn enters the ancient
Druid cell and is aware of ancient time, or in *The Silver Darlings* when Finn "sees"
the Druid priest at the heart of "the house of peace", the ruin of a Druid temple.

in *Sunset Song*, or Chris Guthrie herself and her son Ewan in *A Scots Quair* as a whole. Naomi Mitchison created one of the classic British versions of the mythology in *The Corn King and the Spring Queen* (1931), using ancient Black Sea and Mediterranean cultural opposi-tions as metaphors for the tensions between English and Irish/Scottish cultures. MacDiarmid deployed the mythology in contemporary and autobiographical terms in *A Drunk Man Looks at the Thistle* (1926) when he cast himself as "narodbogonosets" or Godbearer, arguing that "A Scottish poet maun assume / The burden o' his people's doom / and dee to brak their livin' tomb" (MacDiarmid [1926] 1987: ll.1640, 2638–40).

There is no doubting the affirmative and exhortatory quality of many fine texts of the period. MacDiarmid's early lyrics (owing much, it must be admitted, to his predecessors Violet Jacob, Marion Angus and Helen Cruikshank) are magnificent and vital develop-ments, which fuse Scottish Ballad tradition with contemporary Euro-pean aesthetics and forms. His long poems in Scots continually chal-lenge his countrymen to re-think themselves and their country. Neil Gunn and "Fionn MacColla" [Tom Macdonald] used Highland set-tings to embody their exemplary challenges to Scots to reject a fatal-istic response to the defeats and economic difficulties of past and pre-sent – Gunn outstandingly in his magnificent trilogy of Highland his-tory and culture, *Sun Circle* (1933), *Butcher's Broom* (1934), and *The Silver Darlings*, and MacColla in *The Albannach* (1932). Kurt Wittig thought that modern Scottish fiction reached its "highest peak" in Gunn, claiming that "more clearly even than C.M. Grieve [Hugh MacDiarmid] he embodies the aims of the Scottish Renaissance" (Wittig 1958: 333, 339). Naomi Mitchison represented a similarly affirmative case throughout her later Scottish writing, nowhere more strongly than in her epic novel *The Bull Calves* (1947), which, in describing the healing of ancient divisions between Highlands and Lowlands, and Jacobites and Hanoverians, in the period following the Jacobite Rebellions, implied that there was just as great a need for the healing of divisions in modern Scotland.

Yet we need to widen these pre-occupations to include the writ-ers who, despite being major poets or novelists of the period, had very different perspectives. Yes, we can read some of the writing as a rebirth of national language and culture – for example (and arguably more affirmatively than anywhere in MacDiarmid) in some of the work of poet William Soutar. "Birthday" is a magnificent recasting of the journey of the Magi into Scottish terms: Scotland, benighted and wasteland in the beginning, is re-awakened. Three travellers ride through the night, urgent and unspeaking ("nae man spak to his brither"), until, in the mountainous heart of Scotland, in an uncanny snowstorm, they meet with the "snaw-white and siller-bricht" unicorn with the radiant new child of Scotland on its back; purity, rebirth, and vision are restored to their sight, they become allies ("nae man but socht his brither / and look't him in the e'en") vowing to tell all Scotland of their vision. The message is reiterated in "The Whale", with its rediscovery (which MacDiarmid sought in so much of his early poetry like "Gairmscoile" and "Bombinations of a Chimaera") of Scotland's lost essence. The unicorn once again, as so often in Soutar's work, symbolises ancient virtues, and its re-appearance re-invigorates the land, until, by Arthur's Seat, the poet hears the lion roar. Most ambitious of all his poems, Soutar's "The Auld Tree" again takes the medieval dream-poem to envisage a timeless kind of Valhalla garden of all the great poets, moving from the great Makars through Burns and others to pay MacDiarmid a wonderful compliment, associating him with Wallace, the guardian of Scotland, as one of Scotland's great prophets (see Soutar 1988).

If such writers represent the affirmative high-points of "Renaissance", it must be realised that in virtually every case they were shortly to change their tune. In the 1930s MacDiarmid would move to his "poetry of facts" in English, while Soutar, who most positively asserted national and cultural regeneration, would in his later poetry turn away from such overt Renaissance symbolism, seeing Scotland in very different and far less optimistic terms. This is best illustrated in his 1938 poem "Scotland", an enigmatic and disturbing challenge to Scots to discover whether they have or do not have the vision and the shared humanity to confront the future. Soutar here articulates the changing mood of Scottish literature, anticipating how "Renaissance" writers like Gunn, Bridie, and MacColla would after the war retreat from their tradition and rural-based certainties:

Atween the world o licht
And the world that is to be
A man wi unco sicht
Sees whaur he canna see:

Gangs whaur he canna walk:
Recks whaur he canna read:
Hauds what he canna tak:
Mells wi the unborn deid.

Atween the world o licht
And the world that is to be
A man wi unco sicht
Monie a saul maun see:

Sauls that are stark and nesh:
Sauls that wad win the day:
Sauls that are fain for flesh
But canna win the wey.

Hae ye the unco sicht
That sees atween and atween
This world that lowes in licht:
Yon world that hasna been?

It is owre late for fear,
Owre early for disclaim;
Whan ye come hameless here
And ken ye are at hame. (Soutar 1988)

Soutar's poem, while suggesting that Scotland is less than a satisfactory homeland for those at home in it, is nevertheless a challenge to Scots to reject apathy, fear, and disengagement for some kind of "unco sicht", or new vision. Going far beyond this in its denigration of Scottish history and culture, the best-known dissenting voice of the time is that of Edwin Muir in poems like "Scotland 1941" and "Scotland's Winter". In the first poem, Burns and Scott are "sham bards of a sham nation", and Reformation and the industrial revolution have undone Scotland, which has "no pride but pride of pelf", with "smoke and dearth and money everywhere"; the second poem expresses his belief that modern Scots are content with their spiritual permafrost, "their poor frozen life and shallow banishment" from cultural and aesthetic fulfilment. And we remember that MacDiarmid's Drunk Man was unsure at the end of his night's spiritual journey as to whether the symbolic thistle is positive or negative, and the question of whether Scots and Scotland are redeemable remains unanswered: "Auch to Hell, / I'll tak it to avizandum" (MacDiarmid [1926] 1987).

Reading MacDiarmid's principal fellow-poets, we realise that their Renaissance zeal is pretty muted: Goodsir Smith is more pre-occupied with his eccentric personal life and loves than any Renaissance commitment; Sorley Maclean is deeply concerned with what he perceives as his own weakness in the face of international injustice and war, and with his tragic love, whether for actual woman or Gaelic tradition; William Jeffrey is in love with ancient mythology rather than present redefinition; and the sardonic Robert Garioch is unable to conclude any representation of modern Scotland and Edinburgh without the last-line sting of his inimitable reductive idiom (as in his typical mockery of pretentious Scots and Scotland in "Did Ye See Me?", where the inflated diction of the self-promoting public speaker is wonderfully deflated in the final line, when, after being mocked by "the keelies of the toun", he forlornly concludes "I wisht I hadnae worn my M.A. goun!" (Garioch 1977)).

Is the fiction of the time more committed? Setting the positive statements of "Renaissance" against those more negative, it seems to me that the fiction of the period is most often read as diagnosing what the writers felt to be the essential ailments of Scotland through history and in the present. For every *Albannach, Highland River, The Silver Darlings* or *The Bull Calves*, there's a *Sunset Song* as part of a sceptical *Scots Quair*, a bleak insistence on rural and urban despair as in George Blake's *The Shipbuilders* (1935), James Barke's *The Land of the Leal* (1939) or MacColla's *And the Cock Crew* (1945), or hilarious satirical send-up of so-called Renaissance as in Linklater's *Magnus Merriman* (1934), or exposure of the meanness of the average Scottish small town as in Willa Muir's *Imagined Corners* (1931) (with its delightful opening dismissal of essential nationalism in her dry comments on Scotland's wild life, here larks, crows and gulls – "it is doubtful whether they even knew that they were domiciled in Scotland" (Muir [1935] 1987: 2)).

A recurrent phrase and idea in the fiction of Gibbon, MacColla and Gunn is that "it is finished" – in *Butcher's Broom*, in *Sunset Song,* and in classic stories like Gibbon's "Clay", implying that past eras and achievements of older Scotlands, however impressive, valuable and complete, are now over, and irrecoverable. This recognition seems to haunt virtually all the important writers of the time: war, economic realities, and Scotland's overwhelming change from rural to urban realities present complexities that cannot in the end be resolved. With a satirical view from inside the Renaissance movement, Eric Linklater succinctly expresses the would-be affirmative writer's dilemma in his hilarious *Magnus Merriman*, which, for all its humour, is an extended ironic commentary on all aspects of "Scottish Renaissance". The eponymous Magnus aspires to political, literary and agricultural glory throughout the novel; instead, he loses his deposit as a nationalist par-liamentary candidate, his literary ambitions wither, and his farming prospects appear similarly blighted. Linklater exemplifies the pre-dicament of the would-be Renaissance writer, describing how Mag-nus's initial elation regarding his epic Renaissance poem turns sour, as he finds his vision of a resurgent Scotland "elusive as a unicorn":

The satirical half of *The Returning Sun*, then, was when finished a fine gallimaufry. The body of it was the dismal and lifeless condition of Scotland [...] but when he came to write the second half of the poem he found many obstacles: for the latter part was to be constructive, and constructive criticism is regrettably more difficult than detraction [...] He began with an evening vision of the western sea [...] intended to symbolize the returning pride and vigour of Scotland, but how to fulfil the vision and equip it with practical details gave Magnus no little trouble. That renascence should come from the west suggested, of course, a Celtic character for it, and the Celtic ethos was a fine opponent to the decadent commercialism of Scotland and the world at large. But as an Orkneyman Magnus did not wholly trust the Celtic spirit [...] That night he could make nothing of Scotland's renascence [...]. (Linklater [1934] 1990: 202–6)

The drama of the same period, from James Bridie through the Unity Theatre and early Citizens', to the amateur movement led by Joe Corrie, also shows this shift of mood. This is particularly true of Corrie's angry early work, as in his award-winning *Hewers of Coal* in 1937. The same year saw Robert McLellan's *Jamie the Saxt* for the Curtain Theatre, with its ambivalent study of the character of

James VI, and its preoccupation with Scotland's bloody internecine history. McLellan was to spend much of his later energy attacking what he saw as Bridie's betrayal of the principles of Scottish theatre, or later expressing his disillusion – like the poet Robert Garioch – with the bourgeois narrowness of Scotland present, as in *The Hypocrite* (1967). Too often Scottish theatre of the 1930s was dominated by undemanding amateur comedies, and when Scottish theatre did revive in the 1940s it was with plays politically and socially radical like Glasgow Unity's *UAB* (Unemployment Assistance Board) in 1940, or Ena Lamont Stewart's *Starched Aprons* of 1945 (later the celebrated Citizens' production *Men Should Weep*) and Robert McLeish's *The Gorbals Story* of 1946.

The programme of such dramatists, with its acute awareness of Scotland's modern, urban, industrial and essentially Lowland problems, was now far removed from the rural essentialism that underpinned the work of Gunn, Gibbon and MacDiarmid. It anticipated the Scottish novel's post-war rejection of Renaissance values. And even James Bridie, close to Linklater and Gunn in many of his aims for a revival of Scottish theatre in plays such as *The Holy Isle* (1942), is often seen exploring the darker side of Scottish history and character in plays like *The Anatomist* (1931) and *Mr Bolfry* (1943). His 1947 play *Mr Gillie* shares the general post-war mood of disillusion in its study of a well-meaning schoolteacher in a small Lowland industrial town, whose dreams of improving the lot of his pupils are dashed. Bridie here points towards the fiction of writers like Robin Jenkins and George Friel, with their recurrent portrayal of dreamers and would-be improvers, whose ambitions are mocked by harsh Scottish realities and their own failings (see, for example, Jenkins 1958, Friel 1972).

Increasingly, just before and after the Second World War, writers like Soutar, Garioch and Goodsir Smith in poetry, and Gunn, Linklater and Mitchison in fiction, disengaged from issues of national cultural and social rejuvenation. Certainly from the 1950s on Neil Gunn had become something of a metaphysical hermit. Much of the substantial and vital work of the period turned to even more ferocious denigration, as in Edward Gaitens's *Dance of the Apprentices* (1947), with its closure locating its blighted young Glasgow working-class protagonist in a prison cell, and Fionn MacColla's *And the Cock Crew* (1946), with its withering attack on the rottenness of church and state during the Highland Clearances expressing an anger far beyond that of the two other great treatments of clearance, Gunn's *Butcher's Broom* and Iain Crichton Smith's *Consider the Lilies* (1968). Indeed it is hard to find substantial literature of the post-war period that endeavours to carry on Renaissance ideology, although, amidst sceptical and elegiac work like J.F. Hendry's anticipation of lament for Glasgow as dear green place in *Ferniebrae* (1947) and J.D. Scott's *The End of an Old Song* (1954), some brave attempts were made. The outstanding example of this is Naomi Mitchison's ambitious exploration of ancient Scottish internecine animosities, and her plea for reconciliation, now as in the past, in her ambitious *The Bull Calves*. Neil Paterson in his *Behold Thy Daughter* (1950), working like Gunn in *The Silver Darlings* with North-East fisher-folk, created in his heroine Thirza Gair a somewhat glamorised version of Gibbon's Chris Guthrie, and attempts to work within the conventions of the affirmative Renaissance. Mitchison's epic novel of Highland and Lowland reconciliation after Culloden was as much about personal renaissance after the traumas of losing a child and dislocating herself from London to Argyllshire. She too would afterwards become disillusioned in her love affair with Scotland and her attempts to bond with the West Highlands and their ungrateful people, as she shows in the very different and decidedly non-epic *Lobsters on the Agenda* (1952). In the 1960s she refashioned her dream of being matriarch to a Scottish Renaissance to become one with herself in the role of *Mmarona* or tribal mother for the Bakgatlas in Botswana. In her account of this, *Return to the Fairy Hill* (1966), she indicates the extent to which her allegiances have altered in her desire to be buried in a lion's skin in the great kraal where former chiefs have been buried (Mitchison 1966: 212).

The mood of disillusion is found nowhere more strongly than in the novels of the 1950s and 1960s of Robin Jenkins, arguably the greatest of Scottish novelists of the period, and certainly the most prolific voice of post-war Scotland's grey scepticism. Novels such as *Happy for the Child* (1953), *The Cone-Gatherers* (1955), *Guests of War* (1956), and *The Changeling* (1958) mocked Scotland's former glories, forcing readers to focus on the contrast between Scottish icons of romance, war and landscape and the realities of Lowland industrial drabness and the plight of children in Glasgow's slums. He was followed by novelists like Muriel Spark, whose *The Prime of Miss Jean Brodie* (1961) shared his ambivalence regarding Scottish education and its relevance to modern Scotland, while focussing on the very different culture of Edinburgh; and James Kennaway, whose *Tunes of Glory* (1956) and *Household Ghosts* (1961) continued the satire on the central institutions of Scotland in their withering examination of army and aristocracy.

The mood was general. In his preface to *By Yon Bonny Banks: A Gallimaufray* (1961) Maurice Lindsay (who, with Alexander Scott, George Bruce and others such as the publisher Robert Maclellan, can be seen as sustaining what was left of Renaissance aims in the 1950s) was to speak of how his long love affair with Scotland was over. He and Scott, despite continuing with Herculean efforts in supporting Scottish poetry and culture generally, had clearly become somewhat disillusioned. And it is consistent with this that when Scottish literature revived in the mid-1960s with the work of Norman MacCaig, Iain Crichton Smith, George Mackay Brown and Edwin Morgan, it continued to deconstruct and mock what were seen as spurious older mythologies.

With hindsight it can be argued that the values and aims of the Renaissance movement were doomed to failure, given the ideological fall-out of the Second World War. Too much based on Irish Revival, by drawing inspiration from Yeats's astonishing creation of an essentialist rural tradition and mythology for Ireland, and with too great a pre-occupation with rural and traditional Scotland, and too little relationship with the urban and industrial realities of a very different and economically suffering Scotland, it simply didn't connect. Linklater recognised in *Magnus Merriman* that the return to Scots language, land, and myth in the "Renaissance" was seen by most Scots as distrusted irrelevance. And this assessment is supported by the political realities of the period: the Renaissance movement of MacDiarmid and Gunn, for all the scale and richness of its literary achievement, found no echo in terms of parliamentary representation. By the late 1960s and early 1970s, however, when Scotland's major writers were virtually all sceptical with regard to what they saw as the dangers of

narrow nationalism and the emptiness of theories of racial essentialism and mythic inheritance, the Scottish National Party would achieve
major political breakthrough by gaining eleven seats in the Westmin-
ster parliament. It is one of the many paradoxes of Scottish culture and
society that the revival of Scottish writing in the 1960s coincided with
a new distrust of all previous formulations of Scottish character and
history, and, in particular, with a sceptical rejection of an ideology too
closely associated with the ideas of racial consciousness and purity of
Nazi Germany, and far too little associated with the realities and needs
of post-war and increasingly urbanised Scotland.

2.

My second broad proposition is that Scottish cultural and literary criticism, partly in unconscious response to the overdeterminations of the
"Renaissance", too often theorises in ways that unjustifiably minimise
or even efface Scottish achievements. A useful description of such
blinkered or self-justifying editing out or ignoring of Scottish
achievement has recently been presented by Cairns Craig in his
stimulating, if often controversial, study of fiction and the national
imagination, *The Modern Scottish Novel: Narrative and the National
Imagination* (Craig 1999). In his introductory chapter Craig argues
that such cultural erasure is a recurrent feature of Scottish cultural
criticism. He cites three outstanding examples of such erasure, the
second and third of which concern me here. They are, first, Scottish
philosophy and culture's view (and notably that of the philosopher
Alasdair McIntyre) that David Hume and the Enlightenment "erased"
the Scottish philosophy, culture and values which preceded him (a
view Craig sees as a misperception of what Hume and other thinkers
were trying to do, in wishing to create new and what they saw as more
relevant – but still Scottish – cultural traditions); second, the views of
MacDiarmid and Edwin Muir, who, for all their differences
concerning the validity of the Scots language, were in fact very similar
in their conceptions of the limitations of post-1707 Scottish culture;
and finally, the argument of Alasdair Gray (or more specifically, of
his protagonist Duncan Thaw) in a well-known passage in his novel

Lanark: A Life in Four Books (Gray 1981), to which I will shortly return.

What emerges from Craig's analysis is the importance and influence of cultural map-making. In the introduction to his controversial *Contemporary Scottish Studies* (1926), MacDiarmid argued that "the history of the country, either in its cultural or other aspects, is almost wholly unappreciated", and, more specifically, that "from the death of Burns to the end of the late War may, perhaps, be regarded as the most jejune and uninspired period in Scottish literature" (MacDiarmid 1926: 14). So much for Scott, Hogg, and Galt! Unfortunately, given their pioneering and long-lasting cultural influence, neither MacDiarmid nor Muir, since they had so many personal axes to grind, were best suited to making maps that sufficiently appreciated the richness of the cultural landscape. Muir, like his contemporary Grassic Gibbon, regularly and powerfully made Scotland the scapegoat for his personal displacement and unhappiness, as in "Scotland 1941", with its sneering dismissal of "Burns and Scott, sham bards of a sham nation"; and MacDiarmid's self-centred genius all too often judged the worth of his contemporaries in terms of their closeness to his ideals, irrespective of the quality of their work, or sometimes even, one suspects, because they came too close to standing in his light. An example of this can be found in the case of that other fine poet in Scots of the period, William Soutar. MacDiarmid undertook an edition of Soutar's *Collected Poems* (1948), describing Soutar as "a minor classic of our literature" (Soutar 1948: 17), but then omitted several of Soutar's greatest poems, such as "The Tryst", "Birthday", "The Whale", and "The Auld Tree".

MacDiarmid's map of Scottish writing in his own time is outlined in *Contemporary Scottish Studies*, which makes his own particular priorities all too clear: poetry is the premier literary genre, while the novel is a low second. He describes the novel as "a form alien to Scotland": in dismissing Violet Jacob's now highly regarded *Flemington*, for example, he describes the historical novel as "a bastard form, never rising above the bar sinister". Unlike modern criticism, which recognises thematic and formal linkage between Scott, Galt, Hogg, Stevenson, Brown and MacDougall Hay, MacDiarmid does not discern any tradition in nineteenth-century Scottish fiction, valuing Scott's embedded short story of "Wandering Willie's Tale" in

Redgauntlet (1826) (and not the novel itself) so highly as to be willing
to "scrap the whole of the rest of [Scott's] output for a dozen of such
tales" (MacDiarmid 1926: 319). He questions the worth of the "Ste-
vensonian spirit and tradition" carried on by Buchan and Crockett;
MacDonald he lumps in with James Grant and William Black as
"respectable but unexciting" (MacDiarmid 1926: 20), verdicts modern
criticism would find questionable or even bizarre. One does wonder
how many and how much of the authors he assesses he had read.[2]

MacDiarmid's verdicts on Scottish novelists are perhaps unsur-
prising, given his low opinion of fiction in general; more surprising is
his assessment of his contemporaries in poetry. MacDiarmid had experienced the horrors of The Great War, so it is surprising that there is
only the briefest of acknowledgments of the "savagely realistic" quality of the war poets like Kerr, Sorley, and Lee, whose range of comment on the agonies of actual war far exceeds that of MacDiarmid.
And for me, the outstanding and ironically unacknowledged debt
MacDiarmid owes to previous major poets is to the wonderful lyrics
of Violet Jacob and Marion Angus, which explored mysteries of time
and identity in ways MacDiarmid was to develop in his own early
poetry. Writing in 1926 on the poet George Reston Malloch,
MacDiarmid asks "who are the twenty great poets of Scotland? It is
easy enough to name the first ten [...] without being driven to such an
extremity as would place, say, Fergusson [...] in the list" (MacDiarmid 1926: 294). Oddly, MacDiarmid names only three of his first ten,
three Gaels, "Alexander Macdonald, Duncan Ban MacIntyre, Dugald
Buchanan"; though I would guess from reference throughout his work
that the other seven would comprise Dunbar, Henryson, Lindsay,
Douglas, Burns, Byron, and either Davidson or himself (modesty
regarding the inclusion of himself perhaps preventing him from nam-
ing the other six?). His second ten, beyond Reston Malloch himself,
comprises

Dr. Ronald Campbell McFie, Sir Ronald Ross, Lord Alfred Douglas, and Dr Pitten-
drich McGillivray; and of the younger school, Muriel Stuart, Edwin Muir, F.V. Bran-

---

[2] As I argue elsewhere, any broad re-assessment of the "Renaissance" must also
reconsider its problematic relation to later nineteenth-century and *fin de siècle* literary
achievement in Scotland (see Gifford: forthcoming).

ford, John Ferguson, and, I think, William Jeffrey, with Professor Alexander Gray and Rachael A as "runners-up". (MacDiarmid 1926: 132)

Of course it is unfair and all too easy to pick out examples of MacDiarmid's well-known eccentricities of judgement. Great writers are all too often the least reliable assessors of their peers, given their commitment to their own inspiration and art, and MacDiarmid is merely an outstanding example of this kind of critical myopia. What is unfortunate, as with Muir's similar inability to find significant Scottish achievement in literature in Scott and his descendants, is the influence his descriptions of Scottish culture have had until all too recently. Given the lack of other substantial critical assessments of contemporary work, and the failure of Scottish schools and universities to include Scottish history and literature in their curricula (and with the valuable work of literary historians like J.H. Millar, T.F. Henderson and Gregory Smith becoming increasingly dated), the pronouncements of MacDiarmid and Muir, while hardly in accord, set the parameters of discussion regarding Scottish literary achievement in the first half of the twentieth century. More balanced overviews (to my mind) of critics such as William Power – who in *Literature and Oatmeal* (Power 1935) argues much the same case as I put forward here – were overshadowed by the more dramatic statements of the more colourful writers, so that the limitations and exclusions of MacDiarmid and Muir were to a great extent corroborated by provocative and headline-claiming evaluations such as the stimulating but denigratory overview of the literature of "Scotshire" in Lewis Grassic Gibbon's essay "Literary Lights".

The work of the major writers of the "Scottish Renaissance" is characterised overall by its disillusionment with older representations and ideologies regarding Scottish history and culture. What comes across in so many of the major texts is a kind of "positive negativism" (or negative positivism!): negative in its view of the past, more positive in that it seeks to reject that past, to clarify what it perceives as the reality of its focus, and finally, through irony and anger, to change Scottish self-awareness and representation for the better.

What has prevented Scottish literary and cultural history from reaching such a conclusion with regard both to the "Renaissance" and to the period immediately preceding it? Should we conclude by simply blaming MacDiarmid and Muir, together with earlier anglicised de-valuers of Scottish achievement? I do not think so. For all I have argued so far regarding their limitations, it seems to me that we have yet to see clearly the root cause behind Scotland's recurrent erasures and failures of culture. Intriguingly, and with characteristic self-contradiction, MacDiarmid claimed in 1926 that "the Scottish teaching profession – to whom *Contemporary Scottish Studies* appeals – are on the whole the best educated and most open-minded reading public available in Scotland", but then claimed that the range of contemporary literature, art, music and affairs generally was "outwith their ken" (MacDiarmid 1926: 11). Such a flattering claim – his patrons and audience were Scottish teachers – sits oddly with his subsequent criticism of the limitations of the Scottish school curriculum, when he complains that that there are no Scottish texts in the examinations. His curricular criticisms, I suggest, were and are much closer to the mark.

And here, in conclusion, I return to Alasdair Gray and his novel *Lanark*, which is recognised, justly, as one of the finest of recent Scottish – and British – novels, and as one of the key texts, along with the work of writers like Edwin Morgan and Liz Lochhead, in inaugu-rating a new and vital period of contemporary Scottish writing. Nev-ertheless, I believe that at its centre lies a graphic example of my contention that the way Scottish society transmits its past culture to the present is both limited and damaging. Several critics (including myself and Cairns Craig) have identified an important central passage in this respect. It occurs when Gray's main protagonist, the Glasgow artist-as-unhappy-young man, Duncan Thaw, goes with his friend McAlpin to sketch in the Cowcaddens, a poor area behind Glasgow School of Art. In an exchange reminiscent of that between Joyce's Stephen Daedalus and his friend Lynch, McAlpin asks why Glasgow's inhabitants don't notice the magnificence of the city buildings. "Be-cause nobody imagines living here", responds Thaw; he goes on to contrast the experience of living in the city with that of living in Flor-ence, Paris, London – cities familiar to their inhabitants through painting, novels, history books and films. By comparison, Glasgow pales, offering only home, places of work and sport, pubs, streets, cinemas, libraries. Thaw argues that Glasgow offers no cultural enrichment, so that the Glaswegian Scot exercises imagination by escaping to the great cities and histories of the world. "Imaginatively Glasgow exists as a music-hall song and a few bad novels. That's all we've given to the world outside. It's all we've given to ourselves", concludes Thaw (Gray 1981: 243).

Admittedly Thaw's focus is Glasgow and not Scotland; and admittedly he is Gray's creation, just as Stephen is Joyce's in *Portrait of the Artist*, and we must beware of interpreting Gray's satirical treatment of his protagonist as Gray's own view. Craig argues, however, that Thaw is simply wrong:

Thaw is the inheritor of Scottish culture as erasure: the culture which has actually existed in Glasgow, the paintings of the Glasgow boys and the Glasgow girls, the work of designers and architects like Rennie MacIntosh [*sic*], the novels of Catherine Carswell and George Friel, the theatre of James Bridie, have all disappeared in an all-encompassing cultural amnesia. (Craig 1999: 33–34)

Craig then argues that the novel goes on to demonstrate that it is not Glasgow that is unimagined, but Thaw's imagination, "which is so alienated from its own environment that it recognises no other imagination than its own" (Craig 1999: 34). I am not so sure that Thaw, like so many of Gray's similar lonely, loveless, sensitive and perceptive protagonists, does not speak for much of Gray's experience and belief. And there is other evidence in the novel to suggest that Gray's views of Scottish culture resemble Thaw's of Glasgow's. In the novel's idiosyncratic "Index to Dipflags" Gray acknowledges his influences and sources. The list is (deliberately?) unreliable – for example, in the entry on Hugh MacDiarmid, MacDiarmid is quoted as saying "inadequate maps are better than no maps; at least they show that the land exists", the source cited as being the long poem *The Kind of Poetry I Want* (Gray 1981: 493). It is not in that or any other MacDiarmid poem I have read.[3] Taken as a whole, however, the list of background reading tends to support Thaw's more localised view. There is a curious blank area between, on one hand, the local references acknowl-

---

[3] I had intended to use this quotation as highly appropriate in terms of my arguments regarding the remapping of modern Scottish literature. I am indebted to Professor Alan Riach for preventing me from searching endlessly for its source.

edging Gray's contemporaries (or near-contemporaries like Mac-
Diarmid and MacCaig), most of them in Glasgow and amounting to at
least seventeen, including Philip Hobsbaum, Kelman, Lochhead, Leonard and others, and, on the other, the many references to the great
names of world literature, such as Blake, Borges, Bunyan, Carroll,
Conrad, Dante, Joyce, Kafka, Shakespeare, Vonnegut, Wells. True,
there are references to Burns, Douglas Brown, Carlyle, Hume and
MacDonald, but these are the only references to Scottish literature before the twentieth century; and there are no references to any of the
artists and writers Craig identifies as missing from Thaw's "unimagined Glasgow". Writers work from what they are and know, of course,
and there is absolutely no requirement that any Scottish writer need
undertake a course in Scottish literature before writing. But the list
does tend to suggest that Gray's awareness of Scottish culture has
drawn either on the sharing of information with local friends or a
totally admirable self-immersion in the work of great international
writers. What does not appear is evidence of awareness of the kind of
literary background the writers of most nations would have encountered through formal education. Absences from Gray's list of influences include the Makars, the Ballads, the eighteenth-century vernacular revival, Scott, Hogg, Galt, Stevenson, Davidson, Carswell,
Gibbon, Muir, Gunn (whose 1944 vision of dystopian totalitarianism,
The Green Isle of the Great Deep, is one of the few Scottish fantasy
novels to compare with *Lanark*), and Mitchison – so much and so
many, in fact, that I am tempted to argue that just as Thaw takes a narrow view of Glasgow culture before the 1950s, so too does Gray's
novel take a narrow view of Scottish literature as a whole. In this
respect Gray joins a long line of Scottish novelists who believed their
work spoke of their author's lonely creative isolation, among them
Stevenson, Munro, Douglas Brown, and Barrie. Scottish writers
imagine themselves alone, because they work within a national culture
which has little time for the study of its traditions, and which fails to
transmit the information regarding its past achievements.

The root cause of Scotland's failure to recognise its cultural
achievements lies not so much in Scottish critics and their eccentric
judgements, and certainly not in the work of Scotland's many fine
creative writers, but in the grounds and information on which they

make their judgements or fashion their views of Scottish life and society. The fault is surely connected with what MacDiarmid said when he deplored the lack of Scottish history and literature in Scotland's universities, which teach Scotland's teachers, and consequently Scotland's schools. In terms of Scottish cultural and literary awareness, Scottish educationalists reap their scanty harvest of knowledge of Scotland's best writers and texts from deficiencies in their own education, with its past hostility towards Gaelic and Scots, modified now to what is only lukewarm endorsement. Beyond issues of language, both then, as MacDiarmid noted, and now, as we should recognise, there is still a pervasive lack of serious and systematic examination – in general terms – of Scottish history and culture. Scottish schoolchildren are not formally required to read Scottish texts for examination, or to study Scottish history, while the place of Scots language is, to say the least, problematic. It could be argued that even if Scottish history and culture was as limited and narrow as some representations would (in my opinion, of course, wrongly) make out, surely there would then be very good and remedial reasons for examining closely why that should be so, with a concomitant desire to create better? The predicament of the Scottish writer is certainly no longer that identified by Muir in *Scott and Scotland*, where he identified the twin limitations preventing a genuinely Scottish literature as the lack of an organic and supportive tradition on one hand, and the lack of a homogeneous language that could speak for the country on the other. Contemporary Scottish writers like Morgan, Gray, Kelman, Leonard, Lochhead, Galloway and many others now see positive virtue and richness in Scotland's varieties of register and language; with hindsight we realise that Muir's unfortunate Lowland Scottish experience (as with Grassic Gibbon) had predisposed him to find Scottish languages and culture wanting.

The Scottish literary tradition may not have been recognised by Eliot as "major", but nevertheless, however positively negative or negatively positive in its analyses of ailing communities and societies, it is wide-ranging and far more sustaining than has been recognised. It is also a culture of the future, taking its place with the many hyphenated and multi-cultural societies of an increasingly complex world. And given the increasing number of oppositional claims on our literary courses from gender, popular and cultural studies, together with the virtually unmanageable amount of significant literature in the world (in English alone) sooner or later there will be just too much for even "English-English" literature to claim the attention of students world wide. Perhaps at that point of breakdown Scottish literature's tradition of polyphony, fragmented visions, uneasy relations both literal and cultural, will come to seem neither inferior nor irrelevant, and the richness of Scotland's literary traditions, and especially those of the last century-and-a-half, in which Scottish literature took stock of its own and its country's failings, will be seen as a vital part of how Scots tell themselves who they were and who they are.

Bibliography

Craig, Cairns. 1999. *The Modern Scottish Novel: Narrative and the National Imagination*. Edinburgh: Edinburgh University Press.

Daiches, David. 1964. *The Paradox of Scottish Culture: The Eighteenth-Century Experience*. London: Oxford University Press.

Friel, George. 1972. *Mr. Alfred MA*. London: Calder and Boyars.

Garioch, Robert. 1977. *Collected Poems of Robert Garioch*. Loanhead: Macdonald.

Gifford, Douglas. (forthcoming). "The Roots of Renaissance in Nineteenth-Century Scottish Literature". To appear in Carruthers, Gerard, David Goldie and Alastair Renfrew (eds) *Scotland and the Nineteenth-Century World*. Amsterdam and New York: Rodopi.

Gray, Alasdair. 1981. *Lanark: A Life in Four Books*. Canongate: Edinburgh.

Jenkins, Robin. 1958. *The Changeling*. London: Macdonald.

Linklater, Eric. [1934] 1990. *Magnus Merriman*. Edinburgh: Canongate Classics.

MacDiarmid, Hugh. 1926. *Contemporary Scottish Studies*. London: Leonard Parsons.

—. [1926] 1987. *A Drunk Man Looks at the Thistle: The Annotated Edition* (ed. Kenneth Buthlay). Edinburgh: Scottish Academic Press.

Mitchison, Naomi. 1966. *Return to the Fairy Hill*. London: Heinemann.

Muir, Edwin. 1936. *Scott and Scotland: The Predicament of the Scottish Writer*. London: Routledge.

Muir, Willa. [1935] 1987. *Imagined Corners*. Edinburgh: Canongate Classics.

Power, William. 1935. *Literature and Oatmeal: What Literature has Meant to Scotland*. London: Routledge.

Simpson, Kenneth G. 1988. *The Protean Scot: The Crisis of Identity in Eighteenth-Century Scottish Literature*. Aberdeen: Aberdeen University Press.

Smith, G. Gregory. 1919. *Scottish Literature: Character and Influence*. London: Macmillan.

Soutar, William. 1948. *William Soutar: Collected Poems* (intro. by Hugh MacDiarmid). London: Andrew Dakers.

—. 1988. *Poems of William Soutar* (ed. W.R. Aitken). Edinburgh: Scottish Academic Press.

Wittig, Kurt. 1958. *The Scottish Tradition in Literature*. Edinburgh: Oliver & Boyd.

Scotland, Britishness, and the First World War[1]

David Goldie

The popular literature and culture produced and received by Scots during the First World War is better regarded as British rather than Scottish. Authors such as John Buchan, Ian Hay and R.W. Campbell, as well as popular culture such as Variety Theatre, provided a Scottish audience with an identity within the British Empire.
Keywords: John Buchan, R.W. Campbell, Ian Hay, British national identity, First World War.

The tendency of much recent British and American writing about the literary, cultural, and social history of the First World War has been to assume a homogeneous British experience, in which the Welsh and Scottish engagement with the events of 1914–1918 was to all intents and purposes identical with the English. In such work it is commonly assumed that, just as there was a single British economy in the period, albeit with regional variations, so there was also a more or less unified British culture.[2] This is a risky assumption to make without a detailed examination of the relevant sources, and it has come under challenge from a number of writers and researchers engaged in uncovering Scottish specificities and discontinuities within the wider British experience.[3] Elements of such discontinuity do exist and need to be acknowledged, but when Scottish literature and culture are compared with, for example, the culture and literature of Ireland in the period, then it would still seem that there is a pressing case to be made for seeing Scottish culture maintaining a strong British identity. It is the purpose of this essay to press this case, and to suggest that it remains more meaningful to talk about a British rather than a Scottish literature of the First World War.

---

[1] I am grateful to the Arts and Humanities Research Board and the University of Strathclyde for funding a period of study leave during which this article was revised for publication.
[2] See, for example, Marwick 1965, Fussell 1975, Hynes 1990, DeGroot 1996, Robb 2002.
[3] Among these are Royle ed. 1990, Spear and Pandrich eds 1989, Milton 1995, Macdonald and McFarland eds 1999, Spiers 1996.

Two factors particularly apply in saying this. The first is the pressure of a unified war effort, which laid stress on a common British identity. That war has tended to have such a centripetal effect in forcing the margins towards the centre has been a truism of British political life since the Napoleonic Wars, and finds expression in literary terms at least as far back as Shakespeare's *Henry V*. Historically, few things have united Britain more than the perception of a common external threat – a continuing tendency of which the SNP's Alex Salmond had a sharp reminder during the elections to the new Scottish parliament in 1999, when his criticism of NATO bombings in Kosovo contributed to a slump in his party's popularity.

The second factor is the extent to which the literary tradition with which English language writers had to engage in their attempts to comprehend the war had effectively become a British literary tradition (Scottish Gaelic writing is an obvious exception here). This is especially the case of the popular literature and culture on which this essay focuses. Jay Winter has argued that the war helped give legitimacy to popular writing – helping to consolidate the readership of new genres like the thriller while sounding the death knell of the Victorian three-decker novel (Winter 1999). It is important to note the important role played by Scottish writers and publishers in this vitalisation of British popular literature. In the years before the war, Scottish authors such as Robert Louis Stevenson, Sir Arthur Conan Doyle, Neil Munro, J.M. Barrie, and the writers of the Kailyard had been among the most visible authors and reliable best sellers in British popular fiction – a popularity in which they would be followed in wartime by Ian Hay and John Buchan. The English-based Scotsman Andrew Lang had, in his influential reviewing in the British papers, played an important role in popularising the British imperial adventure story before the war. His championing of Henry Rider Haggard and Rudyard Kipling, and his donnish divagations on the virtues of masculine fiction, led C.E. Montague to deride him after the war as the "father and mother of this virilistic movement among the well-read" (Montague 1922: 213). The Anglo-Scottish Macmillan company played a central role in the British Publishers' Association and had been instrumental in establishing the Net Book Agreement in 1899 and the 1911 Copyright Act, as well as publishing important British authors such as James

Frazer and Kipling (Morgan 1943: 151–75).[4] Scottish companies such as Collins of Glasgow and Nelsons of Edinburgh had in the Edwardian period played a significant part in pioneering cheap sevenpenny reprints of living British authors – at a time when the average price of a book was six shillings – as well as publishing works like Collins's one-shilling series on British political issues, *The Nation's Library*, penny libraries of classic British fiction for schools, and threepence ha'penny pocket-size classic novels (Keir 1952: 227–29).[5] *Blackwood's Magazine*, the *Edinburgh Review* and the *Scots Observer* all continued to hold an eminent place in British literary culture – *Blackwood's* in particular enjoying an astonishing ubiquity in every corner of the imperial world.[6] A eulogy to the magazine in *The Times* on 1 February 1913, subsequently emblazoned on the cover of *Blackwood's* during the war and used in its adverts in other journals and newspapers, testified to its singular significance:

"Blackwood's" is an epitome in little of the British Empire – a monthly reminder that its boundaries are world-wide; that it has been won and kept by the public-school pluck of our soldiers and sailors; that in warfare, literature, and art it has a glorious history; that its sons have ever been travellers and sportsmen; and that its politics have still a strong strain of conservative imperialism. Old as it is, "Blackwood's" shows no signs of becoming old-fashioned, because it represents and appeals to all that is best in the undying genius of the race.

Scots had created for themselves a role in British culture disproportionate to their numbers. It could be said that they had achieved this by contributing a distinctive Scots element into the British mix, but, as the example of *Blackwood's* suggests, it might also be argued that these Scots individuals had prospered by (depending upon the terms one prefers) submitting to, colluding with, or playing a leading role in, the construction of a British cultural imperium in which they could trade ideas on advantageous terms. The popular writer necessarily

---

[4] The chairman of the Publishers Association when war broke out was J.H. Blackwood of Blackwood's, who had succeeded Sir Frederick Macmillan in the post in 1913. See Kingsford 1970: 52.
[5] Keir estimates that Collins was, in this period, producing "about 89,000 bound volumes a week" (Keir 1952: 229).
[6] See Finkelstein 1998.

requires to have an eye on the marketplace, and as there was by 1914 little in the way of a distinctive Scottish market, and much more obviously a thriving British and Imperial market, then the value of talking about a Scottish popular literature and culture in the period becomes questionable.

This is not to say that there wasn't a popular literature in Scotland in this period that did retain its particularity – but it tended to do this by having to ignore the war or drive it to the periphery of its vision. Neil Munro's much-loved pre-war stories in the *Glasgow Evening News* of Para Handy, Erchie, and Jimmy Swan continued in wartime. But though Munro experienced the war at first hand as a correspondent on the Western Front for the *Evening News*, his characters view it only from a humorous distance. The main privations his droll waiter Erchie and dapper commercial traveller Jimmy Swan suffer in wartime are rationing, licensing restrictions, and comically-rendered service in the Great War "Dads' Army", the Citizen Training Force.[7] The cook on the *Vital Spark*, Sunny Jim, enlists, but does so only in a way that serves comedy rather than verisimilitude – taking Dan Macphail's place after he has been disappointed in love. We later find out, in the post-war story "Sunny Jim Returns", that he never serves overseas, having moved from one British base to another as the Army's most coveted potato peeler (Munro 1997: 390–94). The war remains a mysterious, barely explicable event occurring in a distant, less comic universe. Something similar happens to another character created for the Glasgow evening newspapers, J.J. Bell's Wee Mac-Greegor, a character who had been appearing in stories in the *Glasgow Evening Times* since 1901, and whose wartime escapades were collected in *Wee MacGreegor Enlists* (1915). But here again, the war is far distant and acts as little more than a plot device – in this case functioning as another obstacle in MacGreegor's long-running on-off relationship with his girl Christina.

But when this demotic, vernacular comedy engages more fully with the war, as it does in R.W. Campbell's Spud Tamson books, the effect is altogether different. Spud Tamson as he appears in the first of the sequence, *Private Spud Tamson* (1915), is the Roman Catholic son

---

[7] See, for example, the stories "Erchie's Work in Wartime", "Coal Rations", "A Wave of Temperance", and "Citizen Soldier", in Munro 1996.

of a rag-and-bone man who lives up Murder Close in Glasgow's Gallowgate. He is one of several incorrigibles and colourful down-and-outs who have joined, for the usual disreputable reasons, the very unheroic Glasgow Militia. The comic idiom and the use of vernacular seem deliberately employed to remind the reader of Munro and Bell. But while Sunny Jim and Erchie and Wee MacGreegor seem resolutely unchanged by war, Tamson is transformed by it. Tamson's Colonel is quite explicit in this, describing his men as "all the same": "in peace times you find him convicted daily for drunkenness, absence, insolence, and a hundred other things, yet in war he is always a hero" (Campbell 1915: 267). Tamson duly confirms this view, turning from a pre-war ne'er-do-well into a sergeant with a Distinguished Conduct Medal. By the book's end he has saved the life of the colonel and won the Victoria Cross and the hand of his beloved for his efforts. The transformation he undergoes, from dissolute life in the provinces to a meaningful, self-respecting identity as a soldier in the national cause, is common to that portrayed in many British books of the war. Charles Murray has the speaker of his "Fae France" echo the point as he acknowledges that at home "mony a yark an' ruggit lug I got to gar me gree, / But here, oonless I'm layin' on, I'm seldom latten be".

This transformation is the paradigm of what is probably the best-selling book by a Scottish author in the Great War, Ian Hay's *The First Hundred Thousand* (1915).[8] This book – published serially in *Blackwood's Magazine* from November 1914 to November 1915 – details the process through which working-class Scotsmen of low self esteem and dubious morality are welded into a cohesive and principled force by their Anglo-Scots officers. This is certainly not portrayed as the imposition of an English discipline on Scottish men (at least not explicitly) – for any number of reasons this would be too crude for books like these, which are written with at least one eye on propaganda value. Neither is it a moralising discourse in which working class Scottish vices are suppressed by British virtues. For Campbell and Hay go out of their way to attempt something a little more subtle – suggesting that the British army works not by suppressing existing characteristics, but rather by channelling them in all

---

[8] For a valuable discussion of the book, see Urquhart 1999.

their diversity into the great work of empire. Britishness doesn't so much cancel out Scottishness as give it a field within which it might be purposively expressed.

Precisely because the enemy is seen to be an efficient, rational-ising Prussianism that subdues the individuality of its functionaries,[9] the wartime fiction of Britishness (of which these examples of Campbell and Hay are typical) employs a rhetoric of voluntaryism, in which regional and personal idiosyncrasy is celebrated. Britishness, in this context, comfortably accommodates the local, the regional, and the national. Hay's Captain Blaikie is allowed to manifest a strong national pride alongside his manifest commitment to the British imperium. "Scotland for Ever!" intones this most anglicised of officers as he prepares on the eve of the Battle of Loos, in which he will be killed (Hay 1915: 282). Hay, indeed, has such confidence in the complicity of his readers to go as far as to recruit, rather impertinently, two historical heroes of Scottish independence to the British cause, renaming for the purposes of his fiction the Argyll and Sutherland Highlanders as the Bruce and Wallace Highlanders.

In attempting to manufacture consent for Britishness in these books, Hay and Campbell draw on an established model of late-Victorian and Edwardian British popular fiction – that of the liminal subject who discovers a strong and assertive individualism through identification with the work of empire and imperial adventure. Camp-bell's Colonel Corkleg and Captain Greens make this explicit in one of the more didactic passages of *Private Spud Tamson*, where they suggest that the ills of slum life, and its attendant threat of socialism, can best be remedied by giving Scottish soldiers and workers a greater share in empire. As Corkleg puts it, "their blood has sealed the bonds of Empire. Let us give their children a share of the Empire's treasure" (Campbell 1915: 270). Spud Tamson becomes the exemplar of this.

---

[9] An essay in *Blackwood's* in 1915, during the serialisation of *The First Hundred Thousand*, argued, for example, that Prussianised Germany, has "turned out millions of well-educated men and women to the same pattern; it has nipped all independence, free-thought, and originality in the bud, and has imposed on all alike a blind and unquestioning faith in the superior, be he officer, official, professor, or statesman, with the necessary result that the German does everything he is ordered to do and believes implicitly in everything he is told by this same higher authority" ("G" 1915: 619). For a range of similar views, see Wallace 1988: 29–42.

After further war adventures in *Sergeant Spud Tamson V. C.* (1918), we find him heading off to Canada and a career in the Royal Canadian Mounted Police in *Spud Tamson Out West* (1924) – "building Britain's greatness o'er the foam", to quote the Robert Service poem with which the book ends (Campbell 1924: 247).[10]

This post-war crossing of the Atlantic to Canada was, of course, taken later by John Buchan, who was perhaps Scotland's most significant contributor to the literature of imperial adventure. His *Mr Standfast* (begun in 1917, published in 1919) offers a prime example of the adaptation of the colonial adventure to the conditions of wartime. It is the novel in which Richard Hannay, the hero of two earlier tales, *The Thirty-Nine Steps* (1915) and *Greenmantle* (1916), makes most explicit the values for which he feels he is fighting. (Hannay is at this stage juggling rather improbably between jobs as a secret agent and a Brigadier in the British Infantry in Flanders.) The key moment in the early part of the novel is his realisation of a vision of the ideal world for which he fights, as he stands on a ridge of the Cotswolds above the ancient Roman Fosse Way:

In that moment I had a kind of revelation. I had a vision of what I had been fighting for, what we all were fighting for. It was peace, deep and holy and ancient, peace older than the oldest wars, peace which would endure when all our swords were hammered into ploughshares. It was more; for in that hour England took hold of me. Before my country had been South Africa, and when I thought of home it had been the wide sun-steeped spaces of the veld or some scented glen of the Berg. But now I realized that I had a new home. I understood what a precious thing this little England was, how old and kindly and comforting, how wholly worth striving for. The freedom of an acre of her soil was cheaply bought by the blood of the best of us. (Buchan [1919] 1981: 21)

This is not merely a standard evocation of Englishness, for it is rather an invocation of an England seen through British and Imperial eyes – the book never lets us forget that Hannay is by birth a Scot and by upbringing a South African. That is to say, Buchan isn't simply mimicking a Rupert Brooke version of Englishness, but is rather

---

[10] Campbell returned to this theme in his *A Prairie Parson* (1925), with the character of Gordon Rollow, an officer in the Scots Greys who becomes a Church of Scotland minister on the prairie and a staunch advocate of British settlement in Canada.

constructing an England that is part of an Imperial Britain of the imagination. This larger sense of an informing Britishness and Imperialism already announced in the central character is reinforced by the novel's geography – and in particular in the journey Hannay makes to Skye through the Western Highlands. In terms of plot development Hannay's travels, which take up a significant part of the first half of the novel, are negligible. The conclusion that might be drawn is that – rather like Humphry Clinker's tour of Scotland – the journey is more important thematically as a way of symbolically binding a unified Great Britain.[11] It gives Buchan an opportunity to engage in the vivid and dramatic portrayal of landscape, at which he is a master, but it also allows him to introduce us to types of honest Scotsmen, like Andrew Amos, who can serve the British cause faithfully while losing none of his integrity and his identity as a Borders radical.

What is perhaps most significant about Buchan's novel is the way it attempts to use literature itself as a means of creating this unified Britain. The novel, as its title suggests, uses Bunyan's *Pilgrim's Progress* as its central structuring device. *Pilgrim's Progress* is both the key to the codes used by the British Agents, and also the allegorical frame within which Buchan invites us to read Hannay's moral as well as physical progress throughout the story.[12] It is significant, then, that Hannay's pilgrimage takes him across a wider Britain. In this it anticipates an inter-war literature that draws powerfully on metaphors of pilgrimage through the British landscape, which takes in writers like A.G. McDonnell and H.V. Morton, and which can be seen in Michael Powell and Emeric Pressburger's *A Canterbury Tale* in the Second World War. It also prefigures the countryside writing of James Ramsay MacDonald, the Scottish leader of the British Labour Party, who shared Buchan's abiding fondness for the English countryside. Ramsay MacDonald would, in the 1930s, travel through these same Cotswolds and describe his journey as having the aspect of a "pilgrimage of grace" as he "passed cottages which were shrines, and

---

[11] For the argument about *Humphry Clinker*, see Crawford 1992: 66–75.

[12] For other examples of the use of Bunyan in the shaping of pilgrimage narratives of the war, see Parfitt 1988: 12–25. Buchan would later describe *The Pilgrim's Progress* as the "constant companion" of his youth, and write of his own Hannay-like devotion to the beauties of the historical landscape of Oxfordshire in Buchan 1940: 17, 168.

went through villages which invited us to return to them as our 'last abode on earth, to pray and die'" (MacDonald 1936: 80).

Yet the notion that Buchan is encouraging us to read the novel through the wider British literary tradition is never very far away – offering support to the general arguments made by Paul Fussell and Samuel Hynes about the significance of literary tradition in helping shape the consciousness of war. No one, for example, could use the phrase "this little England" as Hannay does, without immediately bringing to mind "this England" of John of Gaunt's speech in Shakespeare's *Richard II*. The landscape description, with its evocation of a sleeping timeless England tinged with the vestigial memory of Roman occupation, is one that also calls immediately to mind the England of Rudyard Kipling's *Puck of Pook's Hill* (1906). It might also be argued that it bears similarities to another wartime attempt to invest quasi-religious qualities in the English landscape – that of Rupert Brooke's autobiographical story of 1914, "An Unusual Young Man". Here, the protagonist suddenly realises, with the onset of war, that "the actual earth of England" holds for him "a quality which, if he'd ever been sentimental enough to use the word, he'd have called 'holiness'":

His astonishment grew as the full flood of "England" swept over him on from thought to thought. He felt the triumphant helplessness of a lover. Grey, uneven little fields, and small, ancient hedges rushed before him, wild flowers, elms and beeches, gentleness, sedate houses of red brick, proud unassuming, a countryside of rambling hills and friendly copses. He seemed to be raised high, looking down on a landscape compounded of the western view from the Cotswolds, and the Weald, and the high land of Wiltshire, and the Midlands seen from the hills above Prince's Risborough. And all this to the accompaniment of tunes heard long ago, an intolerable number of them being hymns. (Brooke [1914] 1956: 199)

The way this would be incorporated into a Scottish re-imagining of the English countryside has been suggested already with reference to Ramsay MacDonald. Another example can be found in *England Their England* (1933), written by another child of empire, the Indian-born Scotsman Archie MacDonell. The book's protagonist is Donald Cameron, a Scotsman who we first come across serving in the trenches. After the war he sets out to discover the essence of Englishness and, after several Wodehousian adventures, discovers it, like Brooke's Young Man and Buchan's Hannay, on the side of a hill overlooking a landscape sanctified by history – in this case, St Catherine's Hill above Winchester Cathedral:

Twenty or thirty feet below the grassy deckchair on which Donald was by now half dozing ran the circular trench which the Britons dug as a defence against the Legions. The line of the Roman road was clear, a chalky arrow, as far as the blue horizon. Saxon Alfred's statue might have been as visible through a field-glass as the pale yellow Norman transept of the cathedral was to the eye. The English school, whose motto puts kindliness above flourishment or learning, lay among its water-meads, and all around was the creator, the inheritor, the ancestor, and the descendant of it all, the green and kindly land of England. (MacDonell [1933] 1941: 293)

If further confirmation is required that this is a British as much as an English vision of the English landscape, it's worth looking to the end of Buchan's quest in *Mr Standfast*. As the novel's end approaches, and he has identified his old South African friend as the Mr Standfast of his allegory, his thoughts turn to his future with his girl, Mary – an English rose who quotes Keats in times of stress:

And at the thought of Mary a flight of warm and happy hopes seemed to settle on my mind. I was looking again beyond the war to that peace which she and I would some day inherit, I had a vision of a green English landscape, with its far-flung scents of wood and meadow and garden. … And that face of all my dreams, with the eyes so childlike and brave and honest, as if they, too, saw beyond the dark to a radiant country. A line of an old song, which had been a favourite of my father's, sang itself in my ears:

There's an eye that ever weeps and a fair face will be fain
When I ride through Annan Water wi' my bonny bands again! (Buchan [1919] 1981: 342)

What would otherwise be a difficulty if we accept the separation of English and Scottish literatures – the fact that Hannay celebrates an English landscape by associating it with a Scottish Border ballad – is straightforwardly resolved if we accept the idea of a British literature that Buchan appears to be promoting.

In this, it is possible to see Buchan following closely the example of the British writer who exemplifies a hybridised imperial Britishness in the period, Rudyard Kipling. Time and again Kipling features as a reference point for many of the Scottish writers mentioned. Hannay's exploits in playing what he calls in *Greenmantle*, "the Great Game" of counter-espionage, for example, carry an obvious reference to the "Great Game" of Kipling's *Kim*. And although Hannay is a good deal older than Kim, he shares with him a patchwork imperial identity: Kim is the Irish foster-child of India, while Hannay is the Scottish foster-child of South Africa – a recognition that gives weight, perhaps, to Martin Green's contention in his *Dreams of Adventure, Deeds of Empire* that Buchan might properly be regarded as the Kipling of post-war England (Green 1980: 323).

The journal in which Kipling's literary and political legacy was most clearly manifested, and which serialised the novels of Munro, Hay, and Buchan, was *Blackwood's*. Lord Birkenhead would later characterise "the Service people who read *Blackwood's*" as the "blind idolators" of the Kipling ethos (Birkenhead 1978: 260). That ethos was manifested, both before and during the war, in the monthly tales of colonial life, "From the Outposts", which were very much in the early style of Kipling's *Plain Tales from the Hills*, *Life's Handicap*, and *Soldiers Three*, as well as in impassioned imperialist editorials, "Musings without Method", strongly in the Kipling vein. The wartime work of Campbell and Hay, some of it first published in *Blackwood's*, contains frequent references to Kipling's work. As war broke out, *Blackwood's* was serialising Hay's *The Lighter Side of School Life*, a book which retailed a fictional version of Hay's experiences as a Fettes schoolmaster in a manner reminiscent of Kipling's *Stalky & Co.* (1899) – which had also patently influenced Ian Maclaren's *Young Barbarians* (1907). Campbell's *John Brown: Confessions of a New Army Cadet* (1919) similarly incorporated many of the qualities of *Stalky & Co.* alongside those of *Tom Brown's Schooldays* – not least the emphasis on a robust individualism and a suspicion of overt Jingoism. Campbell's Lieutenant Blase-Bones is appalled to find in the cadets' quarters a novel by "that beastly fellow H.G. Wells" and recommends to the miscreant that "if you feel you want to read, get Kipling and the *Morning Post*" (Campbell 1919: 146).[13] This lieutenant is very much of the same school as Hay's subaltern Bobby Little, whose only books are the "forty or so volumes" of the Service edition

---

[13] Wells was a frequent target for opprobrium in *Blackwood's* editorials during the war. See, for example, "Musings Without Method" 1914, 1915.

of Kipling, released early in the war by Macmillan (Hay 1915: 196).[14]
Campbell collected a volume of verse in the style of Robert Service
(Service, at the time styled "The Canadian Kipling", is another inter-
esting example of the hybrid British imperial writer – an English-born,
Scottish-bred, Canadian emigrant who worked as a stretcher-bearer
during the war) and of Kipling's *Barrack-Room Ballads*, titled *The
Making of Micky McGhee: And Other Stories in Verse* (1916).[15] In
one poem "The Border Breed" he makes explicit one of his models,
beginning the poem, "I crave for the style of Kipling, the touch that
Tennyson made, / To write of the Border gallants who served in a
Scots Brigade" (Campbell 1916: 53).[16] Hay used Kipling again to
illustrate the bonding effect of basic training in *The First Hundred
Thousand* – a work that George Blake would later compare to
"Kipling's chronicles of the old Indian army" (Blake 1956: 19). In
attempting to explain the way in which the men are gradually learning
to merge their identities into the larger unit of the regiment, Hay's narrator draws upon Kipling – incidentally, and perhaps tellingly,
personifying his men as Tommy Atkins rather than as Jock:

Well, when he joined, his outstanding feature was a sort of surly independence, the
surliness being largely based upon the fear of losing the independence. He has got
over that now. He is no longer morbidly sensitive about his rights as a free and independent citizen and the backbone of the British electorate. He has bigger things to
think of. [...] He is undergoing the experience of the rivets in Mr Kipling's story of
The Ship that Found Herself. He is adjusting his perspectives. He is beginning to
merge himself with the regiment. (Hay 1915: 164–65)

The point once again is not that these writers are giving themselves
over to English values. For Kipling must not here be taken simply for
a narrowly English writer. Kipling was, after all, a man who could
describe England as "my favourite foreign country" and was the compulsive explorer of hybrid imperial identities (cited in Birkenhead

---

[14] There were, in fact, only 26 volumes in the Service Kipling, which appeared in
1914–15.
[15] For Service's popularity with British soldiers overseas, see "The Poems of Robert
W. Service" 1916: 306.
[16] According to its publishers, "these verses reveal the discovery of still another
Kipling". George Allen & Unwin Ltd advertisement, *Bookseller* 1916: 513.

1978: 243). He was the creator of Irish, Scottish, and cockney narrators and heroes, and the man whose *Barrack Room Ballads* first came to notice in Britain through their publication in Henley's *Scots Observer*. Taking this into account, it is surely more accurate and meaningful to describe him as primarily a British or an Imperial writer. The Kipling story to which Hay refers, "The Ship that Found Herself", from *The Day's Work* (1898), illustrates this, being a parable of imperial union in which a Scots-built ship makes its first crossing of the Atlantic under the command of a Scottish skipper and the watchful eye of a Scottish engineer.

This sense of a British rather than a specifically Scottish or English cultural identity is reinforced if we look at another area of popular culture that is often argued to have a significant impact on the consciousnesses of war: Music Hall and Variety Theatre. For it's important to note the extent to which, even by 1914, this initially localised entertainment had developed a broad network of national entertainers. An important figure in this was the Edinburgh impresario Edward Moss who had established the significantly-titled "Empire" theatre chain across Great Britain before the war. One of the effects of this national entertainment network was that the routines, songs and patter of many English entertainers were familiar to Scottish audiences, while Scots entertainers had become familiar to the English – and indeed to audiences in the dominions. Perhaps the best-known of the latter was Harry Lauder, who enjoyed great popularity and immediate recognition on both sides of the border and in the wider English-speaking world. In common with a number of popular stars, Lauder reinforced Variety Theatre's reputation for patriotism by taking a vigorous part in recruitment and in civilian and military entertainment.[17] In 1916 and 1917, for example, he appeared in a popular revue in London's West End, singing of "The Laddies who Fought and Won" as he ushered a large detachment of Scots Guards onto the stage. He was a popular troop entertainer too, one of his open-air shows, in June 1917 at Arras, attracting 5000 soldiers in one evening. Lauder's contribution to the war effort was recognised popularly: the 91st Battalion Canadian Militia became known as the "Harry Lauders" because of

---

[17] For a short discussion of the role played by Kipling in this, see MacInnes 1972.

the jaunty angle of their Lauderesque bonnets, while the HLI (High-land Light Infantry) were sometimes known to wags as "Harry Lauder's Infantry". Lauder also won official recognition when he was knighted in 1919 for his contribution to the war effort.

English music-hall stars equally provided songs and patter for soldiers' use. When Captain Wagstaffe in *The First Hundred Thousand* talks ironically of a forced withdrawal, he says "We shall have a cheery walk back, I *don't* think" – a catchphrase that contemporary readers would immediately have associated with the English music-hall comedian Harry Tate. This phrase, like his "Goodbyee" and "How's your father", was ubiquitous among the war's ironists, whether Scottish or English. In song, too, the effect is one of blending rather than of separation. In Campbell's *Private Spud Tamson*, the Scottish soldiers march to their barracks singing music-hall and patri-otic songs. Some sing "My name is Jock McCraw, / An' I dinnae care a straw, / For I've something in the bottle for the mornin'," while oth-ers sing "We're soldiers of the King, my lads, / Who've been, my lads, who've seen, my lads, / The fights for Britain's Glory, lads". And then when they march away, they step off to "'The Cock o' the North', played by the pipers, and followed by 'Stop your ticklin', Jock', drummed out by the band" (Campbell 1915: 71–73). In *The First Hundred Thousand* the men go on a route march and sing a mixture of Lauder's songs, "I Love a Lassie", "Roaming in the Gloaming", and "Its Just Like Being at Hame" and English music-hall favourites, "Hallo, Hallo, Who's your Lady Friend?", "You're My Baby", "Who Were You With Last Night?", and of course that other song of mongrel Britishness, "Tipperary" (Hay 1915: 10–11). Robert Ross recalled officers of the Gordon Highlanders in support in Artois in 1916 singing traditional English songs like "John Peel" alongside Scottish standards such as "My Ain Wee Hoose" and "Auld Lang Syne" (Ross 1918: 198–99). If, as authorities like J.G. Fuller, John Brophy and Eric Partridge suggest, popular entertainment forms played an important part in the way soldiers constructed an oral culture of war, it is clear that, as with literature, there is a good case for describing this properly as a British or British Imperial culture (Brophy and Partridge 1969, Fuller 1990).

There is perhaps little need to claim originality for this argument about a pervasive Britishness in the literature and popular culture of Scotland, because this was an uncontentious fact to many contemporary commentators. To claim that "there is not the remotest reason why the majority of modern Scots writers [of the period] should be considered Scots at all" might be dismissed as an overstatement of the case, were they not the words of Lewis Grassic Gibbon in *Scottish Scene* (Gibbon and MacDiarmid 1934: 189). According to Gibbon, "the chief Literary Lights which modern Scotland claims to light up the scene of her night are in reality no more than the commendable writers of the interesting English county of Scotshire" (Gibbon and MacDiarmid 1934: 199). G. Gregory Smith was less mordant but shared a not dissimilar sentiment in ending his *Scottish Literature: Character and Influence* (1919) with the historically distant character of Sir Walter Scott. Smith's epilogue on modern literature attempts to address the fact that, as he puts it,

modern conditions seem to put the thesis of a well-defined and sustained Scotticism to a very severe test, if not to make it preposterous for any time after the eighteenth century, when the Scot encouraged himself to forget his differences as best he could. (Gregory Smith 1919: 276)

His response is to point rather weakly to what he describes as "some hint of traditional character in the writers of to-day" (Gregory Smith 1919: 285). It was the tepidness of Smith's response to the contemporary state of Scottish letters that encouraged T.S. Eliot infamously to use the past tense in his review of Smith's book "Was there a Scottish Literature?", and which prompted and helped give shape to Hugh MacDiarmid's experiments in nationalist Modernism. MacDiarmid himself was forced to start from the point of acknowledging in 1923 that "there are no Scottish stories today in the sense that there is a Scottish poetry distinct from English poetry. There never has been a Scottish prose" (MacDiarmid [1923] 1996: 43).

To underline the point that the work of most Scottish popular writers in the early twentieth century was inextricably tangled up in a Britishness that it had played some part (perhaps even a disproportionate part) in defining, then, isn't to go against the grain. Rather it is to give the base point from which Scottish Modernism ought properly

to be understood. For Scottish Modernism, particularly as it was manifested in the work of MacDiarmid, found itself weighed down with a
double burden. While much of Modernism sought self-consciously to
separate itself from problems of national identity with a willed internationalism, Scottish Modernism still felt itself compelled to address
specifically "national" problems. While Virginia Woolf could employ
the experiment of Modernism to interrogate the English establishment
from a lofty artistic height in a work like *Mrs Dalloway* or Joyce
could, from his émigré's distance, guy Cyclopean notions of Irishness
in *Ulysses*, a writer like MacDiarmid felt it incumbent upon himself to
define Scottishness and construct its national literary history even as
he was subjecting it to the revision promised by his experimental
technique. In practice he had to take on simultaneously the tasks of
revival and revision that had occupied discrete phases in the development of other national literatures, requiring him, in effect, to be both
antiquarian and iconoclast, founding father and schismatic – a kind of
combination of Douglas Hyde and James Joyce.

It is perhaps this pressure that skewed Modernism in Scotland.
For it to be a viable idea, Scottish Modernism had to show that both
its terms were operative and meaningful, and in order for that to be the
case MacDiarmid had to prove sceptics like Gregory Smith and Eliot
wrong; he had both to furnish his credentials as an international literary moderniser and to instantiate a living Scottish literature, drawing
on its own discrete traditions, that was emphatically not the compromised British literature of the previous thirty years. Under this pressure, Scottish Modernism in the hands of MacDiarmid developed into
an uneasy combination of revolutionary and reactionary impulses,
becoming by turns liberating and repressive, attractively inspirational
and depressingly rebarbative.

The revolution resulted in one of Modernism's major achievements in the British context: the creation, in MacDiarmid's synthetic
Scots, of a language capable of presenting thought and complexities of
feeling in ways previously elusive to the vernacular. But the price that
was paid for this was a belittling reaction, visible in MacDiarmid's
attitudes towards the English and to Scottish popular culture. Where
Gregory Smith had talked of the forgetting of differences between
Scotland and England, MacDiarmid argued that it was essential to a

modern Scottish literature not just to remember, but to exaggerate those differences. This is a practice he adopted vehemently, unattractively, and often unproductively – later going as far as to write that hatred of the English had developed into his "lifework" (MacDiarmid [1943] 1994: 16). While this may be a necessary stage of reaction in the movement towards a national literature, it is perhaps not the ideal base (as MacDiarmid seemed to think it was) on which one might be built. And while other Modernists tended to express anxiety about the threat of a value-deadening popular culture, few went to MacDiarmid's extremes in their castigations. MacDiarmid's vitriolic assaults on figures like Harry Lauder, and his comments on "the current stranglehold of mediocrity in Scotland" and "the moronic character of most of our people", suggest that he had allowed his anxieties about the deadening effects of British popular culture to cloud his better judgement (MacDiarmid [1943] 1994: xiii).

Doubtless several of these less attractive elements derive from MacDiarmid's own particularities, but it is nonetheless arguable that they spring from a more generally held anxiety – an anxiety exacerbated by the popular literature and culture of the war – that the co-option of Scottish literature in the British project had become so complete as to make any declaration of cultural independence almost impossible.

Bibliography

Lord Birkenhead. 1978. *Rudyard Kipling*. London: Weidenfeld and Nicolson.

Blake, George. 1956. *Annals of Scotland 1895–1955*. London: British Broadcasting Corporation.

Brooke, Rupert. [1914] 1956. "An Unusual Young Man" in Hassall, Christopher (ed.) *The Prose of Rupert Brooke*. London: Sidgwick and Jackson. 195–200.

Brophy, John and Eric Patridge. 1969. *The Long Trail: Soldiers' Songs and Slang 1914–18*. London: Sphere.

Buchan, John. [1919] 1981. *Mr Standfast*. Harmondsworth: Penguin.

—. 1940. *Memory Hold-the-Door*. London: Hodder and Stoughton.

Campbell, R.W. 1915. *Private Spud Tamson*. Edinburgh and London: Blackwood.

—. 1916. *The Making of Micky McGhee: And Other Stories in Verse*. London: George Allen and Unwin.

—. 1919. *John Brown: Confessions of a New Army Cadet*. Edinburgh: Chambers.

—. 1924. *Spud Tamson Out West*. London and Edinburgh: Chambers.

Crawford, Robert. 1992. *Devolving English Literature*. Oxford: Clarendon Press.

DeGroot, Gerard J. 1996. *Blighty: British Society in the Era of the Great War*. London: Longman.

Finkelstein, David. 1998. "Literature, Propaganda, and the First World War: the Case of *Blackwood's Magazine*' in Treglown, Jeremy and Bridget Bennett (eds) *Grub Street and the Ivory Tower: Literary Journalism and Literary Scholarship from Fielding to the Internet*. Oxford: Clarendon. 91–111.

Fuller, J.G. 1990. *Troop Morale and Popular Culture in the British and Dominion Armies 1914–1918*. Oxford: Clarendon Press.

Fussell, Paul. 1975. *The Great War and Modern Memory*. Oxford: Oxford University Press.

"G". 1915. "The Blindness of Germany" in *Blackwood's Magazine* (May 1915).

George Allen & Unwin Ltd advertisement. *Bookseller* (October 1916). 513.

Gibbon, Lewis Grassic and Hugh MacDiarmid. 1934. *Scottish Scene: or the Intelligent Man's Guide to Albyn*. London: Jarrolds.

Green, Martin. 1980. *Dreams of Adventure, Deeds of Empire*. London: Routledge and Kegan Paul.

Gregory Smith, G. 1919. *Scottish Literature: Character and Influence*. London: Macmillan.

Hay, Ian. 1915. *The First Hundred Thousand: Being the Unofficial Chronicle of a Unit of "K (1)"*. Edinburgh and London: Blackwood.

Hynes, Samuel. 1990. *A War Imagined*. London: The Bodley Head.

Keir, David. 1952. *The House of Collins: The Study of a Scottish Family of Publishers from 1789 to the Present Day*. London: Collins.

Kingsford, R.J.L. 1970. *The Publishers Association 1896–1946: With an Epilogue*. Cambridge: Cambridge University Press.

MacDiarmid, Hugh. [1923] 1996. "Leaves from a London Scottish Diary" in Calder, Angus, Glen Murray and Alan Riach (eds) *The Raucle Tongue: Hitherto uncollected prose*. Manchester: Carcanet. vol 1.

—. [1943] 1994. *Lucky Poet: A Self-Study in Literature and Political Ideas*. Manchester: Carcanet.

Macdonald, Catriona M.M. and E.W. McFarland (eds). 1999. *Scotland and the Great War*, East Linton: Tuckwell.

MacDonald, J. Ramsay. 1936. *At Home and Abroad*. London: Jonathan Cape.

MacDonell, A.G. [1933] 1941. *England Their England*. London: World Books.

MacInnes, Colin. 1972. "Kipling and the Music Halls" in Gross, John (ed.) *Rudyard Kipling: The Man, his Work and his World*. London: Weidenfeld and Nicolson. 57–61.

Marwick, Arthur. 1965. *The Deluge: British Society and the First World War*. London: Macmillan.

Milton, Colin. 1995. "*A Sough O' War*: The Great War in the Poetry of North-East Scotland" in Hewitt, David (ed.) *Northern Visions: Essays on the Literary Identity of Northern Scotland in the Twentieth Century*. East Linton: Tuckwell. 1–38.

Montague, C.E. 1922. *Disenchantment*. London: Chatto and Windus.

Morgan, Charles. 1943. *The House of Macmillan (1843–1943)*. London: Macmillan.

Munro, Neil. 1996. *Erchie & Jimmy Swan* (intro. and annot. by Brian D. Osborne and Ronald Armstrong). Edinburgh: Birlinn.

—. 1997 *Para Handy: The Collected Stories from "The* Vital Spark*", "In Highland Harbours with Para Handy" and "Hurricane Jack of the* Vital Spark*"* (intro. and annot. by Brian D. Osborne and Ronald Armstrong). Edinburgh: Birlinn.

"Musings Without Method" in *Blackwood's Magazine* (December 1914) 857–66, (April 1915) 565–76.

Parfitt, George. 1988. *Fiction of the First World War*. London: Faber.

"The Poems of Robert W. Service" in *Bookseller* (July 1916). 306.

Robb, George. 2002. *British Culture and the First World War*. Basingstoke: Palgrave.

Ross, Captain Robert B. 1918. *The Fifty-First in France*. London, New York, and Toronto: Hodder and Stoughton.

Royle, Trevor (ed.). 1990. *In Flanders Fields: Scottish Poetry and Prose of the First World War*. Edinburgh: Mainstream.

Spear, Hilda D. and Bruce Pandrich (eds). 1989. *Sword and Pen: Poems of 1915 From Dundee and Tayside*. Aberdeen: Aberdeen University Press.

Spiers, Edward. 1996. "The Scottish Soldier at War" in Cecil, Hugh and Peter H. Liddle (eds) *Facing Armageddon: The First World War Experienced*. London: Leo Cooper. 314–35.

Urquhart, Gordon. 1999. "Confrontation and Withdrawal: Loos, Readership and 'The First Hundred Thousand'" in Macdonald, Catriona M.M. and E.W. McFarland (eds) *Scotland and the Great War*. East Linton: Tuckwell. 125–44.

Wallace, Stuart. 1988. *War and the Image of Germany: British Academics 1914–1918*. Edinburgh: John Donald.

Winter, Jay. 1999. "Popular Culture in Wartime Britain" in Roshwald, Aviel and Richard Stites (eds) *European Culture in the Great War: The Arts, Entertainment, and Propaganda, 1914–1918*. Cambridge: Cambridge University Press. 330–48.

MacDiarmid and Russia Revisited

Alexander Mackay

Hugh MacDiarmid's borrowings from Russian writers take on a progressively cultic aspect as his interest in Dostoevskii, Solov'ev, Chekhov and Maiakovskii gives way to obsessive fascination with the personalities of Lenin and Stalin. His engagement with these writers, particularly in the case of Chekhov, reveals his ostensible "aesthetic internationalism" as motivated instead by an intensifying need to resist English influence, which ultimately disables his programme for aesthetic renewal in Scotland. Keywords: Dostoevskii, Chekhov, Maiakovskii, D.S. Mirskii, Lenin, Stalin, Scottish Renaissance.

"Scottish artists have not written much. They have been unfortunately free from the habit of issuing manifestos." (MacDiarmid 1984: 73)

Critics of all colours, but particularly those who are best disposed towards MacDiarmid, have repeatedly counselled caution in dealing with the publicistic prose he produced in the 1920s. Three provisos are habitually advanced in this regard: first, that MacDiarmid was often working under intolerable domestic and financial pressure; second, that the urge to propagandise was, justifiably or not, consistently stronger than the urge to enlighten; the third, and perhaps most problematic, particularly when taken in conjunction with either of the above, is that MacDiarmid self-consciously embraced conflict and contradiction, variously characterising the Scottish condition, the so-called "Gaelic idea", and of course himself, as locations at which extremes meet in order to produce dynamic syntheses. This and other aspects of MacDiarmid's literary personality make it notably difficult, in general terms, to distinguish the straw targets from the real ones; when we consider in addition, however, that the 1920s also mark the apparent height of MacDiarmid's engagement with Russian literary and philosophical authors, the task of examining the mechanics of how MacDiarmid's encounter with Russia was mediated becomes doubly problematic. On one hand, if we take MacDiarmid at his "Internationalist" word, the contours of his emergent aesthetics cannot be traced effectively in isolation from the European contexts he self-consciously constructs for it; on the other hand, and for the reasons we have outlined, judgement on the weight and significance of any particular strand of European influence must be deferred until we see precisely how its threads are developed in later work, when the storms of the 1920s and 1930s have subsided. It is in the 1920s, however, albeit under the sign of caution, that we must begin.

1. The nineteenth-century legacy

MacDiarmid's determination to advertise his voracious appetite for literary, philosophical and political reading, and the associated habit of littering both prose and poetry with attributed and unattributed quotation, make any exercise in tracing influence deeply problematic. Peter McCarey's *Hugh MacDiarmid and the Russians* (McCarey 1987), which is a detailed attempt to establish relationships not simply of "neutral" influence, but of fundamental co-sympathy with a range of Russian writers and thinkers, is consistently sensitive to the difficulties – and opportunities – this presents. McCarey organises his study on a roughly chronological basis, focussing as much on the contradictions, transitions and slippages in MacDiarmid's engagement with Russia as on similarity and consistency. He also resists the persistent scholarly temptation to treat "influence" itself as the obedient creature of positivism, which is therefore unable to vary in its forms and effects, not to mention its depth. This produces a series of highly differentiated outcomes in the comparative process: McCarey's final chapter, for example, is a convincing statement of the philosophical affinities between MacDiarmid and Lev Shestov, confirming the significance of MacDiarmid's repeated characterisation of Shestov as his "master".[1] We may be entitled to speculate that Shestov's strident irrationalism was as opportune pragmatically as it was philosophically, or

---

[1] Shestov as "master" appears in the poetry on three separate occasions – in "Further Passages from 'The Kind of Poetry I Want'" (MacDiarmid 1993: 1: 622); "In Memoriam James Joyce" (MacDiarmid 1993: 2: 745); "Direadh I" (MacDiarmid 1993: 2: 1170) – and in *Lucky Poet* in 1943 (MacDiarmid [1943] 1972: 402). See also McCarey 1987: 162–200.

to pause at the two men's very different responses to the political terror of the Soviet 1930s, a question to which we will return. We may
also take issue with McCarey's identification of certain passages in
MacDiarmid as "Shestovian": MacDiarmid's recantation of his Drunk
Man's earlier libidinous credo, for example, expressed in "Ode to all
Rebels" – "Hoo could I trust love again if a' / The tender ties twixt us
twa / Like this could be wantonly snapt...?" – is probably more
closely related to MacDiarmid's personal life than Shestovian doubt
(MacDiarmid 1993: 1: 487).[2] Yet none of this detracts too much from
the fact that MacDiarmid was profoundly affected by, in particular,
Shestov's *In Job's Balances*, published in English translation in 1932,
and that the spirit of Shestov, far more than his substantive immediate
influence on *Stony Limits and Other Poems*, stayed with MacDiarmid
for much of his life.

By way of contrast, and this time on the ostensibly stronger
poetic evidence of MacDiarmid's translation of Aleksandr Blok's
"The Stranger" [*Neznakomka*] (MacDiarmid 1993: 1: 88–9; Blok
1960–63: 2: 185–86) and his adaptation of the same poet's "I know
that you will come" [*Predchuvstvuiu Tebia*] (MacDiarmid 1993: 1:
90–91; Blok 1960–63: 1: 94), McCarey's argument is much less a
claim for direct influence or philosophical and poetic affinity than it is
a straightforward critical comparison of two loosely "symbolist" poets
from opposite ends of the European literary firmament (McCarey
1987: 65–114).[3] In the case of both Blok and Shestov the particularities of each object of comparison are not homogenised as aspects of a
common "tradition", nor are the specifics of their relationships to

---

[2] Equally, the lines "To make sex out ethereal and inspiring / Hides the belief that it's
ugly and obscene" and the epigraphs from Petronius, "In his appearance not
overdazzling...", and Jeremiah, "Wherefore are all they happy that deal very
treacherously?" (MacDiarmid 1993: 1: 491, 487) take on a different resonance when
read in conjunction with some of MacDiarmid's recently published letters, in which
he repeatedly returns to his treatment at the hands of his estranged first wife Peggy
and William McElroy. At the height of his agonies, at some unspecified point in 1937,
MacDiarmid imagines McElroy's end "through my hacking off your genitals and
stuffing them down your throat" (MacDiarmid [1937] 2001). The poem was deleted
from first edition of *Stony Limits and Other Poems* in 1934.
[3] MacDiarmid also translated Afanasii Fet's "The Aerial City" [Vozdushnyi gorod]
and Zinaida Gippius's "Her" [Ona]; see France and Glen (eds) 1989: 8–9.

MacDiarmid conflated. McCarey's treatment is designed not to desta-
bilise further what is already shifting and problematic ground by colluding in myth making or by accepting the word of MacDiarmid or of
the poetic text at face value. With regard to Dostoevskii and Vladimir
Solov'ev, however, McCarey's negotiations with these difficulties
reveal a glimpse of the greater problem that lurks beneath the surface
of MacDiarmid's Internationalist persona.

Alongside Lev Tolstoi, Solov'ev and Dostoevskii – one a religious philosopher and metaphysician who occasionally utilised poetic
form, the other a novelist who has been lionised, among many other
things, for his definitive indifference to it – are the dominant cultural
figures to emerge from late nineteenth-century Russia. Their massive
impact on Russia found only a belated echo in Britain, where Dostoevskii was not translated at all until 1881, the year of his death, over
thirty years after his work had first appeared in German.[4] When that
impact came, however, it came in the case of Dostoevskii with an unexpected and unparalleled force. Constance Garnett's translations of
Dostoevskii (1912–1920), in conjunction with critical works like John
Middleton Murry's *Fyodor Dostoevsky. A Critical Study* (Murry
1916), did not only make him as visible as any non-English writer, but
fuelled a veritable cult in his name.[5] The rise of the cult of Dostoevskii
had little to do with questions of poetic form, but rather with his
seeming re-invention of the novel and, more pertinently with regard to
MacDiarmid, with his place in literary Modernism. Sections of the
English literary press were the predictable motor of this cult and of a
burgeoning interest in Russian culture more generally, including the
Adelphi and A.R. Orage's *New Age*, to which MacDiarmid was a

---

[4] Robert Louis Stevenson first encountered Dostoevskii in a French translation of
Crime and Punishment, which prompted the response that "it nearly finished me" and
is "the greatest book I have easily read in ten years [sic]" (Stevenson 1995: 220–22).
In an earlier letter Stevenson writes: "Dostoieffsky is of course simply immense: it is
not reading a book, it is having a brain fever" (Stevenson 1995: 151). There is in fact
every reason to conclude that Dostoevskii's influence on Stevenson was far greater
than it was on MacDiarmid.

[5] Garnett's translation work reached an almost incredible pitch in her twelve-volume
series of Dostoevskii for Heinemann between 1912 and 1920; the first four volumes
were *The Brothers Karamazov* (1912), *The Idiot* (1913), *The Possessed* [The Devils]
(1913), and *Crime and Punishment* (1914). See also Murry 1916.

contributor as well as an avid reader.[6] It was in the pages of the *New Age*, however, that MacDiarmid's interest in Dostoevskii in the broad context of Modernism would be catalysed by altogether different factors: Janko Lavrin's *Dostoevsky and His Creation* (Lavrin 1920) was originally published as a series of articles in the *New Age* in 1918 as "Dostoevsky and Certain of His Problems", and it is this particular mediation of Dostoevskii's vision of the "Russian Idea", along with Oswald Spengler's "canonisation" of Dostoevskii in his *The Decline of the West*, that would seemingly prove decisive.

MacDiarmid's *A Drunk Man looks at the Thistle* (1926) is, to repeat a phrase used earlier, littered with references not so much to Dostoevskii's work, but quite specifically to Dostoevskii himself, or, yet more specifically, to the particular image of Dostoevskii mediated through Lavrin and Spengler.[7] MacDiarmid sees in Dostoevskii the possibility of an irresistible, spiritual nationalism, of which Scotland – or MacDiarmid himself – can only dream. In an address to Hermann Melville, figured on the wanderings of Ishmael, MacDiarmid turns to evocation of Dostoevskii thus:

And, thanks to thee, may aiblins reach
To what this Russian has to teach,
Closer than ony ither Scot,
Closer to me than my ain thocht,
Closer than my ain braith to me,
As close as to the Deity
Approachable in whom appears
This Christ o' the neist thoosand years. (MacDiarmid 1993: 1: 129)[8]

---

[6] MacDiarmid made almost weekly contributions to the *New Age* between April 1924 and July 1926 under the by-line "C.M. Grieve". His contributions after this period become more infrequent, but it is notable that the by-line "Hugh McDiarmid" or "Hugh M'Diarmid" appears from mid-1927 and is reserved for the specific topic of poetry.

[7] Peter McCarey's attempt to link Dostoevskii's "The Dream of a Ridiculous Man" [*Son smeshnogo cheloveka*] to MacDiarmid's "The Bonnie Broukit Bairn" is not only one of only two substantive examples of direct textual influence adduced, it is also extremely tenuous (McCarey 1987: 17–18).

[8] This is the other point at which McCarey detects a textual relationship to Dostoevskii, curiously comparing the sentiment to a passage from *Notes from Underground* (McCarey 1987: 23).

Amid a welter of allusions to the person or image of Dostoevskii,
MacDiarmid famously seizes upon Dostoevskii's Slavophile conception of Russia's historical mission in terms of "the final synthesis of
all mankind". Convinced of the racial affinity of the Celtic races with
the "East", MacDiarmid wishes a similar destiny upon the degenerate
and imperilled Scots:

> But even as the stane the builders rejec'
> Becomes the corner-stane, the time may be
> When Scotland sall find oot its destiny,
> And yield the *vse-chelovek* (MacDiarmid 1993: 1: 134)

This would appear to build upon MacDiarmid's earlier enlistment of Solov'ev in order to bolster his nascent conception of a
"Gaelic Idea", balancing Europe on its Western extremity as the "Russian Idea" does in the East, in the 1923 article "A Russo-Scottish
Parallelism" (MacDiarmid 1969). Solov'ev was also a frequent subject
of attention in the *New Age*, and, specifically, of a series of articles by
the same Janko Lavrin, although these did not appear until 1925–26
(Lavrin 1925–26). And yet, although Solov'ev displays Slavophile
tendencies in his rejection of Western rationalism as inadequate to the
task, this time in MacDiarmid's paraphrase, of "reconcil[ing] the universe to God" (Grieve 1925a), there are problems. On the simplest
level, MacDiarmid appears to be so bedazzled by the high-flown Slav
nationalism of Dostoevskii and (ostensibly, at least) Solov'ev that he is
able to ignore or bracket the theological precept with which it is inextricably bound. MacDiarmid's persistent attribution of many of the ills
afflicting Scottish society to the predominance of the Christian scrip-
tures in Scottish education generally ought to place him at odds with
both Dostoevskii and Solov'ev, neither of whom are able to conceive
of the "Russian Idea" in the absence of an orientation towards the im-
material hereafter of Christian theology (or, in the case of Dostoevskii
at least, a specifically Orthodox theology). MacDiarmid, to give perhaps the most memorable example of his religious aversion, authors
one of Scottish literature's most apt puns when he writes of "Christ as
the worm" in "To Circumjack Cencrastus", and cautions: "For we're
no used to snakes in Scotland here / And h'ae suffered frae Knox on
the heid sae lang" (MacDiarmid 1993: 1: 215). Yet MacDiarmid, even

as late as 1939, is still able to conceive of the need for only a very "slight" modification of Solov'ev's thought:

My poem ["To Circumjack Cencrastus"] envisages [the reconciliation of the lower orders of creation to St. Sophia] (and insists upon the part Scotland should, can and must play in that great task) [...] in purely intellectual – i.e. non-mystical and non-religious terms. (MacDiarmid [1939] 1984: 129)

The implication of this, as McCarey confirms, is clearly that Solov'ev's philosophical system – which conceives of rationalism as inadequate for, rather than opposed to, the Russian Idea, as merely a phase *en route* to the restoration of a higher spiritual unity – is in fact utterly inimical to MacDiarmid's incipient materialism (McCarey 1987: 41, 51). "Non-mystical" and "non-religious" are quite remarkable points of terminus in a devoted reading of Solov'ev, and their use reveals that MacDiarmid is in fact intent on equating the "Caledonian Antisyzygy" with the "Dialectical process", and that Solov'ev's thought is little more than unlikely, and unnecessary, collateral damage.

On another level, we must make the simple point that Dostoevskii is not Solov'ev. MacDiarmid appears initially to have associated the two under the broad heading of the "Russian Idea" and on the basis of their acquaintance during the later years of Dostoevskii's life. His gradual realisation of their very different conceptions of the "Russian Idea" – and of the role played in this distinction by Dostoevskii's Christian utopianism and Solov'ev's gradual rejection of nationalism – is confirmed only by the fact that he jettisons one comfortably in advance of the other. If Solov'ev is forced into an unholy association with dialectical materialism, Dostoevskii has earlier enjoyed the perhaps preferable fate of outright repudiation: the irreconcilability of Dostoevskii – "This Christ o' the neist thoosand years" – with faithlessness has dawned on MacDiarmid long before "To Circumjack Cencrastus", in which he is condemned, along with Christ and all his followers, for "preferrin' Christ to truth" (MacDiarmid 1993: 1: 182). The relationship between Dostoevskii and Solov'ev is in fact perfectly dramatised by a much later claim by Solov'ev's nephew and editor, made only a year before MacDiarmid's death. S.M. Solov'ev, while conceding that Solov'ev's influence is palpable in Dostoevskii's *The*

Brothers Karamazov, argues in his *Zhizn' i tvorcheskaia evoliutsiia Vladimira Solov'eva* [The Life and Artistic Evolution of Vladimir Solov'ev] that his uncle, far from being the one-dimensionally "spiritual" stereotype implied by his identification with Alesha Karamazov, was actually the basis for the characters of *both* Ivan and Alesha, and that "there is considerably more of Solov'ev in the older brother [Ivan]" [причем гораздо больше черт Соловьева в старшем брате] (Solov'ev 1977: 199).

Although it might be possible to recuperate MacDiarmid's interest in Dostoevskii and Solov'ev on the basis of this marvellously schismatic characterisation of the latter, the more compelling conclusion is somewhat different: MacDiarmid's relationships to both, partially revealed by even the briefest comparison of the two, were essentially superficial. That MacDiarmid's borrowings come from a range of sources through which the reception of Dostoevskii and Solov'ev were mediated is unavoidable, but it does have the consequence of preparing the ground for marked incongruities in the "applications" of anyone who, like MacDiarmid, is not especially burdened by the need for circumspection. These incongruities might appear positively harmonious, however, alongside those produced when we move to consider MacDiarmid's relationship to the new Russia that would sweep the world of Dostoevskii and Solov'ev away.

2: Poetry and Revolution

There can be no better illustration of the contradictory responses to the revolutions of 1917 than the later career of Blok, and never more so than in the description of him in an obituary written by another of MacDiarmid's significant Russian "others", Vladimir Maiakovskii. If Blok's poem "The Twelve" [*Dvenadtsat'*] stands as an ambivalent poetic sentinel at the boundary between two epochs in Russian history (Blok 1960–63: 3: 347–59),[9] then Maiakovskii's obituary reproduces that ambivalence at the level of sympathetic human dialogue: Mai-

---

[9] The best available translation of the poem is Sydney Goodsir Smith's Scots rendition, "The Twal", which also has the memorable dedication "Frae Alexander Beak" (Smith 1975: 108–19).

akovskii recounts a conversation with "a thin, stooped figure [Blok] who was warming himself beside a bonfire in front of the Winter Palace [...] in the first days of the revolution"; "I ask him: 'So what do you think?'; 'Good!' said Blok, and then he added, 'They've burned my library in the country'" [Спрашиваю: «Нравится?» – «Хорошо», сказал Блок, а потом прибавил: «У меня в деревне библиотеку сожгли»] (Maiakovskii 1955–61: 12: 21–22).

Although Edwin Morgan argues elsewhere in this volume that MacDiarmid was much closer in his poetic practice to Blok, it is nonetheless true that the central aesthetic principle in MacDiarmid's early attempts to renovate Scottish verse, namely a conviction of the potential *affinity* between Modernist and vernacular experimentation, would appear to place him very close to Maiakovskii (although it should be stated from the outset that the character of the "vernacular" available to Maiakovskii in the Imperial, centralising Russian language was quite different to that available to MacDiarmid at one remove from the centre of "English hegemony"). MacDiarmid famously identifies Maiakovskii as something of a role model, writing in 1926 that "A Scottish Mayakovsky at this juncture would be a Godsend" (MacDiarmid [1926] 1995: 372), and laments his death by suicide in his 1933 poem *In Memoriam Vladimir Mayakovsky*: "O would your nature now from Russia gone / Might reincarnate in a Scottish bard" (MacDiarmid 1993: 1: 1282). MacDiarmid, as ever, is untroubled by the contradictions implied by Maiakovskii's pre-revolutionary call to throw Dostoevskii (along with Pushkin and Tolstoi) "overboard from the Ship of Modernity" [*s Parokhoda sovremennosti*] (Burliuk et al. 1980: 179; 1912), contradictions that run all the deeper when we recall that Maiakovskii is not concerned here with Dostoevskii as a bearer of the Christian message, but rather as a "Classic" – and the classics, as he would later express it, were to be "nationalised". For it is not so much Maiakovskii's attitude to the vernacular, nor any other aspect of his poetic practice, that appeals to MacDiarmid, but rather his spirited iconoclasm, regardless of the object towards which it is directed. More specifically, the role his combatism plays in the construction of a very particular public/poetic persona; Maiakovskii was after all one of the very few major poets of the last century who made a habit in his early days of inviting audiences to discover whether he could fight as well as he could versify. Iconoclasm, a pronounced archetypal masculinity, and, as MacDiarmid makes clear in the same piece from *Contemporary Scottish Studies* on "synthetic Scots", the enlistment of these qualities in the quest for a broad and popular appeal:[10] all of these make Maiakovskii the very *image* of a poet who might indeed prove a "Godsend" for contemporary Scotland. Given the nature of the relationship between "Grieve" and "MacDiarmid", and the former's willed construction of a poetic persona who need not be confined to the page, it is clearly not poetry that is most at issue in this fevered reflection on the unattainable image of proletarian/intellectual perfection glimpsed in, or projected onto, Maiakovskii. That Maiakovskii's pre-revolutionary iconoclasm and aggression find a distinct, if uncomfortable, niche in the cultural politics of the post-revolutionary Soviet state might be considered decisive; in *Lucky Poet*, at a remove of some seventeen years, MacDiarmid reaffirms his admiration for Maiakovskii, and for his

> capacity for using poetry as a weapon in the day-to-day struggle of the workers, with no scruples in using extra-literary means, in organizing rows and literary scenes, in doing everything *pour épater les bourgeois*. (MacDiarmid [1943] 1972: 357).

MacDiarmid, as this brief remark will confirm, remained fond of such expressions long after Maiakovskii's suicide, and long after the Russian bourgeoisie had ceased to be the primary endangered species in Soviet society.

Maiakovskii serves also a particularly important dual function with regard to the figure who ought in one sense to dominate any study of MacDiarmid's relations to Russia – Lenin. Maiakovskii functions for MacDiarmid, on one hand, as a kind of poetic double of Lenin – the educator, propagandist and activist endowed also with lyric voice and epic aspirations – and it is this image, or fusion of images, that will later emerge in MacDiarmid's own writing on Lenin.

---

[10] MacDiarmid cites the following description of Maiakovskii from Mirsky 1926, a book to which we will return: "Mayakovsky is genuinely popular, read by a very wide circle of readers. His appeal is direct and simple, his subjects can interest the most uncultured [...]". The Scotland of 1926 would be a fitting environment for such as Maiakovskii, because, as MacDiarmid immediately tells us, "a sufficiently uncultured public abounds in our midst" (MacDiarmid [1926] 1995: 372).

Maiakovskii also performs a second, more specific function, however, as his poems "Vladimir Ilich!", "Vladimir Ilich Lenin" and "A Conversation with Comrade Lenin" [*Razgovor s tovarishchem Leninym*] are a significant prototype for MacDiarmid's own "Hymns to Lenin". It is tempting on one level to wonder how MacDiarmid might have responded to the pregnant irony of Maiakovskii's dramatic characterisation of Lenin in the last of these as thought personified: "In the enormous forehead / an enormous thought" [В огромный лоб / огромная мысль] (Maiakovskii 1955–61: 10: 17). On a more serious level, however, these poems are the perfect ground for a comparative analysis of the nature of both poets' communist convictions, and of its impact on their poetry. Maiakovskii, of course, enjoyed the "advantage" that his poetry was known to Lenin, and suffered the profound "disadvantage" of writing in a society in which his "progress in communism", as he put it, would be closely monitored. Lenin himself famously expressed dislike for certain of Maiakovskii's poems, although official disfavour, emanating even from the highest levels, was certainly no great distinction in Soviet literary circles, progressive or otherwise.

"A Conversation with Comrade Lenin" is the last of Maiakovskii's Lenin poems, written in 1929, a year before his own death by suicide, and it prompts two important points: the first is that the erection of a cult of Lenin had begun before his death, and by 1929 was already entering a phase in which it would be made to serve as the foundation for the cult of his successor. The second is that, within this context, we can observe profound changes in Maiakovskii's characteristic style of poetic address. Maiakovskii's poetry was consistently marked by the forceful insertion of none other than *Maiakovskii* as poetic persona, often as the subject of direct address, sometimes intimate, at others declamatory. Yet this Maiakovskii is virtually absent from this particular "conversation", and his infrequent incursions are extremely muted. As Peter McCarey describes it: "the Mayakovsky who once threatened God with a knife now declares himself no more worthy than the next man to die for Lenin" (McCarey 1987: 152–53). And it is tempting, as is often the case with Maiakovskii, to read this effacement of his poetic persona as a prefiguration of the imminent destruction of his physical self.

MacDiarmid's relations with God, Christ and Lenin are somewhat different. In "First Hymn to Lenin", Churchill and Beaverbrook are less in comparison to Lenin "than the centurions to Christ", and "Christ's cited no' by chance or juist because / You mark the greatest turnin'-point since him" (MacDiarmid 1993: 1: 297). Lenin is the "truth" that must be preferred to Christ, and has replaced Dostoevskii as the "Christ o' the neist thoosand years". More pertinently, MacDiarmid emerges fully-formed as the Disciple that Maiakovskii has had to toil so long, and without success, to become. Yet "Second Hymn to Lenin" opens with the scandalous assertion that "Ah, Lenin, you were richt. But I'm a poet [...] Aimin' at mair than you aimed at / Tho' yours comes first, I know it." (MacDiarmid 1993: 1: 323). And it ends with a defence and definition of poetry as the ultimate vehicle and manifestation of human achievement, describing it in Leninist imagery as:

Unremittin', relentless,
Organized to the last degree,
Ah, Lenin, politics is bairns' play
To what this maun be! (MacDiarmid 1993: 1: 328)

In between we glimpse the heart of MacDiarmid's attraction to Lenin, the extreme self-projection that moves him to the following:

Wi' Lenin's vision equal poet's gift
And what unparalleled force was there!
Nocht in a' literature wi' that
Begins to compare! (MacDiarmid 1993: 1: 324)

A Dostoevskii, or a Joyce perhaps – Maiakovskii could not rise to such heights – merged with an agent of manifest political destiny: this is the underlying projection of the "Second Hymn". Or perhaps a MacDiarmid? The poem's direct, if somewhat stilted, address, and its engagement with its exalted object on ostensibly equal terms, might be compared to Maiakovskii (when addressing anyone *but* Lenin) or even Burns, were it not for the fact that MacDiarmid's reductiveness is quite without irony. MacDiarmid in fact utilises a solemn egalitarianism ("Betwixt Beaverbrook, say, and God, / Jimmy Thomas or you"

(MacDiarmid 1993: 1: 327)) in order to mask a colossal over-determination of his own self, poetic or otherwise. This process is paradoxically complete in "Third Hymn to Lenin", where reductive irony would be quite out of place in the context of what is the most politically successful, because the most politically *sincere* poem of the three.[11] And yet, frustratingly if altogether characteristically, MacDiarmid shatters the tone of political sincerity by taking the process of identification, of transfiguration of his poetic self, to its disturbing conclusion: "Be with me, Lenin, reincarnate in me here" (MacDiarmid 1993: 2: 895).

Lenin is for MacDiarmid the ultimate, unified persona, onto which every strand of his own motivations can be projected. His relationship to Lenin is the culmination of the essentially cultic regard in which he has previously held Dostoevskii, and which is an element of his relationship with all of the philosophical and literary figures to whom he responds positively. This propensity towards the cult must in turn cast questions of sources and influence in an entirely different light, for the essence of the cult is not the knowledge, understanding or truth that has ostensibly animated MacDiarmid's journey through the Russian tradition; it is rather simulacra of these, constructed at the behest of the individual will of devotee and object of the cult alike. What is particularly interesting about MacDiarmid in this regard is that he is at once prepared to play the role of devotee, yet at the same time harbours manifest ambitions of becoming, in turn, the object of a cult of his own. The figure of Lenin brings together the perilously related elements of vaulting ambition and a sense of functional necessity that define MacDiarmid's actions – and would eventually lead him into one further cultic association on Russian ground.

---

[11] MacDiarmid's other poetry on this theme falls into one of two traps: "The Seamless Garment" (MacDiarmid 1993: 1: 311–14) is artless and patronising, while "The Skeleton of the Future (At Lenin's Tomb)" (MacDiarmid 1993: 1: 386) is cultic in its evocation of "The eternal lightning of Lenin's bones". The latter has been translated into Russian as "Kostiak budushchego" (*Poeziia Evropy* 1977: 1: 164); the excerpts from "The Seamless Garment" that have also been translated into Russian will form part of the ensuing discussion.

3. D.S. Mirskii

Besides the ambitions of their objects and the participation of their devotees, cults also require a history, referents, and agents who will furnish them. In this respect, Lenin, Dostoevskii, indeed all of the authors with whom MacDiarmid has been associated, must cede their place to a much less exalted figure, who was yet the most significant point of mediation between Russian literature and the English literary world of the 1920s, to which MacDiarmid's own aesthetic universe is inextricably – and often paradoxically – bound. Prince Dmitrii Petrovich Sviatopolk-Mirskii was a child of the late-Imperial Russian aristocracy and, almost certainly unbeknown to MacDiarmid, combatant on the side of General Denikin's White Armies in the Russian Civil War. Mirskii managed to escape the Civil War in 1920, and, with his name suitably amended, ended up first in Brussels and then London, where he became a leading figure in the émigré press, taught at the School of Slavonic Studies in London, and contributed to, among others, Eliot's *Criterion* (see Smith 2000). It is, however, for the influential books on Russian literary history he published in the mid-1920s that Mirskii is remembered, books which are partly conditioned by his awareness of the reputation enjoyed by certain writers in Britain as opposed to Russia, thus giving us an oblique insight into the process of reception of Russian literature in early twentieth-century Britain. They also yield a more specific insight into the nature of MacDiarmid's engagement with Russian literature.

Alan Bold has pointed out that Mirskii is one of the earliest sources for an aspect of MacDiarmid's poetic practice that would remain a constant throughout his long career, namely the creative recapitulation of "found" prose elements in unexpected, and unacknowledged, poetic form (Bold 1988: 202).[12] As Mirskii writes of Dostoevskii:

---

[12] Perhaps the best known example of this is MacDiarmid's "Perfect", which reproduces, without attribution, a prose passage from the Welsh writer Glyn Jones's *The Blue Bed*, re-arranged into verse lines. MacDiarmid was joined in his defence of the legitimacy of this practice by the critic Kenneth Buthlay and the poet Edwin Morgan, although MacDiarmid characteristically overstates his defence by later arguing that Jones should have been glad of the "publicity" (see Bold 1988: 423–24).

His doctrine was [...] a democratic Slavophilism, a profound belief that the Russian people (with a big P, and mainly meaning the peasants) was a narodbogonosets – "a God-bearing people" [...]. Pushkin, said Dostoevsky, was Russia's all-in-all (nashe vse), for the very reason that he was a cosmopolitan, or, as Dostoevsky put it, an All-man (vse-chelovek). This Pan-Humanity is the national characteristic of Russia, and Russia's mission is to effect the final synthesis of all mankind. (Mirsky 1925: 48).

Bold's uncontroversial point is that certain of the lines from *A Drunk Man Looks at the Thistle* we referred to above in discussion of Dosto-evskii – "*Narodbogonosets* are my folk tae"; "When Scotland sall find oot its destiny, / And yield the *vse-chelovek*"; "To seek the haund o' Russia as a freen' / In workin' oot mankind's great synthesis..." (MacDiarmid 1993: 1: 134–35) – are not so much suggested by, but rather constructed from Mirskii's prose. Bold is apparently uncon-cerned by the fact that the source of MacDiarmid's fascination with Dostoevskii is never Dostoevskii himself, but rather a range of secon-dary sources like Spengler and Lavrin, among which Mirskii turns out to be the most important.[13] Garnett's literary translations would not appear to be the primary source of MacDiarmid's appreciation of Dostoevskii and, by extension, neither Dostoevskii's "literary world" nor his artistic practice would appear to be as important for MacDiar-mid as the gargantuan literary and spiritual portrait conjured for the imagination by Mirskii or Spengler. Mirskii would prove yet more notable for MacDiarmid, however, in his judgements not of Dosto-evskii, but of Chekhov.[14]

In a 1926 article on the subject of a Scottish National Theatre, which incidentally makes very little of Chekhov's Russianness, but which offers a number of typically MacDiarmidian hostages to fortune in the matter of "Scottishness", MacDiarmid proposes a clear solution to the problem of a "new kind of drama which shall address itself to Scots psychology":

In this connection straight technique will not help. Chekhov is the dramatist who should be studied. His indirect method – his oblique dialogue – his use of irrelevan-

---

[13] Bold also cites Spengler's "canonisation" of Dostoevskii in his *The Decline of the West*, and Lavrin's *Dostoevsky and His Creation*.
[14] I would like to thank Alastair Renfrew for drawing my attention to the impact on MacDiarmid of Mirskii's judgements of Chekhov.

cies consist with the complex, cautious Scots mind. The future of the Scots theatre lies in practically actionless drama, and the employment of expressionist technique to express the undemonstrative monosyllabic subtlety of the Scot. (Grieve [1926] 1995: 254)

This is entirely consistent with MacDiarmid's defence of Chekhov in the *New Age* in the previous year, a defence prompted by some harsh words by none other than D.S. Mirskii in his *Modern Russian Literature* (Grieve 1925b). MacDiarmid takes exception to Mirskii's "*gaffe*" in judging that "to imitate [Chekhov's] dramatic system or even to learn from him is obviously impossible", and considers Mirskii's opinion that "Russian dramatic literature after Chekhov's death is one unrelieved desert" (Mirsky 1925: 91), deserving of a "'Silly Season' prize". This and Mirskii's tendency to

confus[e] his readers with oblique hints of his own undivulged opinions or with unexpiscated fragments of big controversies [...] reduces materially the serviceability of his otherwise respectable, but in no wise brilliant, outline. (Grieve 1925b: 92)

If MacDiarmid is deaf, however, to the more positive things Mirskii has to say about Chekhov in *Modern Russian Literature* – "there can be no doubt as to the greatness of Chekhov [...] we must recognize that he was the greatest writer of his age and of his class" (Mirsky 1925: 85) – something more complex than selective hearing is manifest in his review of Mirskii's next book, *Contemporary Russian Literature, 1881–1925*, in which Mirskii is hardly more restrained on the subject of Chekhov. Alongside reiterations of his global verdict on Chekhov – "His place as a classic [...] is not challenged" (Mirsky 1958: 383)[15] – Mirskii also repeats concerns relating specifically to the plays, the "dominant note" of which is

gloom, depression and hopelessness. [...] They are all in the minor key and leave the spectator in a state of impotent – perhaps deliciously impotent – depression. [...] At any rate, his method is dangerous and has been imitated only at the imitator's immi-

---

[15] Quotations and page references to *Contemporary Russian Literature* (Mirsky 1926) are given from a later compendium edition, *A History of Russian Literature from its Beginnings to 1900* (Mirsky 1958), which incorporates the first two chapters of the earlier book.

nent peril. No play written by an imitator of Chekhov is above contempt. (Mirsky 1958: 382)

Mirskii is, however, at his most unforgiving when comparing Chekhov to the "greats" of Russian literature. Undisputed "classic" he may be, but comparisons with Pushkin, Dostoevskii and Tolstoi provoke indignant response in Mirskii, and never more so than in the following:

Twenty years ago there was no difference of opinion outside Russia as to who was the greatest of Russian writers – Tolstoy dominated Russian literature in a way that no writer had dominated a national literature […] since […] Goethe […]. Since then the wheel of fashion […] has displaced Tolstoy […] and substituted for his the idols of Dostoevsky and, in these last years (strangest of occidental whims), of Chekhov. It is left to the future to show whether the wheel will turn again, or whether the advanced elite of the Western world has definitely reached a stage of mental senility that can be satisfied only by the autumnal genius of Chekhov. (Mirsky 1958: 256)[16]

Yet MacDiarmid, in the same piece in which he has called for a "Scottish Mayakovsky", published on 13 August 1926, elevates Mirskii to the status of unimpeachable authority on Russian literature on the specific basis of *Contemporary Russian Literature* (see MacDiarmid [1926] 1995),[17] and, by November 1926, is moved to describe it as "a model book of its kind. […] I know no parallel to [Mirskii's] feat" (Grieve 1926: 9). The review closes with the statement that "so far as all but a handful of British readers are concerned, this book must be a first glimpse of a whole continent of recent literature" (Grieve 1926: 9), and the bludgeoning implication that the reviewer is himself prominent among that handful.

---

[16] The remainder of Mirsky 1958, i.e. everything preceding the two chapters originally from *Contemporary Russian Literature* referred to above, was originally published as Mirsky 1927b.

[17] MacDiarmid enlists Mirskii's description of Maiakovskii's Futurist colleague Velimir Khlebnikov in arguing for the potential of *zaum'* or "trans-sense" poetry for synthesised Scots verse; it is worth noting, however, that this leads MacDiarmid into one of the most ill-judged criticisms of Burns imaginable, even by his own standards. MacDiarmid laments what Burns might have achieved if only "he had had the attitude to words of a Khlebnikov" (MacDiarmid [1926] 1995: 370); if only he had been born at the dawn of Modernism, witnessed at first hand the epochal crack of the Russian Empire, and perhaps also read Wittgenstein for good measure.

It may be that MacDiarmid's new-found admiration for Mirskii
is explained by relatively subtle but nonetheless fundamental differences in the scope of Mirskii's books: his "Contemporary" Russian
literature deals in some detail with the Revolutionary and post-
Revolutionary period of literary experimentation and rapid social and
cultural change, while his "Modern" Russian literature closes with a
only a very brief appendix on some of the major Symbolist poets of
the pre-Revolutionary period, and hence has nothing to say on the
nexus of Modernism and Bolshevism upon which MacDiarmid's attention is now focused.[18] There is, however, an alternative explanation, which turns on personal rather than literary factors, and which
also, and perhaps crucially, relates to the matter of England more than
it does to Russia.

G.S. Smith has established that a limited correspondence began
around the time of these reviews, but it is not clear exactly when, or
indeed if, MacDiarmid and Mirskii ever met in person (see Smith
1996/97). It is clear, however, that some kind of relationship developed between the two, imbued, at least on MacDiarmid's side, with a
degree of genuine admiration, and which would endure in a curious
form even beyond Mirskii's death in 1939.[19] It is in the context of this
relationship, whether conducted at any stage in person or in correspondence and through the pages of certain literary journals, that a
new element in MacDiarmid's changing view of Mirskii (and Chekhov) emerges. Mirskii published a short essay entitled "Chekhov and
the English" in Eliot's *Criterion* in October 1927, in which he develops a particular aspect of the criticism of Chekhov contained in his

---

[18] MacDiarmid's closing criticism of modern Russian literature is that it "gives us so
few pointers as to the future – so few suggestions as to 'the coming men' [...] No
mention is made of the changed conditions and prospects of literature under the Soviet
government" (Grieve 1925b: 92).
[19] In a letter dated 20 March 1934, for example, MacDiarmid writes: "My dear
Mirsky, It is some considerable time ago since you were living in Gower Street and
we had a correspondence a propos of my poems which I value very highly. I have
some knowledge of your subsequent movements and as you may know my own have
paralleled them to a considerable extent. In other words we have both gone
completely Communist" (MacDiarmid 20 March 1934). This letter has not been
included in MacDiarmid 1996.

books, namely his attitude to language. In *Contemporary Russian Literature*, for example, Mirskii is particularly damning:

Another serious shortcoming is [Chekhov's] Russian. It is colorless and lacks individuality. He had no feeling for words. No Russian writer of anything like his significance used a language so devoid of all raciness and nerve. (Mirsky 1926: 382)

"Chekhov and the English" begins with a familiar profession of surprise at the "cult" of Chekhov among the English intelligentsia "at a time when the Russians (reader and writer) have [...] shelved him as a (probably minor) classic" (Mirsky 1927a: 292). He then goes on to explain the emergence of this "cult" in a manner that would have been horrifying to the MacDiarmid who proposed Chekhov's "oblique" and "actionless" drama as a model for a quintessentially Scottish drama, but which would nonetheless offer obvious compensations in a quite different respect:

Two features attract the English intellectual in Chekhov, the one ethical, the other aesthetical, but both converging towards what may appear a classical *mediocritas*. [...] [This second] attraction of Chekhov is his style, free from anything sharp and glaring, and all bathed in a perfect and uniform haze. (Mirsky 1926: 292–93)

And later:

He had no sense of words – he did not feel them either as symbols (as the logical writer does), or as entities (as the poet does). Nor has his prose distinctness, for its rhythm is such as to blur and mix. Language in his hands becomes an homogeneous and undifferentiated paste. (Mirsky 1926: 296)

It is not difficult to see how MacDiarmid's rejection of Chekhov in favour of the type of writer proposed by Mirskii as his antithesis, the best example of which is Velimir Khlebnikov, is wholly consistent with his own trajectory as a poet, to the point where Mirskii's description of Chekhov would have rendered any association a *de facto* insult. The crowning moment, however, is Mirskii's association of a "homogeneous", "undifferentiated" and even anti-poetic attitude to language with the "uniform haze" of a "classical", and by implication specifically *English* "mediocritas". In his internationalist quest for elements of the continental European tradition that might be adapted

to the needs of a renascent Scottish aesthetics, MacDiarmid had unwittingly stumbled – inevitably, perhaps, among the welter of borrowings of differing degree and motivation – upon an element that
defined him, at least in Mirskii's view, as a typical "English intellectual".

While MacDiarmid's on-going regard for Mirskii is well docu-
mented, Mirskii's opinion of MacDiarmid has until recently been
more difficult to establish. In 1931 MacDiarmid dedicated his "First
Hymn to Lenin" to Mirskii (MacDiarmid 1993: 1: 297), and followed
it in 1955 with a fulsome poetic dedication to "In Memoriam James
Joyce":

A mighty master in all such matters
Of whom for all the instruction and encouragement he gave me,
I am happy to subscribe myself here
The humble and most grateful pupil. (MacDiarmid 1993: 2: 736)

Their correspondence continued after Mirskii's return to Russia in
1932, and MacDiarmid owes his limited exposure in the Soviet Union
directly to Mirskii: in 1933, Mirskii wrote an entry on Scottish literature for the first edition of the *Bol'shaia sovetskaia entsiklopediia* [The
Greater Soviet Encyclopaedia] (see Appendix 1), and, in 1937, he included the excerpt on Lenin from MacDiarmid's "The Seamless Garment" in an anthology of "English" poetry (Gutner ed. 1937: 392; see
also Appendix 2),[20] for which he also compiled biographical notes. On
slightly closer examination, however, these sources do not support
MacDiarmid's version of Mirskii's regard for him. As Mirskii writes
in the encyclopaedia entry:

---

[20] Mirskii's name was removed from the published volume and replaced by that of M.
Gutner, who was one of Mirskii's team of translators. The volume also contains
poems by Stevenson, James Thomson and John Davidson, and a series of biographical
notes, which are revealing even in their opening phrases: Thomson is the "son of a
sailor", Stevenson the "author of adventure novels", while Davidson "committed
suicide", and MacDiarmid, unique among the four, is simply "a Scotsman" (Gutner
ed. 1937: 431, 433, 436, 445). This rare example of the Soviet reception of Scottish
literature, albeit that little emphasis is placed on its Scottishness, is certainly deserving
of closer examination.

In our times there has been a renewed attempt to revive poetry in the Scots dialect, made by the poet Hugh MacDiarmid [...]. MacDiarmid is an original poet-philosopher, not devoid of revolutionary sympathy (two "Hymns to Lenin"), but with a confused world-view. His attempt to revive a Scottish literary language is nothing more than a whim of the intelligentsia. (*Bol'shaia sovetskaia entsiklopediia* 1933: 62: cols.607–8)

In the anthology, Mirskii judges that MacDiarmid's "First Hymn to Lenin" is "a sincere attempt to express sympathy with Communist ideas", but that it also contains "a great deal of philosophical idealism" (Gutner ed. 1937: 445). Worst of all perhaps, as Smith records with some relish, I. Romanovich's translation renders "The Seamless Garment" into an utterly standard literary Russian, poor return indeed for MacDiarmid's fraternal devotion to his partners in the East-West synthesis. Smith's estimation of MacDiarmid as "self-marginalizing" (Smith 1996/97: 56), if based, as it is here, purely on his verse, is perhaps easy to rebut for those who are inclined to do so: Scottish literary studies is unquestionably beyond the stage where the characteristic adolescent cry indexing knowledge to understanding need be offered in defence of the native tradition; indeed, the formulation might be better reversed – "the reason you don't understand our poetry, is because you don't like it". In relation to the broader question of MacDiarmid's aesthetics, however, "self-marginalizing" might even be too kind, and Smith is surely justified in his implication that MacDiarmid is driven here by an increasingly grim "functional necessity", which calls his motivation in engaging with Mirskii, and through him with the Russian tradition, into serious question.

These doubts are not dispelled by the tragic coda to MacDiarmid and Mirskii's relationship. Mirskii was arrested on 2 June 1937, the same year as the excerpt from "The Seamless Garment" was published in Russian, and, on an unknown date in 1939, he perished in the Gulag. The poem MacDiarmid dedicated to Mirskii in 1931, "First Hymn to Lenin", of course contains the following lines:

As necessary, and insignificant, as death
Wi' a' its agonies in the cosmos still
The Cheka's horrors are in their degree;
And'll end suner! What maitters 't wha we kill

To lessen that foulest murder that deprives
Maist men o' real lives? (MacDiarmid 1993: 1: 298)

If this were not enough, MacDiarmid, as late as 1946 at the very least, does not seem to have been aware of Mirskii's fate; in a letter to *The Herald* of 11 November of that year he gives a list of those luminaries who have praised his work, including, among others, "the late W.B. Yeats, [...] the late Lord Tweedsmuir, Mr. Sean O'Casey, Mr. T.S. Eliot", and, unqualified by a more suitable prefix denoting his decease, "ex-Prince D.S. Mirsky" (MacDiarmid [1946] 1984: 784–85).

4. Soviet Aftermath and *Aesthetics in Scotland*

By 1946 the storms that affected MacDiarmid's emergence into public literary life, the accumulation of which drove him for a time beyond the brink of mental breakdown, appear to have abated.[21] He had completed his autobiography *Lucky Poet* (1943), and, a few years later, would embark upon another work that would, amongst other things, emphasise not only that his critical relationship with and reliance upon Mirskii had ceased, but also that his relationship with Russia and its literature had altered dramatically. Neither *Lucky Poet* nor the later work, *Aesthetics in Scotland*, need be subject to – or protected by – the provisos that pertain to MacDiarmid's writings of the 1920s and 1930s, and present themselves as a convenient basis for the reconstruction, on the example of Russia, of the extent and depth of MacDiarmid's aesthetic internationalism.

   Aesthetics in Scotland was written mostly in 1950, but was published, with minor amendments, only in 1984.[22] As well as being insulated from the worst effects of "conflict and contradiction" by distance in time, *Aesthetics in Scotland* has the distinct advantage of being not

---

[21] On MacDiarmid's desperate personal circumstances in the late 1920s and 1930s see Bold 1988: 239–336; also MacDiarmid 2001: 39–174.

[22] It is perhaps significant that *Aesthetics in Scotland* appears towards the end of the period immediately following MacDiarmid's death, during which his centrality to the modern Scottish tradition, critically and artistically, is confirmed by a welter of publications, including Scott and Davis (eds) 1980, Buthlay 1982, Bold 1983, Gish 1984.

only exclusively and specifically concerned with aesthetics, but of embodying some form of *programmatic* statement on the subject. Alan Bold, in his introduction, describes the book as "unusually contemplative [...] and only occasionally exhibit[ing] the fierce polemical anger that characterises most of [MacDiarmid's] published prose" (MacDiarmid 1984: 10); it also allows us "to see exactly how MacDiarmid regarded the aesthetic implications of the artistic revolution he had unleashed on Scotland" (MacDiarmid 1984: 11). In short, *Aesthetics in Scotland* is a much more reliable, retrospective basis for an assessment of the motivations and achievements of the earlier stages of MacDiarmid's cultural and aesthetic crusade. It immediately becomes clear, however, that although MacDiarmid himself may have changed, the perceived lack in Scottish aesthetics which fuelled much of his earlier polemical fire remains substantially intact.

MacDiarmid here does not attribute the roots of the deficiencies of aesthetics in Scotland *directly* to the Calvinist legacy that has often been seen as inimical to developments in painting and, particularly, in theatre, but rather to the stifling predominance of moral philosophy in the Scottish Enlightenment. In a somewhat staggered argument, however, MacDiarmid contends that the disregard for aesthetics demonstrated by writers as diverse as Hume, Dugald Stewart, William and Adam Ferguson, Hugh Blair, Lord Kames and Francis Hutcheson is itself explained by a terrible common affliction, one suffered also by Ruskin, "the greatest writer on art Scotland has yet produced" (MacDiarmid 1984: 43).[23] This terrible affliction, in the words of R.H. Wilenski, is simply "the emotive language of the Bible", a drug forced upon Ruskin until "when at last he was immuned by satiety his power of action was all spent. [...] We shall never know to what extent the obsession impeded his power of thinking" (MacDiarmid 1984: 43). Thomas Reid and William Hamilton are later added to this group, prefacing MacDiarmid's claim that both the perennial lack of an aesthetics in Scotland and contemporary philistinism in general are nothing more than the effects of over-indulgence in "Common Sense";

---

[23] The inclusion of Hutcheson in this roll of ignominy is doubly ironic, given the status of his *Inquiry into the Original of our Ideas of Beauty and Virtue* (1725) as one of the first works of "aesthetic theory" in modern Western culture.

a bold, and genuinely provocative, development of MacDiarmid's earlier diagnosis of the effects of "Knox on the heid".

The post-Enlightenment exception who proves MacDiarmid's rule is A.S. Dallas, an "important and far too little known Scottish writer", whom MacDiarmid has rediscovered by dint of that fact that "I am one of that very few and far between sort of Scotsman sufficiently interested in theories of art to look for and read all I can lay my hands on in this connection" (MacDiarmid 1984: 55). Dallas's *The Gay Science*, published in 1866 (Dallas 1866),[24] is commended by MacDiarmid as a rare and serious attempt at a systematic theory of specifically *literary* criticism, which is itself intriguing, given that a surprising and revealing proportion of *Aesthetics in Scotland* is devoted to the visual arts. MacDiarmid also praises Dallas's acuity in arguing that it is Aristotle's reliance upon the principle of *mimesis* in verbal art that ultimately prevents him from formulating the basis for any kind of "systematic criticism"; and Dallas's insistence upon the significance of the "unconscious mind" for the imaginative process – whether it be regarded as post-Romantic or, as MacDiarmid intends, pre-Freud – is also worthy of note. Dallas is ultimately, however, and perhaps precisely because of these qualities, an isolated exception, whose works had "little effect in their own time", before falling into the neglect from which MacDiarmid seeks to rescue them. MacDiarmid chooses not to attempt to develop Dallas's work, however, and embarks instead on a curious sequence of examples, ostensibly designed to illustrate how the power of the imagination has begun to elude those who would seek to repress its influence on art in Scotland, but which succeeds only in making an all-too-convincing – if unintentional – case for the disrepair into which Scottish aesthetics has fallen (or in which, notwithstanding the influence of MacDiarmid himself, it remains).

---

[24] MacDiarmid gives his initials as A.S., on the basis of the more common spelling of the first name, "Aeneas", as opposed to "Eneas", as it appears on the book's title page and in bibliographical records. Aeneas Sweetland Dallas, born in Jamaica in 1828, studied philosophy under William Hamilton at the University of Edinburgh, and was a member of staff at *The Times*, a career upon which he relied increasingly following the muted response to *The Gay Science*, his major work. The book is available in a number of reprinted editions: 1969, London: Chapman & Hall; 1969, New York: Johnson Reprint Corporation; and 1986, New York: Garland.

In the closing sections of *Aesthetics in Scotland* we are invited to consider the anticipation by Sam Bough – a nineteenth-century Lancashire painter and "rough diamond" (MacDiarmid 1984: 74) – of certain developments in abstract painting; or the fact that Miss Elsie de Wolfe, "the great international de luxe decorator of millionaires' mansions [...] had a Scottish mother" (MacDiarmid 1984: 83), with the implication that this explains her "modern style [...] as recognisable as a signature, with its dramatic use of black and white, Zebra skins, Venetian starred mirrors" (MacDiarmid 1984: 84), a style which had most recently found favour with the film actor Gary Cooper. A digression on the aesthetics of engineering then concludes with a comparison of the "quality of personality" of certain ships, the Lusitania apparently lacking in what its sister ship the Mauretania and the Queen Mary do not, although the latter "has not yet had quite time enough to prove it" (MacDiarmid 1984: 89). More worryingly, at a time when the still Stalinist Soviet Union was experiencing a renewed and only superficially paradoxical wave of repression of Jews, we are also invited to see the Edinburgh Festival as no more than a means by which

some of our better-off people, in compensation for backward cultural conditions and a lost religious ethic, are developing or pretending to develop [...] a supreme talent for refinement just as a certain type of Jew, in compensation for adverse social conditions and a lost national independence, developed a supreme talent for cleverness. (MacDiarmid 1984: 90)

The 1950 typescript of *Aesthetics in Scotland* then concludes, aptly perhaps, with the estimation that "We are a breed of critical simpletons", a sentence removed by MacDiarmid prior to the book's eventual publication; perhaps this is what Alan Bold has in mind by "unusually contemplative".

A quarter of a century into the project of Renaissance this persistent dearth of native aesthetics, and the absurdities into which this perception leads his exposition, provide a perfect retrospective emphasis of the sheer functional necessity of MacDiarmid's earlier aesthetic internationalism. The traces of that internationalism remain in *Aesthetics in Scotland*, in MacDiarmid's reference to Hölderlin's characterisation of the German need to "study the Greeks", for example, not as an automatised basis for Western civilisation, but rather "in order to gain knowledge of themselves" (MacDiarmid 1984: 28). Somewhat more prosaically, MacDiarmid also, after making favourable reference to John Tonge's 1938 book *The Arts of Scotland*, goes on to cite its author's implication of the dearth of such works in Scotland, as compared to the countries of continental Europe (Tonge 1938: x). Again, perhaps inevitably, MacDiarmid makes much more of Tonge's implication than might have been intended, arguing that "Most of these countries have scores of such books to their credit" (MacDiarmid 1984: 30), and that previous attempts in Scotland, in what reads like a portable summation of MacDiarmid's overall view of Scottish aesthetics to that point, had been

little more than unintelligent catalogues of names, diversified with insignificant personalia, chit-chat, comments of the most hackneyed kind, stock platitudes, banal bromides and clap-trap generally. (MacDiarmid 1984: 31)

That MacDiarmid immediately cites with approbation Tonge's characterisation of Edinburgh's New Town as a departure from the "racial norm" of the "Nordic Arts", to which "Celtic Art" apparently belongs, is unfortunate, and it is not quite clear to which of the above categories this sort of remark properly belongs – a "comment of the most hackneyed kind"? A "stock platitude"? Or just "clap-trap generally"?

MacDiarmid in any case almost immediately contradicts this categorisation, arguing that "Gaeldom stands outside Europe altogether. Its affiliations are with the East. And it is not to Worringer's Nordic Arts but to the arts of the East we must look when we seek to understand Gaelic Art" (MacDiarmid 1984: 36). Yet it is never made clear in what exactly the "arts of the East" consist. MacDiarmid at no stage demonstrates any knowledge of the visual arts in Russia, and there is not attempt to invoke his erstwhile interest in such artist-aestheticians as Blok, Chekhov, Dostoevskii, Maiakovskii and Solov'ev.[25] Instead, MacDiarmid goes on to confirm, in a citation of his own *Lucky Poet*, what has become of the Russian influence that

---

[25] Indeed, the only other remaining trace of the Russian cultural environment is a passing reference to Lobachevskii's "discovery of a non-Euclidean geometry" (MacDiarmid 1984: 41).

has been seen as so significant for his emergence as a poet: "The ideas of the East-West synthesis and the Caledonian antisysygy [*sic*] merge into one" (MacDiarmid 1984: 37; MacDiarmid [1943] 1972: 375). All that in fact remains is a vague and overblown sense of racial affinity. Here, in the context of an ostensibly "programmatic" statement of MacDiarmid's aesthetics, there is no substantive link to any of the aesthetic models from the Russian environment MacDiarmid has previously invoked. In a sense, however, it would be surprising if there were, for there is no aesthetics here, either. *Aesthetics in Scotland* has the air of an obligation – self-imposed at that – fulfilled. MacDiarmid's repeated implications of an "artistic revolution" – taken at face value for so long not just by the likes of Alan Bold, but by Scottish literary studies in general – had at some stage to be corroborated by an explicit textual statement. In a typically MacDiarmidian paradox, however, the attempt reveals the very dearth it hopes to correct, and we are left to conclude that the poetic embodiment of particular aesthetic models and experiments in MacDiarmid's most successful early poetry would have been a far more fitting – and convincing – legacy.

On the specific matter of Russia, however, it is to *Lucky Poet* that we must turn for confirmation of the enduring nature of MacDiarmid's engagement, and of an element of his personality to which we have already referred. For MacDiarmid's justification of political murder turns out not to be an isolated exception, exposed with tragic irony in the dénouement of his relationship with Mirskii. It might be argued that MacDiarmid's rhetorical flourish from the "First Hymn to Lenin" – "As necessary, and insignificant, as death [...] What maitters't wha we kill" – is far from placing him out of step with the sentiments of the Left intelligentsia in Britain in 1931. Yet his affection for Stalin's Soviet Union comfortably survives two distinct stages in the exposure of Stalinism to the western Left, the Ezhov-inspired peak of repression of 1937 – MacDiarmid follows through on his "utilitarian" rhetoric with a 1943 call for a "Celtic Union of Soviet Socialist Republics", for example (MacDiarmid [1943] 1972: 26) – and the renewed wave of repression in 1946 with which the Soviet peoples were "rewarded" for the war effort. Compare his "master" Shestov's agonised response to the events of 1937 (see McCarey 1987: 170–71), or indeed Shestov's prior characterisation of death: "the ugliness and agony of death make us forget everything, even our 'self-evident truths'" (Chestov 1932: 241; cited in McCarey 1987: 185).

Worse, however, is the way MacDiarmid once again undermines any defence of purely political commitment by submitting to the cultic impulse that drove his attachment to Lenin, and which now transfers itself all too easily to the person of Stalin, bolstered, in fact, by the accident of Stalin's closer proximity to the source of MacDiarmid's cherished racial myth. In a poetic return to the idea of the East-West synthesis in 1946 MacDiarmid writes: "'Stalin the Georgian,' I have said. We are Georgians all. / We Gaels." (MacDiarmid 1993: 1: 679).[26] MacDiarmid's curious form of Stalinism has, however, already reached almost unimaginable heights in the following:

I would like, say, Stalin a great deal better if [...] he spent his long nights in drunken orgies with his boon companions, his "Desperadoes", and his women – night after night – and yet carrying on his immense work, relentless as steel – "playing poker, quarreling, haggling, and drinking till the sun was well up the sky [...]". (MacDiarmid [1943] 1972: 239)

Thus Stalin outstrips Lenin: not only a racially preferable Georgian, but also a drunkard and womaniser of the mind, but who remains nonetheless, like Lenin and like poetry itself, "relentless". Sydney Goodsir Smith, whom we have already mentioned as the translator of Blok's "The Twelve", brings this new and disturbing projection into fresh perspective in the fifth elegy of his *Under the Eldon Tree*, "Slugabed", where he continues an ironic characterisation of his poetic self as lower even than Oblomov, Goncharov's emblem of the stultified Tsarist past:

O, michtie Stalin in the Aist!
Could ye but see me nou,
The type, endpynt and final blume
O' decadent capitalistical thirldom
        –It took five hunder year to produce me–
Och, could ye but see me nou

---

[26] MacDiarmid, apparently intoxicated by the Soviet Union's heroism during the Second World War, also dedicates the preposterous 1945 poem "Lamb Dearg Aboo" to Stalin (MacDiarmid 1993: 2: 1323–25).

What a sermon could ye gie
[...]
Losh, what a sermon yon wad be!
For Knox has nocht on Uncle Joe
And Oblomov has nocht on Smith
    And sae we come by a route maist devious
    Til the far-famed Aist-West synthesis!
Beluved by Hugh that's beluved by me
And the baith o' us loe the barley-bree– (Smith 1975: 154–55)

MacDiarmid visited the Soviet Union in 1950, and returned in 1957. The cataclysmic events of the intervening period – including the death of Stalin himself, the subsequent exposure not only of his cult, but of the atrocities it masked, and the Soviet invasion of Hungary – appear, however, to have had little effect. MacDiarmid's response to events in Hungary and to the spectre of atrocity under Stalin was to rejoin the Communist Party of Great Britain, at a time when around 7000 members chose to leave (Bold 1988: 411). His published justification of this move includes the following confirmation of his earlier "Hymn" to Lenin:

even if the figures of the enemies of Communism were accurate, the killings, starvings, frame-ups, unjust judgements and all the rest of it are a mere bagatelle [...] the Russian intervention was not only justified, but imperative, if unfortunately necessary. (MacDiarmid 1957)

Which is final proof, if nothing else, that MacDiarmid at least wrote more precisely in verse than he did in prose.

The "barley-bree" that allowed Goodsir Smith to be so indulgent of MacDiarmid's excesses may also have played a significant role in the incident that confirms their longevity, as well as the terminal falseness of his relationship to Russia. In 1962 at the Edinburgh Festival, an event he had disparaged in *Aesthetics in Scotland*, MacDiarmid participated in an International Writers' Conference discussion, during which he dismissed Alexander Trocchi's work as "spurious internationalism" (Bold 1988: 417). In a debate that was ostensibly polarised around the question of "nationalism v. internationalism", Andrew Murray Scott tells us that "MacDiarmid in fact denounced *all* modern fiction", and that Trocchi "found himself in the same camp as the best European and American novelists, whereas MacDiarmid found his support from the official delegates of communist countries" (Murray Scott 1991: 107–8). Murray Scott's slight implication that this source of support was in itself not to MacDiarmid's credit is quite unnecessary, however, when we consider how those delegates might have reacted to MacDiarmid's off-stage reference to Trocchi, William Burroughs and Ian Hamilton Finlay as "cosmopolitan scum" (Murray Scott 1991: 108). Thus, with an expression that drips the blood of those who perished in the Soviet Union's post-war anti-cosmopolitanism campaign, MacDiarmid reveals the enduring depths of his own spurious internationalism.

Appendix 1

Scottish Literature.

Literature in the Scots dialect, one of the northern dialects of *English* [q.v.] (with regard to Scottish literature in Gaelic, see *Celtic Literatures*). The flowering of Scottish literature dates from the period between the "wars of liberation" against the English (the beginning of the 14th century) and the Reformation (the third quarter of the 16th century). Poetry in the local dialect of the south of Scotland existed before this period, but cannot be categorised as a distinct literature.

In the "Golden Age" (14th–16th centuries) the nobility and the towns formed a unified front against England, and orientated themselves towards the continent, towards Flanders and France. The economic and cultural influence of England weakens and Scottish culture develops in a quite different direction to that of England. The first major work of this period is John Barbour's patriotic poem "Brus" (1376). The poets of the 15th century and the beginning of the 16th, the so-called "Makars", achieved an even greater flowering. A mainly allegorical court poetry was cultivated by the nobility, the court and the church, and developed under the dominant influence of *Chaucer* [q.v.]; its founders were King James I ("Kingis Quair"), E. [*sic*] Douglas and D. Lyndsay. The major Scottish poets, Robert Henryson (c. 1425–1500) [*sic*] and William *Dunbar* [q.v.] are, however, distinguished by a certain tendency towards realism and by their greater proximity to the literature of "the low". Henryson's "Testament of Cresseid" and "Fables" are among the best works of this period.

Alongside this court poetry, an anonymous urban poetry also developed, which has come down to us in a number of manuscript song collections, the majority of them satirical or drinking songs. Written *fabliaux* have also survived, e.g. "Thrie Priestis of Peblis", "The Dumb Wyf". In contrast to the court poetry, which adheres to French prosody, this folk poetry employs metres that are close to the metre of the ballads. The flowering of the oral poetry of the ballads also dates from the 15th and 16th centuries, although it has come down to us, almost without exception, in the form of later written records. The ballad emerged in the rural areas and was a reflection, on one hand, of the interests of the more regressive elements of the Scottish nobility, and, on the other, of the peasantry, who remained in patriarchal relations with their feudal masters.

The middle of the 16th century sees the beginnings of the demise of literature in the Scots dialect, due to the fact that the Reformation in Scotland was, to a significant extent, orientated towards England; the English Bible and the works of the protestant leader John *Knox* [q.v.], also written in English, hinder the development of a Scots literary language. The court literature would also soon make the transition to English. The backward socio-economic conditions of the mountainous regions of southern

Scotland allowed the preservation of the ballad, which survived through to the "Romantic renaissance".

In the 18th century, under the influence of a renewed interest in the "folk" poetry of the 15th and 16th centuries, a series of poets – beginning with Allan Ramsay and including R. Fergus [*sic*], H. Bangour [*sic*] and D. Mallet – cultivated a Scots vernacular poetry. But these poets employed the vernacular precisely as such, suitable only for particular genres (the "folk" ballad, the lyric), and without any pretence of cultural autonomy. This poetry has a somewhat amateur and, in significant degree, reactionary-romantic character; the misfortunes of the deposed Stewarts is one of its favourite themes. It is only in the work of Robert *Burns* [q.v.], a poet of the lowland Scottish peasantry, that vernacular poetry reaches more significant heights. There is no basis for distinguishing J. Thomson, Smollet and W. Scott from English literature in general.

In our times there has been a renewed attempt to revive poetry in the Scots dialect, made by the poet Hugh MacDiarmid (pseudonym). MacDiarmid is an original poet-philosopher, not devoid of revolutionary sympathy (two "Hymns to Lenin"), but with a confused world-view. His attempt to revive a Scots literary language is nothing more than a whim of the intelligentsia.

Further reading: Irving D., Lives of Scottish writers, London, 1850; same author, History of Scottish poetry, L., 1861; Smith G.G., Scottish literature (Character and influence), L., 1919; The Cambridge history of the literature [*sic*], ed. by A.W. Ward and A.R. Waller, v. II–The end of the middle ages, L., 1908.   *D. Mirskii*

(*Bol'shaia sovetskaia entsiklopediia* 1933: 57: cols 607–8)

Appendix 2

From "The Seamless Garment"	Отрывок о Ленине
His secret and the secret o' a'	Тайна его – это тайна всех,
That's worth ocht.	Кто работать умеет.
The shuttles fleein' owre quick for	Челнок засновал – значит, нужно
my een	
Prompt the thocht,	Пустить быстрее основу.
And the coordination atween	Нужно уметь сочетать движения
Weaver and machine.	Свои с машиной.
Tha haill shop's dumfoonderin'	Грохот машин меня, чужака,
To a stranger like me.	Сразу оглушит;
Second nature to you; you're	Тебе он привычен и ничуть не
perfectly able	мешает
To think, speak and see	Думать, говорить и видеть
Apairt frae the looms, tho' to some	Не только станки, хоть иным и это
That doesna sae easily come.	Дается с трудом.
Lenin was like that wi' workin' class	Так же вот Ленин легко разбирался
life,	
At hame wi't a'.	В жизни рабочих,
His fause movements couldna been	В движеньях своих он был точнее
fewer,	
The best weaver Earth ever saw.	Лучшего ткача на свете,
A' he'd to dae wi' moved intact	И все, к чему он прикладывал руку,
Clean, clear, and exact.	Удавалось на славу…
(MacDiarmid 1993: 1: 311–12)	(Gutner ed. 1937: 392)

Bibliography

Blok, Aleksandr. 1960–63. *Sobranie sochinenii v vos'mi tomakh* [Collected Works in Eight Volumes]. Moscow & Leningrad: Gosudarstvennoe izdatel'stvo khudozhestvennoi literatury.

Bol'shaia sovetskaia entsiklopediia [Greater Soviet Encyclopaedia]. 1933. Moscow: Sovetskaia entsiklopediia. 62: 607–608.

Bold, Alan. 1983. *MacDiarmid: The Terrible Crystal*. London: Routledge.

—. 1988. *Hugh MacDiarmid*. London: John Murray.

Burliuk, D, et al. 1912. *Poshchechina obshchestvennomu vkusu*. Moscow: G.L. Kuz'min. [pages unnumbered]

—. 1980. "A Slap in the Face of Public Taste" in Proffer, Ellendea and Carl R. Proffer (eds) *Russian Futurism*. Ann Arbor: Ardis. 179–80.

Buthlay, Kenneth. 1982. *Hugh MacDiarmid*. Edinburgh: Scottish Academic Press.

Chestov, Leo. 1932. *In Job's Balances*. London: Dent.

Dallas, E.S. 1866. *The Gay Science*. London: Chapman & Hall.

France, Peter and Duncan Glen (eds). 1989. *European Poetry in Scotland*. Edinburgh: Edinburgh University Press.

Gish, Nancy K. 1984. *Hugh MacDiarmid: The Man and his Work*. London: Macmillan.

Grieve, C.M. 1925a. "Towards the New Order" in *New Age* 36(22): 259.

—. 1925b. "Modern Russian Literature" in *New Age* 37(8): 92.

—. [1926] 1995. "Other Dramatists" in Riach, Alan (ed.) *Contemporary Scottish Studies*. Carcanet. 250–55.

—. 1926. "Contemporary Russian Literature" in *New Age* 40(1): 9.

Gutner, M. (ed.). 1937. *Antologiia novoi angliiskoi poezii* [Anthology of New English Poetry]. Leningrad: GIKL.

Lavrin, Janko. 1920. *Dostoevsky and His Creation*. London: Collins. [Originally Lavrin, Janko. 1918. "Dostoevsky and Certain of His Problems" *New Age*, 22(12): 229–30; (22)13: 252–54; (22)14: 272–73; 22(15): 288–90; 22(16): 312–14; (22)17: 327–29; 22(18): 354–56; 22(19): 372–74; 22(20): 389–90; 22(21): 410–12.]

—. 1925–26. "Vladimir Solovyov and The Religious Philosophy of Russia" in *New Age* 37(24): 283–84; 37(25): 295; 37(26): 308–9; 38(1): 9–10; 38(2): 21–22; 38(9): 104–5; 38(10): 118–19.

McCarey, Peter. 1987. *Hugh MacDiarmid and the Russians*. Edinburgh: Scottish Academic Press.

MacDiarmid, Hugh. [1926] 1995. "Towards a Synthetic Scots" [13 August 1926] in Riach, Alan (ed.) *Contemporary Scottish Studies*. Carcanet. 368–73.

—. 20 March 1934. [Letter to D.S. Mirsky]. National Library of Scotland, MS 26078, f. 1.

—. [1937] 2001. "To William McElroy" in Grieve, Dorian, Owen Dudley Edwards and Alan Riach (eds) *Hugh MacDiarmid: New Selected Letters*. Manchester: Carcanet. 139–40.

—. [1939] 1984. "Letter to Helen Cruickshank, February 1939" in Bold, Alan (ed.) *The Letters of Hugh MacDiarmid*. London: Hamish Hamilton. 129.

—. [1943] 1972. *Lucky Poet: A Self-Study in Literature and Political Ideas*. London: Jonathan Cape.

—. [1946] 1984. "Letter to *The Herald*" in Bold, Alan (ed.) *The Letters of Hugh MacDiarmid*. London: Hamish Hamilton. 784–85.

—. 1957. "Why I Rejoined" in *Daily Worker* (28 March): 2.

—. 1969. "A Russo-Scottish Parallelism" in Glen, Duncan (ed.) *Selected Essays of Hugh MacDiarmid*. London: Jonathan Cape. 38–43.

—. 1984. *Aesthetics in Scotland*. Edinburgh: Mainstream.

—. 1993. *Complete Poems* (eds Michael Grieve and W.R. Aitken). 2 vols. Manchester: Carcanet.

—. 1996. *The Raucle Tongue: Hitherto uncollected prose* (eds Angus Calder, Glen Murray and Alan Riach). Manchester: Carcanet. vol. 1.

—. 2001. *Hugh MacDiarmid: New Selected Letters* (eds Dorian Grieve, Owen Dudley Edwards and Alan Riach). Manchester: Carcanet.

Maiakovskii, Vladimir. 1955–61. *Polnoe sobranie sochinenii v trinadtsati tomakh* [Complete Works in Thirteen Volumes]. Moscow: Gosudarstvennoe izdatel'stvo khudozhestvennoi literatury.

Mirsky, D.S. 1925. *Modern Russian Literature*. London: Oxford University Press.

—. 1926. *Contemporary Russian Literature, 1881–1925*. London: Routledge.

—. 1927a. "Chekhov and the English" in *Criterion* 6(4): 292–304.

—. 1927b. *A History of Russian Literature from the Earliest Times to the Death of Dostoyevsky (1881)*. London: Routledge.

—. 1958. *A History of Russian Literature from its Beginnings to 1900*. New York: Vintage.

Murray Scott, Andrew. 1991. *Alexander Trocchi: The Making of the Monster*. Edinburgh: Polygon.

Murry, John Middleton. 1916. *Fyodor Dostoevsky: A Critical Study*. London: Secker.

Poeziia Evropy. 1977. Moscow: Khudozhestvennaia literature.

Scott, P.H. and A.C. Davis (eds). 1980. *The Age of MacDiarmid: Essays on Hugh MacDiarmid and his Influence on Contemporary Scotland*. Edinburgh: Mainstream.

Smith, G.S. 1996/97. "D.S. Mirskii and Hugh MacDiarmid: A Relationship and an Exchange of Letters (1934)" in *Slavonica* 3(2): 49–60.

—. 2000. *D.S. Mirsky: A Russian-English life, 1890–1939*. Oxford: Oxford University Press.

Smith, Sydney Goodsir. 1975. *Collected Poems*. London: John Calder.

Solov'ev, S.M. 1977. *Zhizn' i tvorcheskaia evoliutsiia Vladimira Solov'eva* [The Life and Artistic Evolution of Vladimir Solov'ev]. Brussels: Zhizn' s Bogom [subsequently re-published as Solov'ev, S.M. 1997. *Vladimir Solov'ev: zhizn' i tvorcheskaia evoliutsiia*. Moscow: Respublika.]

Stevenson, Robert Louis. 1995. *The Letters of Robert Louis Stevenson* (eds Bradford A. Booth and Ernest Mehew). New Haven and London: Yale University Press. vol. 5.

Tonge, John. 1938. *The Arts of Scotland*. London: K. Paul, Trench & Trubner.

Flying with Tatlin, Clouds in Trousers: A Look at Russian Avant-Gardes

Edwin Morgan

Russian avant-garde poetry has been a formative influence on the poetry of Edwin Morgan. Blok, Maiakovskii, Khlebnikov and Kruchenykh have inspired Morgan's own forward-looking and sonically innovative poetry.
Keywords: Aleksandr Blok, Velimir Khlebnikov, Aleksei Kruchenykh, Vladimir Maiakovskii, Edwin Morgan, Futurism.

During the last years of the Soviet Union I wrote a poem for the opening of the East-West conference at the old Third Eye Centre in Glasgow (now the Centre for Contemporary Arts); the Third Eye Centre, unlike its successor, gave literature a high profile, and those who remember it do so with fondness and regret. Its director, Chris Carrell, was a man of vision and energy, with excellent contacts in Russia and Eastern Europe, and he organised a number of remarkable events that encouraged a commerce of ideas between Scotland and Russia. The conference I wrote the poem for was called "New Beginnings", and was meant to celebrate the heady days of *perestroika* and *glasnost*; the poem, until now unpublished, is called "New Beginnings and Old Memories":

I shall never know who he was, that socialist
    slipping my conservative parents' net in '32,
leaving me those stunning copies of *USSR in Construction*
    to pore over and be caught for ever by the future.
Also I do not forget the wartime letters
    from my friend George who joined the navy,
survived the blizzard-battered convoys to Murmansk
    while I was scraping the desert from my mess-tin.
Enough of war; and let construction be reconstruction,
    watch Perestroika skimming in her troika
like Mungo's mother over the old badlands, rocks
    of bureaucracy, sands of censoriousness,
bogs of dogma, let the horses whinny and get a whiff
    of good bread high free blue bright heady air.
And it's a double troika, it's a sixareen,

Art, music, poetry, dance, film, drama,
with a bareback juggler, criticism – good god – yes,
     criticism, discussion, the opening of the doors
of perception, the necessary *glaz* and *golos* of Glasgow's   [eye; voice]
     glasnost, with a clown or two to crown it;
to get it all going, with the sound of ravishing harmonies,
     the flutes of Glasgow District Council, the clarsach
of Strathclyde Regional Council, the bagpipe of the Scottish
     Arts Council, the cor anglais of the Arts Council
of Great Britain, the balalaikas of Visiting Arts
     and the drums of the Foreign and Commonwealth Office:
a welcome, to soviets and councils and people
     east and west, to celebrate all our new beginnings.

The poem refers at its beginning to the year 1932, when I was twelve,
and when I first got sight of copies of the multilingual Russian propaganda magazine *USSR in Construction*. The magazine, as its title suggests, was very Constructivist, with emphasis on Soviet achievements
in architecture, engineering and film, well illustrated with photographs
bled off the page (this seemed frightfully modern), and with a general
optimistic and, if you like, Futurist tone. Both the photographs and
tone chimed with my own feelings during the 1930s, a decade which
coincided with my teens. I was studying for my "Higher" in Art at
school, and I was much attracted by modern architecture, and by Le
Corbusier in particular. Even today I have a sinking of the heart when
I see on TV high-rise buildings being demolished. Since Le Corbusier
had a big influence on the modernisation of Russian architecture, all
this helped to bolster my interest in Russia; but it also made me look
at Glasgow.

The much-maligned 1930s, once you had got over the hump of
the Great Depression at the beginning of the decade, were in many
ways a period of prosperity and innovation. Modern style came to
Glasgow for the first time since Rennie Mackintosh. The Beresford
Hotel, the Odeon Cinema, the Cosmo Cinema, the Kelvin Court flats,
the Lumex lamp factory, the Bennie Railplane, and most of all the
Empire Exhibition in Bellahouston Park – all these were not just modern but modernist. The three hundred-foot Tait's Tower at Bellahouston might well have appeared in Moscow or Berlin at that time. When
the Empire Exhibition opened in 1938 (and I had a season ticket), I

was studying Russian at Glasgow University and, although I enjoyed my Pushkin, I was also immediately drawn to the sense of modernity in early twentieth-century Russian arts, particularly as I found there an entirely different sort of modernity from what I had supposed to be "modern" in the works of Ezra Pound and T.S. Eliot – a left-wing modernity not devoted to rearranging the past, but rather to adumbrating the future. I found it thrilling, and tried to find out as much as I could about it.

Tait's Tower, I discovered, might have been a modest cousin of Vladimir Tatlin's Monument to the Third International in Russia, which was to be twice the height of the Empire State Building in New York, but was never built. The models and drawings for Tatlin's Tower depict a structure that is both Constructivist and Futurist, consisting of inter-locking spirals, cylinders and cubes – complex, abstract, but also functional. It would have contained offices, a radio station, printing presses, and a huge external screen for public information. Lack of the necessary technology meant it was never put up, though Tatlin's models won prizes at international exhibitions. Tatlin tried again in the late 1920s with what he called his *Letatlin*, a sort of glider for the masses (*Letatlin* was a pun on his own name and the Russian verb *letat'*, to fly; this project also came to nothing, though the machine was made and underwent field trials near Moscow). The *Letatlin* had curved, organic-looking wings reminiscent of Leonardo da Vinci's drawings for a manned flight machine. Although it failed as a practical proposition, its value lay in its expression of Soviet millenarianism, of the feeling that artists and engineers should combine forces to make future life better than present life. I couldn't help thinking of George Bennie's railplane, the rocket-like elevated railway system, which you could see for many years slowly rotting away near Milngavie, and which certainly would have worked if anyone had taken it up; like so many things invented here, it was developed elsewhere, in Germany and America, and we are left with hardly even the memory of Bennie the inventor (and hardly even with the word "railplane", once familiar, but now only to be found in the best dictionaries).

It was through reading about a colleague of Tatlin, Vladimir Maiakovskii, that I began to appreciate the extent of the Russian avant-garde; but the upheavals of the years before and after 1917 are perhaps better illustrated, at least initially, in the example of Aleksandr Blok. There had been a great ferment of ideas in Russia before the Revolution, from at least 1910, but the Revolution released and channelled energies through all areas in the arts – literature, painting, film, architecture, photography, graphic design, theatre, even ceramics. Already a major poet prior to 1917, and the most significant figure in the dominant Symbolist movement, the refined and recessive Blok was shaken into a kind of second life, brief though it turned out to be, the most notable product of which was his long poem "The Twelve" [*Dvenadtsat'*]. Revolutionary in both style and content, with street language, broken rhythms, cinematic montage effects, and more than a touch of futurism, it was translated into Scots by Sydney Goodsir Smith as "The Twal" for his book *Figs and Thistles* (1959), and printed with its original Russian title and a dedication to Hugh MacDiarmid. It's a vigorous translation, and the howling winds and blafferts of snow of the original seem to fit well into the Scottish, especially at its end:

Wha's yonder, wi the Reid Flag? There!
Can ye see the man? It's mirk as hell!
Wha's yonder, rinnan by the hooses?
In the shadows dernan his sel?

Och, never heed – I'se get ye yet!
Surrender, man, for your ain guid!
– Nou then, brither, ye've been tellt!
Come out! – Or we shoot!

Crak tak-tak! – Nocht but the echo
Dinnles frae ilka hoose…
Nocht but the gowlan cavaburd
Lauchs frae the snaw-wreithe in the close!

    Crack-tak-tak!
    Crack-tak-tak!…

And sae thae mairch with sovereign tread…
At their heels the stairvin tyke…
The bluid-reid standart at their heid…
And, skaithless frae their bullets' flicht,

Seen by nane i' the snawblind nicht,
Throu the storm wi lichtlie pace,
Aa besprent wi pearls o ice,
His croun a white nimbus o roses,
Aye at their heid there mairches – Jesus. (Smith 1975: 118–19)

– Кто там машет красным флагом?
– Приглядись-ка, эка тьма!
– Кто там ходит беглым шагом,
Хоронясь за все дома?

– Все равно, тебя добуду,
Лучше сдайся мне живьем!
– Эй, товарищ, будет худо,
Выходи, стрелять начнем!

Трах-тах-тах! – И только эхо
Откликается в домах...
Только вьюга долгим смехом
Заливается в снегах...

         Трах-тах-тах!
         Трах-тах-тах...

...Так идут державным шагом –
Позади – голодный пес,
Впереди – с кровавым флагом,
     И за вьюгой невидим,
     И от пули невредим,
Нежной поступью надвьюжной,
Снежной россыпью жемчужной,
     В белом венчике из роз –
Впереди – Исус Христос. (Blok 1960–63: 3: 358–59)

Hugh MacDiarmid was an almost exact contemporary of Maiakovskii, knew about him, referred to him now and again in his work,
and certainly admired him, but was probably much closer in spirit to
Blok. Like Blok, he was basically a symbolist, and MacDiarmid's
Scots version of Blok's poem about an unknown woman, "Neznakomka", which begins "At darknin' hings abune the howff", is a
memorable poem (see MacDiarmid 1993: 1: 88). MacDiarmid was an
eccentric homespun avant-gardist, and aspects of his poetry have a
quasi-futurist quality that owes nothing to the Russian, but is

nonetheless interesting in its own right. Although MacDiarmid was
not inward with Maiakovskii's poetry as he was with Blok's, did not
try to translate it and in fact knew very little about it, he was clear
about the importance of Maiakovskii as a political poet and as a poet
of the Revolution. MacDiarmid was also at that time an avowed
Communist, and thought that Scotland could do with such a writer and
fighter as Maiakovskii. MacDiarmid wrote an elegy on Maiakovskii
after his death in 1930, which although not a very good poem makes
some important points:

In Memoriam Vladimir Mayakovsky

O would your nature now from Russia gone
Might reincarnate in a Scottish bard;
Some influence from you, some knowledge of your life
By genius's intuition be bestowed usward;
For there are thousands inarticulate here
In Glasgow in the worst slums that Europe knows
That could they speak, with poet's power endowed,
Of your great voice would ring like echoes.
Alas! By your suicide far more is lost
Than Scotland's ever had of what it needs the most,
Or's ever like to have save so by death transferred
A man's tones are at last among our toy-angels heard.
(MacDiarmid 1993: 2: 1282)

The emphasis here is on giving a voice to the inarticulate in society,
which Maiakovskii certainly did (though he did other things as well).
The poor ought to be empowered, and one way of doing this is for a
poet to identify, and identify with, their problems. In Scotland, in
Glasgow, MacDiarmid argues, this is not being done. What Scotland
lacks is "your great voice", and Maiakovskii's voice was indeed great,
both physically and metaphorically. In the closing line he emphasises,
in his macho way, the maturity and strength of "a man's tones", which
he can't hear in Scotland among our "toy-angels". (Who are they?
Edwin Muir might be one!?)

    In my own case, I was attracted to Maiakovskii for both political
and aesthetic reasons. He genuinely believed in the possible transformation and betterment of society and wanted to put his art at the service of his society, but without giving an inch to the philistines who

accused him of producing work that might not be immediately understood by ordinary people. This was a heroic stance, which at times
tore him apart, but I admired it; it made me want to learn as much as I
could about the background to his poetry, and indeed of his other
work, in theatre and cinema, for example. Like Maiakovskii, I was
greatly interested in language, and this set me fast on the track of the
Futurist movement with which Maiakovskii was identified, before and
after the Revolution. The Futurists believed that language was not ex-
empt from revolution in society, and ought to prepare itself to extend
and develop its instrumentation away from ideas of correctness or tradition or acceptability. At one level, spoken language, street language,
should be drawn into serious literary contexts; at another, writers
should be able to invent new words and to regard neologisms as a tool
for exploration and discovery, and for the general dumfoonering of
hidebound conventional critics. As Maiakovskii wrote, "Innovation,
innovation in materials and methods, is obligatory for every poetical
composition" [Новизна, новизна материала и приема обязательна
для каждого поэтического произведения] (Mayakovsky 1970: 56;
1955–61: 13: 116); and, in one of his poems, "Poetry – all poetry – is
a journey into the unknown" [– Поэзия – вся! – езда в незнаемое]
(Maiakovskii 1955–61: 7: 121). Maiakovskii was a signatory to the
Futurist Manifesto of 1912, "A Slap in the Face of Public Taste",
which reported that "the past is crowded" [*proshloe tesno*] and ad-
vised poets to throw Pushkin and other famous masters "overboard
from the Ship of Modernity" [*s Parokhoda sovremennosti*]; it also de-
clared the poet's right to "to enlarge the scope of the poet's vocabulary with arbitrary and derivative words" (Burlyuk et al. 1980: 179).[1]
This iconoclasm was a sign of the times: similar things were being
said in Italy by Marinetti, the leading Futurist outside Russia. But I
knew that Maiakovskii had a high concept of art behind the iconoclasm, a concern for structure, even if it was structure of a new kind.
Some of his poems, which at first sight look like sprawling free verse,
are in fact based on a free but definite metrical beat, and rhyme is
hardly ever given up, though it may be hidden or disguised in carefully engineered ways. I liked that, and to some extent it set him apart

---

[1] Translation modified: "на увеличение словаря в его объем произвольными и
производными словами" (Burliuk et al. 1912: pages unnumbered).

from the other Futurists; I also, in a different way, liked the more extreme experiments that came out of the Futurist movement, experiments that were condemned in Russia after 1930. Much of this work was almost forgotten because works were not reprinted, but has re-emerged and received much attention in recent years, partly because it was prophetic of things like concrete poetry, language poetry and sound poetry, and partly also because linguists are now more reluctant to rubbish the idea that all aspects of a language have meaning, including its sounds and its morphological units.

The Futurists talked a lot about *zaum'*. In a dictionary, this might be translated as "nonsense", but the Futurists weren't having that sort of nonsense. *Zaum'* properly means "beyond sense" or "transrational", and the Futurists' aim was to release the hidden powers of language. One of them, Aleksei Kruchenykh, had a slogan, "*slovo shire smysla*" – "the word is broader than its meaning" –, and I know I felt instinctively that this must be true. I began to translate some of the Futurist poems written in *zaumnyi iazyk*, transrational language, including those of Velimir Khlebnikov, the most important of the *zaum'* poets. One of his poems, "Incantation by Laughter" [*Zakliatie smekhom*], probably written in 1907 or 1908, might be called a sound-poem, and is built up on imaginative extensions of the word "laughter" [*smekh*]. I translated it, using the same means, into Scots under the title "Gaffincantrip":

Och, unsneck, snicherers!
Och, unsnib, snicherers!
Gar thaim smicker wi smirlin, gar thaim smirkle skirlinlie,
Och, snicher smirtlinlie!
Och, the snorkstock o the besnorkit – the smue o the besmuit snicherers!
Och, snocher snowkilie, smirl o the snirkit snirters!
Snowkio, snorkio,
Smirl and snitter, sneeterers and sneisterers,
Snicherikins and snocherikins.
Och, unsneck, snicherers!
Och, unsnib, snicherers! (Morgan 1996: 335–36)

О, рассмейтесь, смехачи!
О, засмейтесь, смехачи!
Что смеются смехами, что смеянствуют смеяльно,
О, засмейтесь усмеяльно!

О рассмешищ надсмеяльных – смех усмейных смехачей!
О, иссмейся рассмеяльно смех надсмейных смеячей!
Смейво, смейво,
Усмей, осмей, смешики, смешики,
Смеюнчики, смеюнчики.
О, рассмейтесь, смехачи!
О, засмейтесь, смехачи! (Khlebnikov [1930] 1986)

Some of the Futurists believed that if they could unlock the semantics of sound, they could produce a genuine world language, and this linked up with the visionary aspect of communism. Analogies can perhaps also be found in James Joyce's *Finnegans Wake* and MacDiarmid's *In Memoriam James Joyce*. As Kruchenykh wrote in 1921: "Transrational works may result in a universal poetic language which is born organically, and not artificially like Esperanto" (cited in Markov 1969: 345–46).[2]

Maiakovskii was too socio-politically calibrated to take his Futurism as far as Khlebnikov and Kruchenykh recommended, but he did invent words and he obeyed the Futurist desire to reinvigorate all literary expression through surprise, daring, shock, hyperbole, and an almost surrealist deployment of metaphor and simile. He kept his feet on the earth, but he wanted to amaze his readers and hearers. He was, as the title of one of his poems suggests, a "cloud in trousers" [*oblako v shtanakh*]. Is that funny? There is a great deal of humour and high spirits all through his poetry, but you never forget the underlying tensions and loneliness, and indeed anguish, of his stance *vis-à-vis* society and convention. In "A Cloud in Trousers", a long poem written in 1915, he uses the most extraordinary imagery to present a sense of his own vulnerability in an unhappy love affair. Raindrops on the window-pane howl and grimace like Notre Dame gargoyles. A fire brigade draws up to put out a fire in the room – it's his heart, you can smell the burning flesh. As he looks out, taxis bristle in his throat like

---

[2] Translation modified. "Заумные творения могут дать всемирный поэтический язык, рожденный органически, а не искусственно, как эсперанто". The original was first published in 1921 and later appeared in many of Kruchenykh's books; it is here cited from Kruchenykh 1923. It is slightly ironic that a typographical error has produced the word "eksperanto" in Kruchenykh's text, which reads like one of the neologisms of which he was so fond.

fishbones. The earth is fat and greasy like Rothschild's mistress. A
carriage passes, dripping with the cud of its inmates' dinners. At the
end, the universe falls asleep like a dog with its paw curled round its
huge ear infested with ticks – the stars.

It's a love poem, and it's a city poem. Involvement with the
modern city was one of the things that drew me to Maiakovskii. Glasgow was a small city in world terms, but it had to be written about, it
had to be made articulate, and I got good vibrations from poets like
Whitman and Hart Crane and Maiakovskii. One of Maiakovskii's
short poems, written in 1913, was much discussed, and sometimes
condemned because it appeared to be using Futurist techniques to
write about something that ought to be straightforward – a poet writing in an urban environment. But to Maiakovskii, what he had to say
was important, and he thought it could be understood. Think about it,
he used to say. The poem is called "A vy mogli by?", which might be
translated as "Yes but can you?" or "Yes but could you?". I translated
it into Scots as "Ay, but can ye":

Wi a jaup the darg-day map's owre-pentit –
I jibbled colour fae a tea-gless;
ashets o jellyteen presentit
to me the great sea's camshach cheek-bleds.
A tin fish ilka scale a mou –
I've read the cries o a new warld through't.
But you
wi denty thrapple
can ye wheeple
nocturnes fae a rone-pipe flute? (Morgan 1972: 19)

Я сразу смазал карту будня,
плеснувши краску из стакана;
я показал на блюде студня
косые скулы океана.
На чешуе жестяной рыбы
прочел я зовы новых губ.
А вы
ноктюрн сыграть
могли бы
на флейте водосточных труб? (Maiakovskii 1955–61: 1: 40)

A glass of tea, a plate of jelly, a tin fish hung up to advertise a shop –
poetry must come from these and things like them. William Carlos
Williams would have agreed. I agreed. But there were worries in Russia (not now, but at the time): how could anyone, with a dainty throat
or not, use a rone-pipe as a flute? I suppose one answer is that the hero
of James Kelman's *A Disaffection* (1989) can do it; but what Maiakovskii is suggesting is that your throat must not be too dainty to take
on the streets and all that that implies.

Streets, cars, trains, subways, skyscrapers – all this was a new
world for poetry to enter. Maiakovskii loved cars and bought himself
one, to the displeasure of some of the comrades. He also went to
America, the home of modernity, and wrote about it in both prose and
verse. He was thrilled and excited by New York, with which and in
which he had a love affair, and was especially stunned by Brooklyn
Bridge; indeed, his poem on that monument to engineering technology
is one of his best. It's also one of those I translated into Scots, and I
always liked it because it shows both the Futurist and the Constructivist strains at work together. There is an attractive fantastic element
– the poet goes onto the bridge like a conqueror, bestriding a cannon
with its snout in the air like a giraffe – but its main thrust is to praise
the workmanship of the bridge, which has created a solid, lasting object that is both useful and beautiful, both down-to-earth and visionary, an object such as a good poem should be:

It's as prood I am
              o this
                    wan mile o steel,
my veesions here
                    tak vive and forcy form –
a fecht
        for construction
                    abune films o style,
a strang
        trig-rivetit grid,
                    just whit steel's for! (Morgan 1972: 61)

```
Я горд
        вот этой
               стальной милей,
живьем в ней
               мои видения встали –
борьба
        за конструкции
                       вместо стилей,
расчет суровый
               гаек
                       и стали. (Maiakovskii 1955–61: 7: 85)
```

That steel-like strength is in Maiakovskii's poetry, and obviously there is an appeal to anyone like myself brought up in an area of steel-making and shipbuilding. Well-made things, whether from bridge-builders, or Maiakovskii, or W.S. Graham on the Clyde, are good. Urban Futurists are, of course, quite capable of enjoying a day by the sea, as described in Maiakovskii's poem in praise of the Black Sea health resort of Eupatoria. The poem is full of Futurist play on the word Eupatoria, which I have tried to maintain in the Scots translation:

```
O for the souch o the seas
                       and the glory o
the breeze
        that waffs owre Eupatoria!
(By-ordnar kindlike
                 in its peripatorium
it kittles
        the cheek o the haill Eupatorium.)
We'se lie
        on the *plage*
                 and plouter at the sandy-pats,
broichin and bronzin
                 wi the broon Eupadandycats
Skellochs
        and splish-splash
                       and the skraich o rollocks!
The joukin swankies,
                 the Eupajollocks!
Smeek-black broos
        o Karaite Jews
```

wi their skyrie bunnets
                    and Eupataptoos!
And him,
            fair pechin for as dark a skin
puir Muscovite –
                    Eupataryan!
Aawhere, roses
                on jimpy shanks,
and joyfu weans
                    at their Eupajinkajanks!
Ilka seikness
                cries Kamerad
                            uncondeetional
to the glaury plaisters
                    Eupamedeecinal.
Ilka kyte
            kests twa stane to Kilquhanity
in the rummle-and-pummle
                            o Eupatorianity.
It's a peety
            for aa the ither
                        sanatoria.
Man, there's juist nae place
                    like Eupatoria. (Morgan 1972: 70)

Чуть вздыхает волна,
                    и, вторя ей,
ветерок
            над Евпаторией,
Ветерки эти самые
                    рыскают,
глядят
            щеку евпаторийскую.
Ляжем
        пляжем
                    в песочке рыться мы
бронзовыми
                евпаторийцами.
Скрип уключин,
                всплески
                            и крики –
развлекаются
                евпаторийки.
В дым черны,
            в тюбетейках ярких

караимы
        евпаторьяки.
И сравнясь,
           Загорают рьяней
Москвичи –
        евпаторяне.
Всюду розы
          на ножках тонких.
Радуются
        евпаторенки.
Все болезни
         выжмут
            горячие
грязи
       евпаторячьи.
Пуд за лето
         с любого толстого
соскребет
        евпаторство.
Очень жаль мне
          тех,
            которые
не бывали
        в Евпатории. (Maiakovskii 1955–61: 9: 228–29)

Bibliography

Blok, Aleksandr. 1960–63. *Sobranie sochinenii v vos'mi tomakh* [Collected Works in Eight Volumes] Moscow and Leningrad: Gosudarstvennoe izdatel'stvo khudozhestvennoi literatury. vol. 3.

Burliuk, D., Alexander Kruchenykh, V. Mayakovsky, Viktor Khlebnikov. 1912. *Poshchechina obshchestvennomu vkusu.* Moscow: G.L. Kuz'min.

Bûrlyuk, D., et al. 1980. "A Slap in the Face of Public Taste" in Proffer, Ellendea and Carl R. Proffer (eds) *Russian Futurism.* Ann Arbor: Ardis.

Khlebnikov, Velimir. [1930] 1986. "Zakliatie smekhom" in *Tvoreniia* [Works] (ed. M.G. Poliakov et al.). Moscow: Sovetskii. 54.

Kruchenykh, Aleksei. 1923. "Deklaratsiia zaumnogo slova", in *Apokalipsis v russkoi literature* [Apocalypse in Russian Literature] MAF seriia teorii, № 1. Moscow: MAF.

MacDiarmid, Hugh. 1993. *Complete Poems* (ed. Michael Grieve and W.R. Aitken). 2 vols. Manchester: Carcanet.

Maiakovskii, Vladimir. 1955–61. "A vy mogli by?" in *Polnoe sobranie sochinenii v trinadtsati tomakh* [Complete Works in Thirteen Volumes]. Moscow: Gosudarstvennoe izdatel'stvo khudozhestvennoi literatury. 1: 40.

——. "Bruklinskii most" in *Polnoe sobranie sochinenii.* 7: 83–87.

——. "Evpatoriia" in *Polnoe sobranie sochinenii.* 9: 228–29.

——. "Kak delat' stikhi" in *Polnoe sobranie sochinenii.* 13: 81–117.

——. "Razgovor s fininspektorom o poezii" ["A Talk with the Taxman about Poetry"] in *Polnoe sobranie sochinenii.* 7: 121.

Markov, Vladimir. 1969. *Russian Futurism: A History.* London: MacGibbon & Kee.

Mayakovsky, Vladimir. 1970. *How Are Verses Made?* (tr. G.M. Hyde). London: Jonathan Cape.

Morgan, Edwin. 1972. *Wi the Haill Voice: 25 Poems by Vladimir Mayakovsky* (tr. Edwin Morgan). South Hinksey: Carcanet Press.

——. 1996. *Collected Translations.* Manchester: Carcanet.

Smith, Sydney Goodsir. 1975. *Collected Poems.* London: John Calder.

The Return of the Repressed

Sarah M. Dunnigan

The notion of a Scottish literary tradition epitomised by the twentieth-century Scottish Renaissance, and formed by Calvinist cultural paradigms, is built on the repression and occlusion of what is "other" to it. In particular, the literature of pre-Reformation Scotland is occluded and excluded in the construction of an "authentic" Scottish literary tradition.
Keywords: Cairns Craig, Edwin Muir, Renaissance literature, Reformation, Scottish Renaissance.

"the idea which had appeared before consciousness as the vehicle of this irreconcilable wish fell a victim to repression, was pushed out of consciousness with all its attached memories, and was forgotten." (Freud)

"There has been a forgetting of our past with the result that modern-day Scotland lacks proper cultural roots." (James MacMillan)

To suggest that Scottish literature has been created by the agency of "repression" might seem paradoxical; to imply that the "tradition" of Scottish criticism is defined by its repressive impulses may appear unduly pessimistic. Processes of elision or exclusion are perhaps inevitably part of the formation of an assertive literary and critical identity. This essay, however, suggests that certain Scottish identities, whether aesthetic or critical, are *deliberately* built on exclusion or, in Freud's phrase, "pushed out of consciousness"; and that the subject of what is here termed "repression" is eloquent of certain unexamined "anxieties" within mainstream Scottish criticism. This is illustrated by exploring several acts of cultural remembrance and "forgetting" from the two Scottish "renaissance" periods (the late-sixteenth and early-twentieth centuries), which, it is argued, are echoed in an influential contemporary narrative about Scottish literary history. The apparent entanglement of different literary periods within this essay is therefore intended to reveal certain perspectives that have formed, and continue to form, the critical looking-glass of Scottish cultural and literary commentary.

The first instance of "repressive desire" is drawn from the *ballat buik* which was compiled by one George Bannatyne in the 1560s. This was a manuscript of over four hundred leaves of Scottish poetry from the fifteenth and sixteenth centuries, divided into five sections containing religious, moral, comic, and erotic poems and, in conclusion, a collection of "fabillis".[1] Bannatyne's "choice" of Scottish poetry is unique and fascinating, but not well known enough to literary historians outside the early modern field.[2] And yet, for eighteenth-century Scottish anthologists, antiquaries, and archivists, it stood as the single, prodigious effort of a youthful merchant-poet to preserve and promulgate a national poetic heritage within a period of crisis;[3] to some degree, it is an elegiac or memorialising artefact. By 1568, the last temporal inscription found in the manuscript,[4] Mary Stewart, Queen of Scots, had been deposed, and what was to prove a troubled protestant regency instituted. Politically, these acts sealed a decade of violent reform, which had opened with parliament's declaration of the national establishment of the protestant faith without royal sanction. Bannatyne's anthology evidently displays sympathy with the new doctrinal climate,[5] excising (with two exceptions) all allusions to the fallen sovereign, Mary, and by renaming or simply excluding from the religious section subjects such as the Holy Name, the Seven Words on the Cross and, above all, Marian contemplations such as the Compassion of Our Lady and the Rosary. Both heavenly and earthly queens were silenced in accordance with new political and religious exigencies.

---

[1] For the manuscript's historical context, see MacQueen 1970; Lynch 1990; MacDonald 1986, 1993; van Heijnsbergen 1994.

[2] The manuscript is overwhelmingly but not exclusively devoted to Scottish poetry; see: Fox and Ringler 1980; Brown 1903–4; Hughes and Ramson (eds) 1982: ch.2; Kratzmann 1989.

[3] For identification of Bannatyne and his family, and analysis of the context and coterie of the manuscript, see van Heijnsbergen 1994.

[4] For analysis of the "1565" elision, see Fox 1968; the date of 1568 appears on the first leaf of the Draft MS; on ff. 97r, 290v, 298r, 375r. On f. 290, 1565 appears, then emended to 1568 (similarly on f. 298 "1566" "overwritten" to "1568"). "1562" is found on f. 90; hence Fox concludes that most of the manuscript was copied between 1562 and 1565, and that "1568" denotes the year of completion.

[5] For detail see MacDonald 1983, 1984, 1992.

The intertwining of literary and political cultures itself is hardly unusual in this period, but the apparent instances of "censorship" or omission on Bannatyne's part constitute clear "editorial" gestures towards the politicised, protestantised circles that comprised the manuscript's audience or readership. They are expressive of the wilful desire to erase, entomb or rather to repress the remarkably recent past, and to endorse a present in the process of reform. Yet the "sins" of the past are not so easily expiated. The manuscript's fourth section ostensibly contains poetry of love; but a sizeable part is devoted to poems that both excoriate and praise women. In literary terms, this can be explained by the enduring popularity of the *querelle des femmes* controversy, which, for over three hundred years in Europe, had fostered a diversity of rhetorical debate about the nature of woman. Bannatyne may have eagerly sought to imbue his anthology with fashionable literary polemics. Yet, ironically, in those poems which articulate the defence of women, the model of perfect womanhood is found in the Catholic Regina Maria:

ffor in reuere[n]s of the hevy[n]nis queen
We awcht to wirschip all weme[n] yat bene

ffor of all creaturis that evir wer get and born
Thus wot ye weill a woma[n] was the best
By hir sone wes recouerid the bliss that we had lorne
And thruch hir sone sall we come to rest
And bene ysavit gife that our self lest
Quhairfoir methinkis gif ye haif grace
We ochtin weme[n] honor in every place ("All tho that list": ll.160–68)[6]

As a consequence, this section of the manuscript seems both censored and yet unexpurgated, the locus of a residual Mariology as well as of its suppression (see Dunnigan 2002: ch.2; Newlyn 1992). The presence of the Blessed Virgin within an evidently protestantised text may be explained in a number of ways, the most obvious being that the influence of reformed practices within the cultural sphere were not imposed rapidly (the manuscript apparently ends, after all, only in

---

[6] Attributed erroneously to Chaucer; Fox and Ringler suggest this may have been copied from Thynne's 1532 Chaucer (Fox and Ringler eds 1980: xxxvii).

1568) or with a degree of absolutism. In a wider sense, there is evidence of the Reformation acceptance, even "rehabilitation" of Marian devotion, rather than its absolute destruction. The Virgin remained as the supreme model of faith in the word of God (*sola fide*), and as the guarantor of the reality of the Incarnation and of Christ's humanity (see Pelikan 1996: 19–20). The Marian presence in Bannatyne's fourth part also forms a counterpart to the predominantly Christological nature of the manuscript's religious section proper. But what Annabel Patterson terms "the hermeneutics of censorship" (Patterson 1984) – in the Bannatyne context the transformation of Catholic into Reformed devotion – is peculiarly complex. After all, only a year earlier, the *Gude and Godlie Ballattis* had been printed in Edinburgh, which crystallised the new popular art of protestant worship (see *Ane compendious buke* 1567). The shadow of the Virgin which haunts this section of the Bannatyne manuscript is therefore the emblem of a Reformation which, by the late 1560s, was well-entrenched but by no means absolute, unchallenged, or unqualified. Bannatyne's manuscript speaks also of the desire to fashion an image, a monument, or perhaps simulacra of "Scotland", or at least some kind of nationally inspired *florilegium* or anthology; but it emerges as partial and incomplete, haunted in subtle ways by "the Other" which it has sought to repress.

This example of the Bannatyne manuscript serves as a way of illustrating the psychoanalytically inflected resonance of this essay's use of the term "repressed", intended to evoke the practice of forgetting or ignoring of unresolved conflicts, unacknowledged desires, or the "traumatic" past. While drawing on specific and, in the case of the earlier Renaissance period, possibly more obscure or less well-known literary moments, the essay is essentially concerned with the "haunting" of Scotland's national, critical psyche. Cairns Craig, writing about Edwin Muir's version of Scottish history and of contemporary historical narratives of Scotland in *The Modern Scottish Novel: Narrative and the National Imagination*, contends that the "Scottish predicament" can be epitomised as

the total elision of the evidence of the past and its replacement by a novelty so radical that it is impossible for the individual to relate it to his or her personal memories. And impossible, therefore, for that environment to be "related" as a coherent narrative. The

constant erasure of one Scotland by another makes Scotland unrelatable, un-
narratable: past Scotlands are not gathered into the being of modern Scotland; they are
abolished. (Craig 1999: 21)

This essay endorses such a notion of perpetual "erasure", but suggests,
in contrast, that the impulse to bring about "a coherent narrative" – a
cultural story or literary version of the past which Scottish criticism
tells itself – is intimately related to the question of desire. It is vital to
comprehend the "psychic" content of the critical, no less than the literary, work. One way of accomplishing this is to uncover some
strange and surprising affinities in the creation of Scotland's "Renaissances".

Since the early part of the last century, Scotland has managed,
somewhat hubristically, to possess two "Renaissances". This is well
before the eminent art-historian, Erwin Panofsky, proposed the idea of
not one but many individual, temporally different "renascences" (Panofsky 1960), and even longer before post-structuralist and new histori-
cist approaches to early modern English literature fashioned a pseudo-
democracy in questioning the contours of a centralised Renaissance
(when, in fact, Scotland, unlike Ireland, still largely remains ignored).
Posing the question of when precisely each of these "Renaissances"
began and ended may well be akin to debating the number of angels
that can dance on the point of a pin: while Denis Saurat's essay of
1924 bestowed the term on MacDiarmid and the writers of *Northern
Numbers* and *Scottish Chapbook*, others might posit beginnings in the
1880s and 1890s; and the first Scottish "Renaissance" may encompass
as great a span as the period c.1500–1750.[7] It is neither possible nor
necessary here to debate the precise temporal contours of either
period, but rather to emphasise the interesting fact that the same category – whether used as a chronologically or culturally defining term –
is used without eliciting critical comment or question.

While one may take this as yet another instance of Scotland's
marvellously self-inventive capacity for paradox and dualism –
apropos of T.S. Eliot, Edwin Muir, and above all G. Gregory Smith –
it most probably arises from the fact that, as R.D.S. Jack notes,

---

[7] This is the historical compass given in Heijnsbergen and Royan (eds) 2002: ix.

the emergent discipline of Scottish Literature, in striving to forge a separate identity, has chosen effectively to erase the years between James VI's assumption of royal power in the late sixteenth century and Allan Ramsay's initiation of the so-called 'Vernacular Revival' in the early eighteenth. (Jack 1997: 66)

For the majority of Scottish cultural critics, there is only one Renaissance, which, unlike the rest of Western Europe, happened in the twentieth century. This may be dismissed as a minor quibble made by the disaffected over what constitutes Scotland's "true renaissance", but it is intended in the present context as a serious critique of Scottish criticism's limited horizons and limited powers of self-questioning. Despite the recent habit of alluding to Scotland's seeming "plurality" – an apparent state of Bakhtinian *heteroglossia* – it might still be argued that Scotland's apparently inventive self-fashioning actually rests on the desire for a shining singularity of self-definition: the single, essentialist definition which occludes and excludes all others that impinge upon or confuse the desired clarity. The composer James MacMillan made a similar point in a speech that provoked controversy and outrage at the Edinburgh Festival in 1999: "This tendency to restrict, to control and to enforce conformity and homogeneity is an obsessive and paranoid flaw in the Scottish character" (MacMillan 2000a: 16). MacMillan was speaking about what he passionately perceived to be the ineradicable sectarianism and bigotry of Scottish society. He identified "obsessive attempts, historically and contemporaneously, to periphalise and trivialise the Catholic experience in Scotland" (MacMillan 2000a: 16). MacMillan's arguments merit a separate examination that is not possible within the scope of the present essay. Instead, I wish to use his argument about the Scottish marginalisation of Catholic experience, artistically rendered, as one way of elucidating what I would term the "inferior" medieval and Renaissance literature within the Scottish critical psyche. If Scotland's imagination is conceived to be protestant, and in particular lent the doctrinal cast of Calvinism (as Cairns Craig's recent work argues), then such a "master-narrative" has no room for what is so potently "other". If there is little room for, or accommodation of, the artistic and cultural languages of Catholic Scotland or of a "Scottish Catholic imagination" (however one might begin to elucidate it), then pre-Reformation literature is first to disappear from the Scottish critical horizon. It is therefore ironic that it was in the second Renaissance period that medieval culture was perceived to have any role or potential in renewing Scotland's literary vision (see Parkinson 2002).

Much of the non-fictional writing of the twentieth-century Renaissance and its genuine polemical quality needs to be reassessed. There have been many critiques of Edwin Muir's (in)famous thesis about the irreparable failure of the Scottish imagination and its roots within linguistic schism. Yet what is rarely pointed out is the fascination of Muir and other writers associated in different ways with this artistic period for the medieval past. In the writing of Muir, MacDiarmid, and others, one witnesses a serious and concerted effort to resurrect in aesthetic, intellectual, and spiritual terms a part of Scotland in which current critical narratives invest little interest. Muir's essay on Robert Henryson is an obvious but interesting example:

Henryson's poetry has two main virtues; one the property of his age, the other more specifically his own [...] He lived near the end of a great age of settlement, religious, intellectual, and social; an agreement had been reached regarding the nature and meaning of human life, and the imagination could attain harmony and tranquility. (Muir 1949: 7)

It can be argued that this instance, and many others, are merely contentious acts of imaginative "beatification". Muir perceives in pre-Reformation Scotland a phantasmic image of wholeness, purity, and unity; a purely illusory wholeness which is simply part of Muir's underlying poetics of loss, mourning, and melancholia.[8] The idea of "the medieval", unduly simplified, performs an act of compensation and consolation for the lack within Muir himself, through which he projects onto contemporary Scotland a version of Joyce's "cracked looking-glass" Ireland. And one can find both Muir and MacDiarmid guilty of fashioning their own partisan image of medieval Scotland, largely composed of the trinity of William Dunbar, Robert Henryson, and Gavin Douglas (although MacDiarmid included in his *Golden Treasury* of 1940 the Bannatyne manuscript, and even a piece by arch-

---

[8] On Muir's work as a whole see, for example, Aitchison 1988, Knight 1980, McCulloch 1993.

Marian polemicist George Buchanan; MacDiarmid's anthology is as
biased as any other but is fruitfully eclectic).

What is not often perceived, however, at least to a sufficient degree, is the extent to which the preoccupation with the medieval in
these "second Renaissance" writers is also sympathy for (inevitably) a
Catholic imagination, perhaps surprisingly so, given the notorious
anti-Irish bias of some Renaissance writers (see McIlvanney 2001). Of
course, in Muir and others, no explicit doctrinal statement of alle-
giance is found to compare with those of Fionn MacColla, an ardent
convert, and Compton Mackenzie, especially in his *Catholicism in
Scotland* (1936), and his *Catholic Barra*, published in John Lorne
Campbell's *Book of Barra* (also 1936), about the faith and culture of
Scotland's indigenous Gaelic Catholicism.[9] *Catholicism in Scotland* is
an eloquent and reasonably scholarly work, which prefigures Mac-
Millan's arguments in a striking number of ways. Mackenzie takes
issue with readings of Scottish culture, art, and history that serve only
to endorse Scotland's protestant identities. The project was suggested
to Mackenzie by James Leslie Mitchell [Lewis Grassic Gibbon],
though in the dedication to Gibbon, who died before the book's completion, Mackenzie confesses that, "unwilling to involve myself in the
odium of religious controversy", he wished "to substitute Jacobitism
for Catholicism" (Mackenzie 1936b: 8).

It is easy to criticise the passions of Mackenzie, MacColla and
others as tendentious and distorting, guilty of their own form of
essentialism. One might argue that the Catholic sympathy, perhaps
even empathy, of the "second Renaissance" writers, whether merely
implicit or intensely felt, was only a kind of Yeatsian perception of
homogeneity: on the model of Ireland, Catholicism was intrinsically
associated with the nation-state. Yet it is the often contradictory artistic and cultural energies of this period, which ironically has served to
obscure the original Renaissance, which permitted the imaginative
exploration of another historical identity: the "second Renaissance"

---

[9] "I have drawn particular attention to the Catholic history of Barra because the
religious question is unfortunately still a dominant political issue in Scotland, and it is
useful to remind some of my fellow-countrymen both in the north and in the south
that the Catholicism of the Highlands and Islands, which was the faith of Wallace and
Bruce, is as essentially Scottish as the Established Church" (Mackenzie 1936a: 25).

may be seen as one of the few sustained or collective moments in Scotland's literary history, when "the Other" Scotland – medieval, Catholic – was allowed to return and inform freely the state of contemporary critical and intellectual debate. Ultimately, perhaps, this "other" found its best expression as an aesthetic trope. It is interesting that the only other significant period in Scottish cultural history when the literary iconography of the medieval is adopted is the early eighteenth century, when figures such as Archibald Pitcairne, the Ruddimans, Allan Ramsay, and James Watson are motivated, in part, by Jacobite, and implicitly Catholic, if not Episcopalian sympathies.

What has been suggested thus far is the existence of an aesthetic and intellectual sensitivity to, or cognisance of, a deeper cultural history in the later Renaissance. Yet the period is also renowned for presenting another historical narrative, or version of history. Embedded in the writing of Muir and others is the "catastrophic" or rather traumatic reading of Scottish culture and history, which sees the Reformation as the nation's crown of thorns. The poem "Scotland 1941" has become Muir's canonical expression of anger at John Knox and the Calvinist Reformation, which constituted a singular and overwhelming act of aesthetic desecration:

But Knox and Melville clapped their preaching palms
And bundled all the harvesters away,
Hoodocrow Peden in the blighted corn
Hacked with his rusty beak the starving haulms.
Out of that desolation we were born (Muir [1941] 1989: ll.8–12).

Muir confesses in his autobiography and letters that the process of writing his biography of Knox permitted a kind of personal purgation, but also one at a kind of "national" psychic level:

I came to dislike him more and more, and understood why every Scottish writer since the beginning of the eighteenth century had detested him: Hume, Boswell, Burns, Scott, Hogg, Stevenson. [...] Though dead for three centuries and a half, he was still too close for me to see him clearly. (Muir [1954] 1993: 226)

It was more particularly written for the purpose of making some breach in the enormous reverence in which Knox has been held and is still held in Scotland, a reverence

which I had to fight with too in my early days ... and which has done and is doing a
great deal of harm. (Muir 1974: 66)

The following can perhaps be seen as the culminating statement of
Muir's perception of the Knoxian cultural trauma:

What Knox really did was to rob Scotland of all the benefits of the Renaissance.
Scotland never enjoyed these as England did, and no doubt the lack of that immense
advantage has had a permanent effect. It can be felt, I imagine, even at the present
day. (Muir 1929: 309)

Cairns Craig neatly summarises the Knoxian tragedy for Muir: "Knox
becomes the embodiment of a culture of erasure" (Craig 1999: 16). He
places Muir's statement in the context of the late-nineteenth-century
reaction to the previously hagiographic Scottish biographies of Knox,
"challenged first by Andrew Lang and then by almost everyone who
wanted to escape from the world of Victorian puritanism, seen as one
of the logical outcomes of Knox's Reformation" (Craig 1999: 18).
One might also add that anti-Knoxian feeling had always been implicit
in a fairly constant stream of Marian writing – writing in defence of
the cause of Mary, Queen of Scots – from her death to the periods of
high Romanticism and Victorianism. A pro-Marian stance need not
necessarily imply a firm doctrinal position (Roman Catholic), but
rarely would the positions of both Mary and Knox be advocated
simultaneously. Muir's position may also have been influenced by
late-nineteenth-century Catholic aestheticism.[10]

It is not the intention of the present essay to determine whether or
not the Reformation was an artistic and spiritual calamity for Scotland, although one objective means of assessment is David Mac-
Robert's catalogue of material destruction by the Reformers (Mac-
Roberts 1962: 415–62). The debate remains open, renewed by Mac-
Millan's assertion that "[t]his cultural revolution involved a violent
repudiation of art and music from which it could be argued we have
not fully recovered" (MacMillan 2000a: 14). But there are clear dangers in adopting the Muir-like "traumatic" reading of the Scottish sixteenth century; indeed, a "traumatic reading" of Scottish history, as

---

[10] For similar views of Scottish medieval literature to those espoused by Muir, and
explicit sympathy with those views, see Moncrieff 1960: esp. 60–64.

Robert Welch says in the context of Irish history, is "catastrophic", and "for that reason, satisfying" (Welch 1993: 2; discussed in van Boheemen-Saaf 1999: 12), since one easily becomes guilty of the sin of omission in condemning the last four decades of that century and the next, as Muir does partly, to the status of an artistic wasteland. Most recently, Robert Crawford has pointed out the flaws in Muir's argument:

Muir's view of the Reformation is not straightforwardly wrong, but it is oversimplified and damaging. Accepting it can lead to a sense of pained isolation for the Scottish poet whose formation is protestant. If poets work with images, runs this argument, then the Scottish Reformation smashed images and so is hostile to poetry. (Crawford 2000: 190)

If Calvinism is a "religion which outraged the imagination" according to Muir, then it still helped foster an indigenous print culture in Scotland, and fired the literary and spiritual souls of seventeenth-century Scottish women who produced, paradoxically and even miraculously, the Calvinist version of female Catholic mysticism. Crawford has also argued for the existence of a protestant aesthetic in modern Scottish writing. Muir is easily chastised, even though in his defence one can argue that his dereliction of this period sprang from a coherently argued artistic (and utopian) vision. And it is a perhaps an unwanted or ironic effect that Muir's anti-Calvinist argument reinforced Calvinism as *the* essentialist or key Scottish identity, even though at the same time it seeks its annulment.

But, in the twenty-first century, why should we still give credence to the belief that the Reformation has left any lasting imprint upon Scottish artistic consciousness? One can produce other epochal dates in Scottish history which may arguably be of equal, if not more, cultural consequence. One compelling piece of evidence that there has been a lasting effect is the vigorous media and public response to James MacMillan's speech (MacMillan 2000b: 265–70). Another is the way in which Craig uses the premise that "Calvinism [. . .] was the foundation [. . .] of [. . .] Scottish identity" in order to articulate a particular aesthetic narrative or paradigm (Craig 1999: 37). In historical terms, this is undeniably true. As Craig notes:

Calvinism was the foundation of key institutions – religion, education – through which Scottish identity was shaped [...] whether for or against Calvinism's conception of human destiny, no Scot could avoid involvement in the imaginative world that Calvinism projected. (Craig 1999: 37)

The series of literary responses Craig charts in his work are evidence of, and reaction against, "the enduring legacy of Calvinism itself". Craig makes clear that "[i]f there is a stress in my argument on the Calvinist inheritance of Scottish culture, that is not to ignore the significance of other religious and intellectual traditions" (Craig 1999: 35). His argument is harnessed to particular ideas of Scottish intellectual modernity and its shaping of a modern fictional aesthetic, and it is also alert to the pitfalls of constructing "[a]ny version of a tradition" (Craig 1999: 35). Despite this, his influential work still posits the notion of enduring intellectual and aesthetic "tradition(s)", which at once achieves the elision of both the pre-Reformation era, and all non-protestant identities. This is symptomatic of the devaluing of the early period in the main current of Scottish literary and cultural criticism. In terms of recent anthologies, a useful index of current cultural tastes, there is evidence that this is being redressed. Significant collections in this respect are Jack and Rozendaal's *The Mercat Anthology of Early Scottish Literature* (Jack and Rozendaal 1997, 2000); and the pre-fourteenth-century medieval era has been superbly represented in Thomas Clancy's *The Triumph Tree* (Clancy ed. 1998).[11] Robert Crawford and Mick Imlah's *The New Penguin Book of Scottish Verse* also allows considerable inclusion from the medieval period (Crawford and Imlah eds 2000). In terms of general critical histories, though, the early periods are under-represented. There are, of course, a sizeable number of essay collections devoted, at least in part, to late-sixteenth and early-seventeenth-century Scottish literature.[12] One may also argue that the critical moment has passed for the writing of generalist literary histories. But it still remains true that the first "Scottish Renaissance" has fallen into a critical chasm, estranged from the "traditions" or continuities which critical

---

[11] See also the fascinating collection, Bateman, Crawford and McGonigal (eds) 2000, and Clancy and Márkus (eds) 1995.

[12] See most recently Mapstone and Wood (eds) 1998; Houwen, MacDonald and Mapstone (eds) 2000; van Heijnsbergen and Royan 2002.

orthodoxy still places at the heart of Scottish literary narratives. The explorations of this essay can therefore be brought full circle, since the neglect of the earlier Scottish Renaissance corpus persuasively arises from the persistent devotion to "writing the nation" – to seeking out, and accordingly investing in, a particular version or image of "Scotland". The original Renaissance does not conform to current critical conceptions of the narrative that has come to represent, imperfectly and partially, the narrative of "Scottish literature". R.D.S. Jack has suggested that the critical obfuscation of post-1603 Scottish literature rests on an aesthetic of essentialism:

the "death" of so much early Scottish literature is due to its prioritising the very characteristics of poetry, artifice, fantasy and linguistic virtuosity with which a paradigm based on prosaic naturalism, realism, Scots alone, and extrinsic values of Scottishness has most difficulty in coping. (Jack 1997: 77)

Theo van Heijnsbergen and Nicola Royan argue that

one of the attractions of Scottish texts from the sixteenth to the early-eighteenth centuries [is] in their own context, namely their capacity to articulate critical perspectives that are crucially different from – and thus interrogate – those conceptualized and canonized in more received models of interpretation. (van Heijnsbergen and Royan eds 2002: x)

The desire of contemporary critics to seek out defining narratives of nationhood pays little regard to the complex vision of literary nationhood articulated in the first Renaissance, when in fact the Renaissance image of nationhood is more complex and subtle than conventional accounts of Scottish literary history usually concede. The first Renaissance period also offers a subtle illustration of the "repressive" impulse. Despite their historical difference, Scotland's two Renaissances uncannily share a similar prescription for cultural self-renewal. If MacDiarmid advocated that the nation become incarnate through the refusal of English linguistic and literary paradigms, then so did James VI, sovereign author of the Jacobean or "Castalian" Renaissance of the 1580s and 1590s:

Ze may maruell paraduenture, quhairfore I should haue writtin in that mater, sen sa mony leimit men, baith of auld and of late hes already written thairof in dyuers and sindry languages: I answer that nochtwithstanding, I haue lykewayis writtin of it, for twa caussis: The ane is As for the[m] that wrait of auld, lyke as the tyme is changeit sensyne, sa is the ordour of Poesie changeit. [...] quhat I speik of Poesie now, I speik of it as being come to mannis age and perfectioun, quhair as then, it was bot in the infancie and chyldheid. The vther cause is. That as for thame that hes written in it of late, there hes neuer ane of thame written in our language. For albeit sindrie hes written of it in English, quhilk is lykest to our language, zit we differ from thame in sindrie reulis of Poesie, as ze will find be experience. (James VI [1584] 1955: 67)

James's treatise is ironically itself an imitative work, closely emulating earlier French and Italian defences of the vernacular.[13] Written by an eighteen-year-old king anxious to strengthen his power, it is a flawed work, arguably of greater interest symbolically than technically. The Renaissance vision imagined by James, and largely carried out by poet-courtiers such as Alexander Montgomerie and William Fowler, who were more artistically gifted than the king himself, was circumscribed by particular sovereign dictates. Yet the imaginative image of "Scotland",[14] or the national literary utopia to which the Jacobean Renaissance aspired, can be considered symptomatic of later narratives of nationhood: it too is animated in part by the ideological desire to erase or silence a troubling aspect of the past. In James's case, it was the need to exorcise the ghost of his mother, Mary, Queen of Scots, and her faith (Mary was executed three years after James's treatise appeared in print). For the Renaissance dreamt of by the devout Catholic queen's son would, in theory at least, be a distinctly protestant Renaissance. His treatise is therefore a work of vulnerability as much as one of putative empowerment.

James's *Essayes of a Prentise in the Divine Arte of Poesie* (1584), in which the treatise was first printed, is deeply influenced by the French protestant poet, Guillaume de Salluste Du Bartas (1544–1590). James produced a partial translation of Du Bartas's *L'Vranie on Muse Celeste*. Another symbolic commemoration of Du Bartas's importance was the translation of *La Judit,* "le triomfi de la foi", originally published in 1574 at Bordeaux by Thomas Hudson, an English musician at the Scottish court. In 1591, James published a

---

[13] In particular, Du Bellay 1549; see Jack 1967.
[14] While one can argue that the treatise projects a "national" poetic vision, its locus is also very firmly that of the Jacobean court.

partial translation of Du Bartas's *La Seconds Sepmaine, on Enfance du Monde,* entitled *The Furies.* Adherence to a protestantised "sacred Muse" by the courtier poets who composed James's intimate literary coterie could be considered expedient for any political or artistic advancement. Emulation of the Pléiade poet, Pierre de Ronsard (1524– 1585), for example, might conceivably have crypto-Catholic connotations.[15] While Alexander Montgomerie is deeply indebted to Ronsard's erotic poetry, James largely eschews the loyal Catholic poet, attacked by Calvinist pamphleteers in the 1560s, with whom his mother shared aesthetic and spiritual affinities. Ronsard, briefly resident at the Scottish court in the reign of Mary of Guise, was allegedly poetic tutor to Mary in France; she is the dedicatee and subject of many of his eulogies and ceremonial verse. Only two quatrains in alexandrine metre survive, clearly intended for Ronsard; instead she sent "'un buffet de 2000 ecus, surmonte d'un vase elaboure en forme de rocher, representant Le Parnasse' et portant cette inscription: 'A Ronsard, L'Apollon de la Source des Muses'" (Bodleian MS Add.c.92, f. 22v). Ronsard is perhaps too Marian a writer for James to emulate wholeheartedly.

Yet, despite the ways in which the Jacobean Renaissance appeared poised to institute a "protestant aesthetic", the actual writing produced by the king's coterie suggests that it was often doctrinally transgressive, slipping from monarchical restraint. Indeed, it is in the paradoxical inheritance of the medieval Catholic poet, Petrarch, that perhaps both the strength and the fragility of James's attempt to create a "Reformed" Renaissance is seen. When one writer, William Fowler, translates Petrarch's *Trionfi* – the "triumphe of chastnes, deathe, and fame" over earthly love – James praises its resurrection of cultural "nationhood".[16] This offers a striking parallel to the predicament of Renaissance Spain where, as Ignacio Navarrete points out in his study, *Orphans of Petrarch,* an acute sense of cultural inferiority led Spanish poets to respond to perceived crises in the national lyric tradition by

---

[15] See Dunnigan 2002: ch.3.
[16] See the sonnet printed in Meikle (ed.) 1914: 18.

continuously rewriting and reappraising Petrarch's work.[17] Petrarchan lyric and the Spanish empire therefore became metonymically associated. Similarly, the example of Petrarch offered Scottish poetry rich opportunities to create a "national lyric tradition", but one which was never as ideologically "pure" as the king might have wished.

Given such complexities, it would appear that the overlooked Renaissance period offers fertile ground for contemporary critical investigations of "nation and narrative". It also gives the lie, in part, to any sense, *apropos* of Muir and others, of Calvinist domination or a firmly entrenched protestantised literature. Scotland may remain as an example of a "Northern" Renaissance country, which shared more affinities with the Low Countries than with Spain. But there is other evidence to consider which renders impossible the idea of any untroubled homogeneity. The king who was tutored and enclosed by a Protestant regime in his early life, married a queen who later converted and was allowed to practise her closet devotions, and himself loved Esmé Stewart, Duke of Lennox, his French Catholic cousin who was condemned and exiled from Scotland by the machinations of ultra-Protestants (see Bergeron 1999; Dunnigan 2002: ch.3). There is evidence of what might be termed a "Counter-Reformation" aesthetic sensibility in Scottish literature. Edwin Muir would, or should perhaps, have been interested in Alexander Montgomerie, a convert suspected of covert Catholic counter-plotting, proclaimed as the supreme lyricist of the Jacobean court by James, but ultimately exiled from it. His poetry is haunted in all kinds of ways by his spirituality. In the seventeenth century, the major writers are largely Episcopalian – William Drummond, Alexander Craig. The former's devotional writing is more akin to Richard Crashaw than George Herbert and aesthetically has more in common with a Counter-Reformation European baroque.[18] In *John Knox: Portrait of a Calvinist*, ironically, Muir was prepared to concede that

---

[17] Navarrete also explores the idea of "cultural belatedness" in Spanish Renaissance poetics, which again has interesting parallels with anxieties within Scottish lyric writing of the period; see Navarrete 1994: 13ff.

[18] For advocacy of Drummond, see Jack 1993: 13.

[w]hatever was done in literature during this time came from the opponents of Calvinism or from men out of sympathy with it; Drummond of Hawthornden's poetry and his still nobler prose work, *A Cypress Grove*, some fine verses by Montrose, and Sir Thomas Urquhart's great translation of Rabelais. (Muir 1929: 307)

Each of these writers has the potential to unravel narratives of the Scottish imagination that have yet to be told.

This essay has sought to trace some flawed and imperfect attempts by literary "Scotland" to sculpt an image of itself which in some way convinces the beholder of some semblance of "authenticity". This seems always to have involved some form of "repression": whether, as with James, of a troubling Marian and Catholic past; or in the case of Muir and others, of the culture which post-dated the pre-Reformation culture unified in spirit and art (that is, the later Marian and Jacobean periods, and the seventeenth century). And lastly it suggests that the "repression" which has returned to haunt the present critical map of Scottish literature bases its cultural and aesthetic assumptions only on certain historical and religious events. The consequence is that only certain incarnations of Scotland are validated, or given greater overall importance than others. (This also has linguistic parallels in the persistent tensions between literature in Scots and English, and in Gaelic.)

This is not to suggest that current critical discourses in Scottish literature are "sectarian". Since that is an almost unimaginable claim to make of any other European (and English) literature at present, it would cast Scottish literature in the bleakest of lights. Rather my contention is that, despite assertion and celebration of Scottish literary and critical "plurality" ("Scotlands", not "Scotland"), there persists a sense in which some cultural roots are remembered more than others, to use MacMillan's phrase from the epigraph to this essay. Perhaps (all) that means is that we acknowledge more openly in Scottish criticism the different kinds of desires we invest in the literary work, or, in Mary Jacobus's sense, bring to the "scene of reading" (Jacobus 1999); that we admit to the complex role of cultural memory in the articulation of identity; and that we recognise the convergence and divergence of different desires over the "same knot of understanding". Scottish literature still needs to relinquish its investment in the idea of "tradition(s)", bound up with ideas of "authenticity", in order to ensure that certain aesthetic narratives or literary periods are not eclipsed. Once we make our confessions, then perhaps we can begin some kind of reparation.

Bibliography

Aitchison, James. 1988. *The Golden Harvester: The Vision of Edwin Muir*. Aberdeen: Aberdeen University Press.

"All tho that list of wemen evill to speik" in Ritchie, W. Tod (ed.). 1928–34. *The Bannatyne Manuscript writtin in tyme of pest 1568*. Edinburgh and London: Blackwood. 4: 64–70 (275r-76v).

Ane compendeous buke, of Godlye psalmes and spirituall psalmes and spirituall sangis, Newly translated out of Latine into Inglis. 1567. Edinburgh: John Scot for Thomas Bassandyne.

Bateman, Meg, Robert Crawford and James McGonigal (eds). 2000. *Scottish Religious Poetry from the Sixth Century to the Present: An Anthology*. Edinburgh: St Andrew Press.

Bergeron, David M. 1999. *King James and Letters of Homoerotic Desire*. Iowa City: University of Iowa Press.

van Boheemen-Saaf, Christine. 1999. *Joyce, Derrida, Lacan, and the Trauma of History*. Cambridge: Cambridge University Press.

Brown, J.T.T. 1903–4. "The Bannatyne Manuscript: a Sixteenth-Century Poetical Miscellany" in *Scottish Historical Review* 1: 136–58.

Clancy, Thomas Owen (ed.). 1998. *The Triumph Tree: Scotland's Earliest Poetry*. Edinburgh: Canongate.

Clancy, Thomas Owen and Gilbert Márkus (eds). 1995. *Iona: The Earliest Poetry of a Celtic Monastery*. Edinburgh: Edinburgh University Press.

Craig, Cairns. 1999. *The Modern Scottish Novel: Narrative and the National Imagination*. Edinburgh: Edinburgh University Press.

Crawford, Robert. 2000. "Presbyterianism and Imagination in Modern Scotland" in Devine, T.M. (ed.) *Scotland's Shame: Bigotry and Sectarianism in Modern Scotland*. Edinburgh and London: Mainstream. 187–196.

Crawford, Robert and Mick Imlah (eds). 2000. *The New Penguin Book of Scottish Verse*. London: Penguin.

Du Bellay, Joachim. 1549. *Deffence et illustration de la langue francaise*.

Dunnigan, Sarah M. 2002. *Eros and Poetry at the Courts of Mary Queen of Scots and James VI*. Basingtoke: Palgrave.

Fox, Denton. 1968. "Some Scribal Alterations of Dates in the Bannatyne Manuscript" in *Philological Quarterly* 42: 259–63.

Fox, Denton and William Ringler. 1980. "A description of the Bannatyne Manuscript" in Fox, Denton and William Ringler (eds) *The Bannatyne Manuscript: National Library of Scotland Advocates MS 1.1.6*. London: Scolar Press. ix-xvii.

Fox, Denton and William Ringler (eds). 1980. *The Bannatyne Manuscript: National Library of Scotland Advocates MS 1.1.6*. London: Scolar Press.

van Heijnsbergen, Theo. 1994. "The Interaction between Literature and History in Queen Mary's Edinburgh: the Bannatyne Manuscript and its Prosopographical Context" in MacDonald, A.A. et al. (eds) *The Renaissance in Scotland: Studies in Literature, Religion, History and Culture Offered to John Durkan.* Leiden: E.J. Brill. 183–225.

van Heijnsbergen, Theo and Nicola Royan (eds). 2002. *Literature, Letters and the Canonical in Early Modern Scotland.* East Linton: Tuckwell Press.

Houwen, L.A.J.R., A.A. MacDonald and S.L. Mapstone (eds). 2000. *A Palace in the Wild.* Leuven: Peeters.

Hughes, Joan and William Ramson (eds). 1982. *Poetry of the Stewart Court.* Canberra: Australian University Press.

Jack, R.D.S. 1967. "James VI and Renaissance Poetic Theory" in *English* 16(1967): 208–11.

—. 1993. "Scottish Literature: the English and European Dimensions" in Brink, Jean R. and William F. Gentrup (eds) *Renaissance Culture in Contact: Theory and Practice.* Aldershot: Scolar Press. 9–17.

—. 1997. "'Translating' the Lost Scottish Renaissance' in *Translation and Literature* 6: 66–80.

Jack, R.D.S. and P.A.T. Rozendaal (eds). 1997, 2000. *The Mercat Anthology of Early Scottish Literature 1375–1707.* Edinburgh: Mercat Press.

Jacobus, Mary. 1999. *Psychoanalysis and the Scene of Reading.* Oxford: Clarendon Press.

James VI. [1584] 1955. *Essayes of a Prentise* in Craigie, James (ed.) *The Poems of James VI of Scotland.* Edinburgh and London: Blackwood. 1: sig. K.ijr–K.ijv.

Knight, Robert. 1980. *Edwin Muir: An Introduction to his Work.* London: Longman.

Kratzmann, Gregory. 1989. "Sixteenth-Century Secular Poetry" in Jack, R.D.S. (ed.) *The History of Scottish Literature.* 4 vols. Aberdeen: Aberdeen University Press. 1: 105–24.

Lynch, Michael. 1990. "Queen Mary's Triumph: The Baptismal Celebrations at Stirling in December 1566" in *Scottish Historical Review* 69: 1–21

McCulloch, Margery Palmer. 1993. *Edwin Muir: Poet, Critic, Novelist.* Edinburgh: Edinburgh University Press.

MacDonald, Alasdair A. 1983. "Poetry, Politics, and Reformation Censorship in sixteenth-century Scotland" in *English Studies* 64: 410–21.

—. 1984. "Catholic devotion into Protestant lyric: the case of the Contemplacioun of Synnaris" in *Innes Review* 35: 58–97.

—. 1986. "The Bannatyne Manuscript: A Marian Anthology" in *Innes Review* 37: 36–47.

—. 1992. "Censorship and the Reformation" in *File: A Literary Journal* 1: 8–16.

—. 1993. "The printed book that never was: George Bannatyne's poetic anthology (1568)" in Hermans, J.M.M. and K. van der Hoek (eds) *Boeken in de late Middeleeuwen.* Groningen: Egbert Forsten. 101–10.

McIlvanney, Liam. 2001. "The Scottish Renaissance and the Irish Invasion: Literary Attitudes to Irishness in Inter-War Scotland" in *Scottish Studies Review* 2 (2001): 77–89.

Mackenzie, Compton. 1936a. "Catholic Barra" in Campbell, John Lorne (ed.) *The Book of Barra*. London: Routledge.

—. 1936b. *Catholicism in Scotland*. London: Routledge.

MacMillan, James 2000a. "Scotland's Shame?" in Devine, T.M. (ed.) *Scotland's Shame: Bigotry and Sectarianism in Modern Scotland*. Edinburgh and London: Mainstream. 13–24.

—. 2000b. "I Had Not Thought About it Like That Before" in Devine, T.M. (ed.) *Scotland's Shame: Bigotry and Sectarianism in Modern Scotland*. Edinburgh and London: Mainstream. 265–70.

MacQueen, John. 1970. "Introduction" in *Ballattis of Luve*. Edinburgh: n.p. xi–lxix.

MacRoberts, David. 1962. "Material Destruction Caused by the Scottish Reformation" in MacRoberts, David (ed.) *Essays on the Scottish Reformation 1513–1625*. Glasgow: J.S. Burns. 415–62.

Mapstone, Sally and Juliette Wood (eds). 1998. *The Rose and the Thistle. Essays on the Culture of late Medieval and Renaissance Scotland*. East Linton: Tuckwell Press.

Meikle, Henry W. (ed.). 1914. *The Works of William Fowler*. Edinburgh and London: Blackwood.

Moncrieff, George Scott. 1960. *The Mirror and the Cross: Scotland and the Catholic Faith*. London: Burns & Oates.

Muir, Edwin. 1929. *John Knox: Portrait of a Calvinist*. London: Jonathan Cape.

—. [1941] 1989. "Scotland 1941" in *Collected Poems*. London: Faber and Faber.

—. 1949. "Robert Henryson" in *Essays on Literature and Society*. London: Hogarth Press.

—. [1954] 1993. *An Autobiography*. Edinburgh: Canongate Classics.

—. 1974. *Selected Letters of Edwin Muir* (ed. P.H. Butter). London: Hogarth Press.

Navarrete, Ignacio. 1994. *Orphans of Petrarch: Poetry and Theory in the Spanish Renaissance*. Berkeley: University of California Press.

Newlyn, Evelyn S. 1992. "The Political Dimensions of Desire and Sexuality in Poems of the Bannatyne Manuscript" in McKenna, Stephen R. (ed.) *Selected Essays on Scottish Language and Literature. A Festschrift in Honour of Allan H. MacLaine*. Lampeter: Edwin Mellen Press. 75–96.

Panofsky, Erwin. 1960. *Renaissance and Renascences in Western Art*. Stockholm: Almquist and Wiksell.

Parkinson, David. 2002. "Dreams in the Clear Light of Day: Older Scots Poetry in Modern Scotland" in van Heijnsbergen, Theo and Nicola Royan (eds) *Literature, Letters and the Canonical in Early Modern Scotland*. East Linton: Tuckwell. 138–50.

Patterson, Annabel M. 1984. *Censorship and Interpretation: The Conditions of Writing and Reading in Early Modern England*. Madison, Wis.: University of Wisconsin Press.

Pelikan, Jaroslav. 1996. *Mary Through the Centuries*. Yale: Yale University Press.

Welch, Robert. 1993. *Changing States: Transformations in Modern Irish Writing*. London: Routledge.

Reflections on Lukács and Adorno: Some Co-ordinates for the "Scottish Literary Tradition"

David Miller

For the early Lukács, irony is the key trope of modern literature; autonomous art ironically counterpoints the cultural and economic demands of the society which it represents. Adorno develops this idea in his critique of art which might attempt to unironically affirm its authenticity and spontaneity. To speak of a Scottish literary tradition therefore deprives "Scottish literature" of its constitutive irony, and resubordinates it to national culture and economy.
Keywords: Theodor Adorno, George Lukács, Marcel Proust, C.K. Scott Moncrieff, irony.

It might seem odd to suggest that the debate between the two Marxist intellectuals Theodor Adorno and Georg Lukács can best be discussed in terms of their respective attitudes to a trope. Given the liberal platitudes that tend to haunt leading Marxists, one has come to expect the debate to focus on attitudes to the state apparatus, the role of the vanguard party, or the role of class and so forth. Nevertheless, the fact that Lukács' later works appear so binary and constrained, and are thus so objectionable to Adorno, is not a consequence of dispute over such issues. The tension and antagonism between the work of the two writers is in large part due to Lukács' banishment of a previously sophisticated use of irony. As we shall see, questions relating to the repudiation or acknowledgement of irony have ramifications that reach far beyond the merely rhetorical.

1. Lukács, Irony and History

In his early works such as *Soul and Form* and the slightly later *The Theory of the Novel*, Lukács argues that the development of the "form" of the novel is the result of a change at the level of human consciousness. The novel, in contrast to the epic, reflects the transformation and modifications of "man's" way of defining himself in terms of an all-embracing awareness of "each individual destiny".

Because existence no longer carries the substantive weight of the "consecration of the absolute" that was present in "epic" existence, this awareness registers as itself a "metaphysical homesickness" and thus Being is aware of its relentless "becoming" (see Lukács 1974: 91–151; 1978: 62–83). As Paul de Man makes clear, however, Lukács' theory is not merely "sociological", rather it is truly "philosophical" (de Man 1983: 53). The distinction Lukács makes between epic and novel is a distinction between the Hellenic and the Western mind, and the basis for this distinction is a three-fold dialectic. Theoretically, Lukács follows Hegel's *Phenomenology of Spirit* in maintaining that alienation is an intrinsic characteristic of reflective consciousness that functions with much the same dynamics as the "lordship and bondage" relation (Hegel 1977: 111–19). Put simply, the extension or intensification of consciousness is curiously bound-up with the self's estrangement from itself. Or to put in another way, any intensification of self-awareness is bought at the price of an increased alienation from some putative integral unit. The labour of this act of recognition is partly the return of the original labour necessary for our abstraction from the brute determining forces of nature. Once again following Hegel, Lukács places this "alienated" state of consciousness in relation to the intrinsic desire for "totality" and this need expresses itself as a kind of re-intensification of isolation, an "overflowing interiority". This desire or need for "totality" operates as a force, a kind of subconscious drive (Lukács' term is "longing"), operating at the level of general "historical development" (see Lukács 1978: 62–74). For the early Lukács, the novel emerges out of a dialectical relationship between the desire or need for "totality" and man's actual alienated state. This relationship is however "ever-suspended", as the desire for "totality" is self-evidently registered as the force of a non-presence. Whereas, according to Lukács, the Hellenic world possessed totality in the mechanisms of its body politic, it lacked the acute self-consciousness implied in the generally alienated condition of "modern" Western existence: what is lacking historically in the Western condition is precisely the "totality" the Hellenic world possessed. The Hellenic world has "totality" but no individuality; the bourgeois world has individuality but no "totality". In the case of the bourgeois world, the primary social realm within which this social "lack" or existential deficiency can be recognised and deployed as a productive absence is art. Freed from its subaltern role in religious ritual and released from the degraded utility of economic production, the *relative* freedom of the artwork with regard to the organisation of its material permits it to demand the "totality" that society can never possess.

The means by which the force of this non-presence establishes a degree of determinate leverage on alienation is through irony, for irony is the figure by which the determining force of absence is registered. An ironic literary language allows the novel to establish itself as a genre that mediates between social experience and historical desire. It is the use of irony as a figure and as a concept that permits Lukács to move beyond an idea of the novel as a mere passive imitation of reality. Lukács in fact conceives of mimesis not as an inert speculum, but as an active reflection. In contradistinction to the traditional Horacian doctrine of *ut pictura poesis* in which the literary work of art aspires to a static beauty analogous to sculpture or painting, Lukács' early works promote a theory in which the novel has an active role in history itself. One can discern, therefore, that for Lukács the validity of literary art exists not at the level of quiescent mirroring, but as an artistic form of self-reflection, which operates at a higher stage of "abstraction" and "self-awareness" in which "the ironic language of the novel is the self-correction of the world's fragility" (Lukács 1978: 75). Unlike merely sociological or empirical theories of literature, this awareness or higher level of abstraction is not reducible to the cultural norms of which it is part: art, in these terms at least, must operate at a more acute level of abstraction than culture. Culture is here posited as the realm of socially symbolic forms that exist primarily to impart a sense of social integration and "wholeness" and ethical coherence. But this apparent "wholeness" is false, masking the exploitative divisions and *dis*-integration of "bourgeois" existence. Art, in other words, begins in culture, but is not reducible to it.

We can also see, however, that to remove irony from the basis of such a theory would be to limit severely its conceptual options. Further, if one is constrained to accept that certain privations, both of intellect and of body, are assumed to have been transcended (as Lukács *apparently* did with regard to the Soviet Union of the 1930s), then irony, especially when conceived as that figure which mediates between longing and absence, becomes somewhat suspect. The banishment of the concept of irony in the later work of Lukács attests to a state of affairs in which criticism has become wilfully blinded to its own insights by virtue of the pact it has made with its own historical present.

Significantly, for our purposes, the banishment of irony is particularly evident in the one work where Lukács focuses directly on a Scottish author. *The Historical Novel* was first published in Moscow in 1937 and, taken as a whole, constitutes a fairly unequivocal statement of the extent to which the dialectical theory has begun to rigidify (Lukács 1962). Here Lukács takes the novels of Walter Scott as the primary example of a form of literary compromise in which the ambivalent and ironic condition of novelistic discourse is replaced by a more organic notion of a "symbolic concentration" of "dramatic forces of composition".[1] The dialectic between alienation, totality and irony is replaced in *The Historical Novel* by a more dualistic theory based on entropy and a concentration of compositional elements symbolically located within characters and dramatic scenes. The whole concept of an ironic form of ultimately deferred concretion, which operates at the level of inner-necessity and self-reflection, is here replaced with a merely specular and passive version of reflection. A previously active and subtle concept of mimesis is replaced wholesale with a conventional notion of "reflection" as a kind of passive pictorial "image", and this novelistic mirror "image" in turn reflects a "progressive" stage of societal development. Put simply, *The Historical Novel* presents the novels of Walter Scott as a particular "concrete" moment of "historical" reflection in the general progressive movement of history as such; dialectical reasoning has been replaced with the traditional philosophical concept of truth as correspondence. Initially, one might want to say that it is a peculiar *critical* theory that makes literary aesthetics so singularly representative of historical progress. One would have expected the privileged index of social advance to

---

[1] In addition to Scott, the novels of Fenimore Cooper and Manzoni are enlisted as positive examples of the classic historical novel. These "positive" examples of historical authenticity are then valorised over the "pseudo-monumentality, exoticism and decadence" of Flaubert, Nietzsche and Baudelaire (see Lukács 1962: 230–50).

belong with much more material social developments such as literacy levels, life expectancy, democratic participation and so forth. However, the fact that the "historical novel" is made the locus of *concretised* dialectical historical forces points to an aestheticisation of history via the novelistic. A *successfully* progressed history would surely not need certain generic novels to justify its existence. The historical reality would be justification enough. Oddly, perhaps, the method that produces this miraculously balanced "novelised" history lesson must first of all become less sinuous: thus the very rigid "formalism" Lukács himself purports to "despise" can be sensed more acutely in his later work than in his earlier stereotypically "idealist" and "aesthetic" writings such as *Soul and Form*. This yoking together of formalism and historicism evident in *The Historical Novel* seems to be the reaction of a genuinely critical discourse under extreme pressure to conform to political expediency, while attempting at the same moment (to its credit) to retain some kind of theoretical coherence. The performance is not altogether convincing, however, and, in the estimation of the Marxist philosopher Ernst Bloch, Lukács had by this time descended to that brand of "schematic sociologism" his own earlier work had done so much to undermine (Adorno et al. 1990: 20, 64). Bertold Brecht, typically, was more outspoken, claiming that in this period Lukács wrote like an "apparatchik" whose "every criticism contained a threat".

For our purposes, one can be sure that the choice of Scott over more "historically" problematic works such as those of Sterne or Hoffmann, for example, is certainly not random, but is made quite judiciously in order to sustain a flawed theoretical position: in *The Historical Novel*, the novelist of successful historical compromise fits the compromised theory. Indeed, this is exactly the argument of the first part of the book: as far as Lukács is concerned, the composite and compromised nature of Scott's writing best exemplifies the historical success of the bourgeoisie in its advancing period. It may be "true", as Lukács informs his readers, that in comparison with Goethe and Pushkin, Scott appears slight and superficial, but he is nonetheless more "representative" and "typical" of a "resultant [...] historical necessity". Thus Lukács approves of Scott's "middle-of-the-road heroes and composite characters", as representative of a "successful" and "conscious" bourgeois history (see Lukács 1962: 64–73). In effect, the "inner" dialectical contradictions of history are replaced with an *ex post facto* "resultant" social fact, of which Scott's "historical novel" is a mirror. In the novels of Scott, Lukács implies, history as consciousness and history as event have combined in some totalised equilibrium.

In less circumspect hands than those of Lukács, as we shall see, this type of "symbolic" concretion becomes the basis for the consecration of a tradition. Lukács himself, however, refrains from taking this seemingly logical next step, perhaps all too aware of the stark contrast with his earlier writings. In the essays collected as *History and Class-Consciousness*, for example, an idea such as cultural "tradition" with its "pseudo-holiness", cult of origins, totemic undertones and hagiography is posited as the very pseudo-history that art, as a supreme act of self-consciousness, exists to oppose (Lukács 1968: 16). The Lukács of the mid-1930s has effectively brought his dialectics to a standstill and it is no accident that he enlists the writings of Scott in order to do so. What began as "the irony of the novel that is the self-correction of the world's fragility" is then replaced, full-circle so it seems, by a "self-corrected history" reflected in a novel form apparently devoid of any true pathos or irony. No longer "fragile", world history appears redeemed and this redemption is certainly not abstract, but securely concrete. The ontological "homesickness" of *Soul and Form* and of *The Theory of the Novel* is domesticated as a kind of social and historical "homecoming" in *The Historical Novel*.

2. Adorno

The kind of "progressive" and peculiarly integrated history posited here by Lukács leaves little room for the registering of disaster, reversal or failure. One consequence is that Lukács "theory" inevitably fails adequately to convey the possibility of a historical catastrophe such as Fascism. For Theodor Adorno, on the other hand, the "totality" and "concretion" apparently present in the discourse of the historical novel is both false and is, moreover, infested with the desperate ironies with which art, philosophy and criticism must not only identify, but must also engage. For Adorno, the idea of a successful and progressive history mirrored by successful artistic composition is disastrous for dialectical criticism and amounts to little more than a kind of grand teleological *apologia*; or, in other words, it implies a "criticism" that has ceased to be critical. In effect, the critical enterprise has become a theory of art that has thus capitulated to official "culture". In doing so, the theory helps to turn the work of art into a product that is both politically palatable and fit for cultural consumption. This is the terminal destination of the reconciliation and compromises promoted in Lukács' later work, which Adorno identified as "extorted" and coerced, as false reconciliations more akin to ideology than to critical reflection *per se*. The later work of Lukács, according to Adorno, tends to import progressive "historical" categories into the analysis by moral fiat in the manner "of a philistine film censor, who wants to blame the presentation for what is present" (Adorno 1992: 1: 226).

So what, we are entitled to ask, does Adorno propose by way of an antidote? What, contrary to the now prevalent tendency to disavow any definition of the artwork on pain of accusations of elitism, is his alternative *concept* of the work of art? Our contemporary (anti)elitism of the mediocre, which authorises the cultural pundit to state, in all too dreary and well-rehearsed phrases, that we no longer know what art is, might not quite imply, as Hegel once predicted, that art no longer has the *right* to exist; but it does imply a limp capitulation to what merely *is*. In contrast to this accommodated and accommodating position, for Adorno, art (albeit in the form of anti-art) exists precisely because the "free" life of the subject does *not*, a position he summarises as follows: "What is reflected in aesthetic transcendence is the disenchantment of the world" (Adorno 1992: 1: 32). From *Negative Dialectics* to the *Aesthetic Theory* therefore, the whole concept and practice of literary transcendence involves a complicated double movement. It is a movement in which alienation, once freed from rigid economic subordination, *promises* to become the index of a condition in which the self-leverage implied by "alienation" (the same alienation we first encountered in the work of the early Lukács), might produce an uncoerced subjectivity. This is the promise of "freedom" in which an uncoerced "alienated" subject succumbs only to those determinations that emerge from the subject's engagement with the "object" of its own consciousness. For Adorno therefore, the work of literary art is a kind of "sublime joke"; forever holding out the promise of an autonomy and a felicity that it, as a product of exploited surpluses, can never materially deliver. The self-realisation of literary art's "doubled" condition (what, in relation to literary art, Paul de Man would later term the necessary "*dédoublement* of *all* truly literary language" (de Man 1983: 225)), produces a kind of ironic melancholy, austere and at the same time vaguely ridiculous. Literary art becomes a metaphor of revelation that knows itself only as a metaphor, and although its true subject is the decomposition and possible disappearance of meaningfulness, the literary artwork still clings tenaciously to the possibility of meaning. For Adorno, therefore, the existence of the literary work of art in an increasingly administered culture is not so much a paradox, as it is a form of supreme irony. This irony is both the condition of art's internal formal relations and crucially, an index of its relationship to the social existence of which it is a part.

It is worth remembering here that the irony Adorno deploys is not a failed and platitudinous notion of irony as plain self-mockery, and neither is it merely an all-too-familiar lack of seriousness and ambition. It is the literary equivalent of a philosophically austere negation of negation, coupled to a Kierkegaardian notion of an undermining of one's own claim to absolute mastery over the object of analysis: it is that form of irony in which complacency rather than concepts are destroyed. We can immediately see how alien this is to that contemporary form of non-ironic "irony" that actually confirms our complacency in the ultimate "plurality", "relativity" and "ambivalence" of all concepts and social values. Adorno is as far from postmodern scepticism as it is possible to be. Adorno remains faithful, despite his rigorous and austere adherence to a form of critique without platitudes, to the idea of a non-metaphysical transcendence that art, by its very existence, implies. For Adorno, the reduction of art to mere cultural product is not only an index of political and historical failure, but is also a symptom of a loss of critical nerve. For if, as in Hegel, art reaches its relative autonomy by liberating itself from its own subordinate role in totemic ritual and symbolic culture, then art's *reduction* to culture represents a re-subordination. As far as Adorno is concerned, uncritical valorisations of culture as such, are representative of the commodification and domestication of criticism. Adorno's desire for historical transcendence is no less insistent than it is in Hegel: it is just that the Hegelian "Absolute" is faced with the bill for its own failure. In this regard, Adorno's writings are close to what Jacques Derrida has termed "a Hegelianism without Reserve" (see Derrida 1978: 251–77). A mode rather than a method as such, it is an approach in which the supreme dialectal method of Hegel's *Science of Logic* is turned against the far too complacent and idealist conclusions of the method itself.

Certainly, for Adorno, "auto-referentiality" is not equivalent to self-reflection, and this will have far-reaching implications for contemporary critical theory. In the first instance, what Fredric Jameson has called "the ubiquitous auto-referentiality" of much postmodern culture can be seen to be bereft of the acute self-criticism Adorno describes, to the point where we are entitled to question whether "postmodern irony" is actually "irony" at all (Jameson 1998: 33–42). Irony implies parody not pastiche, for irony is the means by which absence is intimated yet deferred. Irony surely implies criticism, inasmuch as it must always imply an absence. One effect of ignoring or misunderstanding the axiomatic ground of irony is that the disenchantment of the world implied by a dialectical use of irony will be reversed, and irony will become an index of its own authenticity. A culture industry that manages to colonise the use of irony and dialectics in such a way will banish active self-criticism just as effectively as if it was being carried out by governmental decree. A reduction of the theoretical density of irony goes hand in hand with an attenuation of its potential critical capacities. This is a procedure with which we are now very familiar; the demands of an irony-allied critical discourse are replaced with a more "useful" terminology: irony is "hybridity", "plurality", "ambivalence", "ambiguity" etc., dialectics becomes "system", dogmatic logic, or ludicrously, the gulag. One possible result of this type of non-ironic "critical" discourse, as with the Lukács of the 1930s, is a re-enchantment of the present; the primary point of difference, according to Adorno, is that in the "West" we are at least able to say so.

In his essay "The Artist as Deputy", Adorno presents the prose artist as a figure who "walks the fine line between aesthetic form and reflection on art in provocative fashion"; and this double internal tension becomes, in the hands of the true artist, a latent but "inherent" force, capable of resisting "the stubborn antithesis of committed and pure art" (see Adorno 1992: 1: 90–110). This "antithesis" between "pure art" and "committed art" is a baleful product of the "culture industry", an industry that demands stereotypes, platitudes and schematic binary formulas. The useful polarities of the cultural pundit deliberately and ceaselessly mask the "deeper social and historical content" that operates at the level of the "formal immanence of the work of art". It goes almost without saying that Adorno is not advocating a return to a literary criticism based on the inalienable, eternal and "universal" ideas that lie at the heart of idealist philosophies of art. On the contrary, his task is to decipher, in allegorical fashion, the immensely complex affinities between formal tensions and "historical change" that lie beneath the surface textures of the work of literary art. Adorno also thus implies that the text which lacks such deep tensions and affinities, cannot, by definition, be considered a work of art. Any work that is demanding and deserving of critical attention avoids and confounds any shortcut to critical praxis that might allow the critic a sense of security or self-satisfaction. The alternative is, however, perhaps even more pernicious, and consists in the blithe attribution of equal amounts of ambivalence and ambiguity to all literary works, which are then placed securely beyond any form of plausible and secure analysis. For Adorno, this kind of "criticism" in particular is a betrayal of intellectual labour, a kind of neurotic symptom, a repetitive gesture that shadows the system of commodity production it seeks to embarrass: it is ultimately unproductive and just as fetishistic as its projected opposite. The critic is thus neither "connoisseur" nor "partisan" and s/he is required to establish "absolute intimacy" with a work with which intimacy is at least possible and worthwhile. Like the artwork's relation to its own material, the critic must become intimate with the latent significance of forms in order to pass "through mediations" to "magnificent self-awareness". And "such an intensification of specialisation becomes a form of universality in which (as in Hegel's system) every particular instance is implied in the intricate contours of every single concept" (Adorno 1992: 1: 101–3).

In its non-capitulation to technology on its own terms, the artwork appears peculiarly "archaic" as well as "modern"; "a work of artisanship", as opposed to the mass production of the factory floor and the production line. The fact that the artwork may ultimately fall prey to the system of consumption is no reason for it to capitulate to the system's method of production. The intimacy implied between producer and product that still resonates in the work of art exists as a kind of rebuke to the reified conditions of production that characterise the commodity object. The artist must alienate himself and re-establish intimacy with the object of his/her production in order to resist a form of reification that threatens to equalise production in general. The artist becomes an instrument in order to prevent the work from becoming instrumentalised.

Adorno follows Marx and Hegel in defining the "individual" as a "historical subject" and not a natural entity (Adorno 1992: 1: 241). For Adorno, therefore, the subject matter of a mature art is the possible or actual dissolution or continuance of this "historical subject". The artwork is the arena in which the currents of any possible advance or retreat in human "freedom" may be discerned. Of course, the artwork does not constitute that "freedom", nor less does it guarantee an autonomous realm fit for individual development; rather, the modernist artwork registers the condition of its failure as an actual historical entity. The truly modernist artwork exists as an austere index of the missed chances that make up a degraded history. The moment art becomes a justification or compensation for this irretrievable loss it relegates itself to the status of the culinary, and becomes ripe for speedy absorption into the culture industry.

As outlined above – and similar in many ways to the early Lukács – Adorno's writings on art and literature employ a concept of limitless dialectical irony. But this concept entails its own negation. For irony is not only an epistemological category, it is also a rhetorical one and, as such, it swerves away from definition. It is difficult, therefore, to define what irony is in the context of the literary artwork; it may only be possible to say what it does. Its "negative capability" applies also to its own dialectical movement. The irony implied in the work of literary art is not only a moment of interruption or disillusion in narrative confidence, it is more than a moment of parabasis (de Man 1996: 163–84). It is a continual or permanent state of parabasis, in which conceptual categories and tropological ones are constantly confronting each other. The supreme example of this condition is the work of Proust, in which the seemingly never-ending sentences become non-sentences; in which, in turn, the moment of semantic definition seems delicately and supremely suspended. The literary artwork is always reaching beyond itself in a sort of state of magnificent suspension. The kind of critical negative dialectic indicated in Adorno's writings on aesthetics thus implies the "beyond" of aesthetics as a rigidified body of strictly philosophical principles. However, Adorno's mode is more anti-aesthetics than non-aesthetics, representing as it does a kind of theoretical accompaniment to Schoenberg's anti-music and Beckett's anti-drama. The intimacy with the art object is too acute and too prolonged for any merely *contemplative* epistemological distance to hold determinate sway.

3. The Scottish Literary Tradition

It will be immediately clear that Adorno's formulations constitute, among much else, a challenge to the very basis of an expression such as the "Scottish Literary Tradition", or even, by extension, "Beyond *Scotland*". At the most basic level, the idea of a specifically "Scottish" mode of *artistic* as opposed to cultural expression must be deeply troubling. The reduction of the literary to a national principle implies for Adorno a return to cultic roots, pseudo-theological symbolism, and ancestor worship – everything that art has struggled to free itself from in the era of Modernity. At its worst, such reductionism lends itself to the valorisation of the *Volk*, and a terror of this type of "aesthetic" pseudo-populism understandably haunts Adorno's later work. It was never lost on Adorno that by holding fast to a notion of "national" or patriotic literature, the literary itself inevitably suffers a kind of trauma. It is forced back upon a "symbolic theological doctrine", in which the "fissure between the mediate and immediate" upon which art relies is eventually abolished (Adorno 1999: 95). In other words, what is abolished is precisely the *necessary* irony with which this essay began.

Even if we leave aside for a moment the specificity of the "Scottish", we must still deal with the problematics of "tradition". At least one plausible definition of tradition is that it represents the transformation of history into elements fit for social or ideological usefulness. Adorno does not propose an outright denial of this utility, especially as far as the social and political realm is concerned. The notion of a symbolic recuperation, or what Paul Ricoeur has called the "hermeneutics of affirmation or recovery" (in contrast to the slightly more shop-worn "hermeneutics of suspicion"), may well be utterly necessary with regard to social memory and political optimism (Ricouer 1984: 17–35). However, in order to prevent this "need" from becoming self-gratifying, art – as art – must remain antagonistic to its mollifying trends. There may certainly be "traditional" culture or cultures, but whether such a thing as traditional *art* is desirable or even possible is quite another matter. Adorno is, at the very least, sceptical: for him, art is the "beyond" of culture (or at least the beyond of any given culture).

Any attempt to examine critically, to build or defend the notion of a "Scottish literary tradition", must therefore function within, and explicitly acknowledge, the demands of irony and disenchantment towards the concepts of "tradition" and "the culture industry" we have so far discussed. This is not to say, however, that such attempts should not or cannot be made. To say that there may be no concrete and productive concept that can be made to fit the term "Scottish Modernism" is *not* to say that there are no Scottish literary modernists. It is just that the particular work of an artist does not always slide into the general cultural vision in the seamless manner some cultural patriots would seem to desire. I would like to offer a brief discussion of the work of one "Scottish" literary modernist by way of exemplification.

The writings of Proust meant a great deal to Adorno. *À la recherche du temps perdu* in particular is one of the indelible reference points for his thinking on art and literature. In Proust's "novel", Adorno sensed not only the tension of artistic expression at its limit, but also the contours of a deep conceptual engagement with language and art. As Adorno writes: "Proust has played a central role in my intellectual development for decades, and I simply could not imagine him absent from the continuity of my concerns" (Adorno 1992: 2:

312).[2] There is, however, a much more compelling reason to embark upon a discussion of Proust and Scottish literary modernism in the light of Adorno, which once again turns on significant absence.

The profound nature of the debt owed to C.K. Scott Moncrieff is nearly always passed over in silence in discussions of Scottish literary modernism. There may be fairly straightforward reasons for this, one of which is the persistent disregard for the genuinely *literary* achievements of the translator. As George Steiner writes in *Language and Silence*:

> Though translation is probably the single most telling instrument in the battle for knowledge [...] the translator himself is often a ghostly presence. He makes his unnoticed entrance on the reverse of the title-page. Who picks out his name or looks with informed gratitude on his labour? (Steiner 1997: 270)

Put simply, it was the scholarship, creativity and courage of Scott Moncrieff that first provided English-speaking readers with access to Proust's contribution to European modernism. If Proust exists as a reference point in the Anglophone world for thinking on art and literature, then this is in large part due the intricate but also immense efforts of Scott Moncrieff. This indifference to the figure of Moncrieff and to the extraordinary subtlety of his literary achievement is not simply an "ethical" matter regarding due recognition; it also raises necessary and difficult questions about the very nature and possibility of a "Scottish modernism".

If Moncrieff has been ingrained into the literary landscape so completely that he has ceased to be visible, to the point where he can be termed a "ghostly" presence, then he is confirmed in his twilight by a form of literary amnesia we must be careful to refrain from calling peculiarly "Scottish". Existing between transposition, translation, literature and commentary, and bound in a delicately complex and ironic register, Moncrieff's achievement is one of "high" modernism's

---

[2] This connection alone might have furnished enough of a pretext for a brief discussion of Proust's "modernism" in relation to the "Scottish" context. We must add, however, the fact of the curious non-presence of Proust as a literary and intellectual reference point in the landscape of "Scottish modernism". Alasdair Gray, for example, may be "like Joyce" or "like Huxley", James Kelman may well be "like Kafka" or "like Sartre", but nobody it seems is ever "like" Marcel Proust.

lasting artworks. By bending the syntax of English to the demands of Proust's paratactic sentences in such a manner as to retain Proust's "metaphysics of language", Moncrieff managed to push at the conceptual boundaries of translation. Indeed, Moncrieff can be said to be one of the few writers who exemplifies the "task" of the translator as understood by Walter Benjamin (Benjamin 1992: 70–83); he conducted a true literary transposition. In terms of "literary" personality and in the nature of his work, Scott Moncrieff exists as an image of literary non-coincidence; or, to extend Steiner's phrase a little, Moncreiff's name and achievement exist *in* the "language of silence". This non-coincidence deploys itself as an elegant and delicate otherness, which inserts itself between the contours of our habitual modes of thinking. And so Moncrieff's accomplishment persists, in true anti-binary form, in the absolute liminality of his name and the seductive intermediality of his literary achievement.

There is a painting of Moncrieff in the Royal Portrait Gallery in Edinburgh. The apparent homage is, however, surreptitious: the portrait is in the "military" section. Evidently, Moncrieff's military achievements (he was wounded on the western front in the First World War) are more significant than his literary ones. The face looks directly at the viewer, the head is slightly inclined, the skin is pale pink and the hands, resting on the knees, are solidly calm and seem large and slightly out of proportion. The figure sitting, but not in repose, appears small in frame, but athletic under the regimental dress uniform. The eyes are large and dark, without melancholy but also without joy, without bitterness or anger. The initial impression is that the eyes are curiously expressionless, but this is only momentary. The eyes appear to eschew expression, but they are not blank; the look is in fact an almost paradoxical one of tenderness combined with austerity. The totality of the framed image implies a strange discipline: a discipline not based upon tradition or acknowledged rules, but upon absences. There is a military belt without holster and without weapon; the uniform carries no obvious insignia. The right hand, bearing a delicately ornate ring, extends and holds a silver-topped walking cane: this cane – a compensation for a wound, or the tool of the Parisian *flâneur*? The figure seems fixed in delicate kinetic indecision, ready to move, saddened but not surprised at being squeezed by the indiscretions of cultural administrators, between Douglas Haig and the surrender of the German fleet. Despite the incongruity of its position, to which the portrait itself seems indifferent, the portrait's composed unselfishness should not disguise the cruelty of the betrayal perpetrated against it.

Little mentioned, even less acknowledged, despite the enormity of the debt the art of literature owes, C. K. Scott Moncrieff is, at best, a marginal figure in Scottish "culture" and literature, especially today. The boastful self-misunderstanding implicit in the spatial organisation of the paintings in the gallery merely reflects this. And yet the invocation of Moncreiff's name, and its indissoluble association with the name of Proust, reminds us not only of his achievement, but also that the compound Moncrieff/Proust or Proust/Moncrieff has always seemed to imply both author and non-author. As a semantic unit it presents itself both as a surface emblem of master and slave, but also as the "beyond" of host and parasite. Scott Moncrieff is always "inside" and "beyond" Scotland. The rest, as they say, is just culture.

Bibliography

Adorno, Theodor. 1992. *Notes to Literature* (tr. Shierry Weber Nicholsen). 2 vols. New York: Columbia University Press.

—. 1999. *Aesthetic Theory* (tr. Robert Hullot–Kentor). London: Athlone Press.

Adorno, Theodor, Walter Benjamin, et al. 1990. *Aesthetics and Politics*. London: Verso.

Benjamin, Walter. 1992. *Walter Benjamin: Illuminations* (tr. Harry Zohn, ed. Hannah Arendt). London: Fontana Press.

Derrida, Jacques. 1978. *Writing and Difference* (tr. Alan Bass). London: Routledge.

Hegel, G.W.F. *Phenomenology of Spirit* (tr. A.V. Miller). Oxford: Oxford University Press.

Jameson, Fredric. 1998. *The Cultural Turn: Selected Writings on the Postmodern*. London: Verso.

Lukács, Georg. 1962. *The Historical Novel* (tr. Hannah and Stanley Mitchell). London: Merlin Press.

— 1968. *History and Class Consciousness: Studies in Marxist Dialectics* (tr. Rodney Livingstone). London: Merlin Press.

—. 1974. *Soul and Form* (tr. Anna Bostock). London: Merlin Press.

—. 1978. *The Theory of the Novel* (tr. Anna Bostock). London: Merlin Press.

de Man, Paul. 1983. *Blindness and Insight: Essays in the Rhetoric of Contemporary Criticism*. London: Routledge.

—. 1996. "The Concept of Irony" in *Aesthetic Ideology*. Minneapolis: University of Minnesota Press. 163–84.

Ricoeur, Paul. 1984. "The Creativity of Language" in Kearney, Richard (ed.) *Dialogues with Contemporary Continental Thinkers*. Manchester: Manchester University Press. 17–35.

Steiner, George. 1997. *After Babel: Aspects of Language and Translation*. Oxford: Oxford University Press.

The Whereabouts of Literature

Edna Longley

Some contemporary Scottish criticism tends to misread Irish writing as a homogeneous national-ethnic resistance to the United Kingdom. This misrepresents the subtleties of both Irish and Scottish literature. The position of writers in Northern Ireland, for example, is a clear instance of such overlooked complexity.
Keywords: John Hewitt, Edwin Muir, Hugh MacDiarmid, W.B. Yeats, Irish literature.

"I myself never quite understood the meaning of the 'Celtic movement', which we were said to belong to. When I was asked about it, I used to say it was a movement meant to persuade the Scotch to begin buying our books while we continued not to buy theirs." (Lady Gregory [1913] 1972: 21)

This will be a comparative look at how some modern Irish and Scottish writers and critics conceive the locus of "literature" itself: the place where it is created and/or mediated. I will mainly consider poets' horizons, and how poetry is invoked by the kind of criticism concerned to locate poetry in a national context, and the nation in a poetic context. Perhaps the "nation" attracts poets because it seems to reproduce older relations with community and audience. Equally, the nation may disappoint when it fails to deliver those collectivities on the poet's terms – hence the trope of withdrawal from Ireland or Scotland as an environment where poetry cannot survive.

Thus one of W.B. Yeats's poles is to situate his ideal place of creation and reception "Beyond the fling of the dull ass's hoof" (epilogue to *Responsibilities*). Edwin Muir's well known dismissal of Edinburgh as literary metropolis – "a blank" (Muir 1936: 12) – resembles critiques of Belfast and Dublin by Muir's Irish contemporaries (more on Belfast later). Dublin is often a blank or hell in Patrick Kavanagh's writing rather than the literary utopia which his sonnet sequence "Temptation in Harvest" (1945) can still residually envisage as "the City of Kings / Where art, music, letters are the real things". In "From Monaghan to the Grand Canal" (1959), Kavanagh berates himself for having accepted "the stuff that was being produced in Dublin" as "the final word in painting and letters". And although elsewhere he idealises London as the place of intelligent reception, here he condemns the "big market in England for the synthetic Irish thing" and the "American literary market" as "Another villainous maw opened for things Irish-and-proud-of-it" (Kavanagh 2003: 274, 276). Kavanagh's and Muir's self-protective Edens ultimately constitute the inner sanctum where poetry survives. This locus occasionally merges with the prelapsarian or utopian nation: in *Scottish Journey* Muir calls the Border ballads "an unchanging pattern of the Scottish spirit" (because "older than Protestantism") (Muir 1935: 46). More often, however, it resists national claims as hostile to the spirit of art. In his poem "Innocence", Kavanagh designates his own unchanging ground as the space between "whitethorn hedges". A similar structure was physically enacted in the 1980s saga of Ian Hamilton Finlay and the war of Little Sparta.

I initially stress this Irish-Scottish trope of poetry's withdrawal (with its angry and paranoid aspects) because contemporary brands of literary-critical nationalism tend to forget or rebuke or sublimate it. For instance, Scottish critics promulgate a strangely upbeat version of Yeats's Irish world. And when Ireland and Scotland misread one another's textual nuances, the misreading may repress awkward commonalities. Thus the well-chosen title of Graham Walker's book on Ulster and Scotland, *Intimate Strangers* (1995), covers some literary-critical rhetoric too. It also covers the fact that "Scotland and Ulster" is a less popular literary and political theme than "Scotland and Ireland". Just as Scotland's Britannic and imperial self-confidence once shut out the insecurities of the "Ulster Scot", so work on Scotland's devolutionary selfhood or self-image makes the Celtic Tiger a more attractive beast than the neighbouring monster of sectarianism (Walker 1995: ch.1; Walker 2002). Patterns of literary intercourse between Ireland and Scotland parallel patterns of economic competition and emulation, both under the union and in these post-Ukanian days. In an abiding contradiction, they exhibit the double desire to create a local literary metropolis and to impress London. Instances of Dublin and Edinburgh or Glasgow preferring to impress one another are rarer.

Here are some examples. In 1845, thanking Thomas Davis for *The Spirit of the Nation*, Samuel Ferguson said: "When I see how we are all working, I hope to see Dublin at least a better Edinburgh" (cited in Denman 1990: 63). Yeats in his early crusading years cited Edinburgh as his devolved metropolitan model, while Burns became his model of the national poet who unites quality with popularity: a kind of redeemed, proto-symbolist Davis. He resented D.P. Moran's taunts that there was "no Anglo-Irish poet [...] who can talk straight to the heart as Burns talked to the heart of Scotland", and that "what the country requires [...] is an Anglo-Irish Burns, and not an Anglo-Irish mystic" (Kelly and Shuchard 1994: 19–20). By 1919 Dublin/Ireland was doing so well that Gregory Smith, in *Scottish Literature*, felt obliged to question its place on the archipelagic map. We should not forget that Smith's concept of the "Caledonian Antisyzygy" involves an effort to disentangle aspects of Scottish literature from an Irish-identified Celticism – though without consigning them to unsexy Saxonism. Smith protests:

The consideration of this second element [delight in the grotesque and uncanny] has generally been narrowed down to argument about its Celtic origin. The problem does not press on us as it did upon Renan and Matthew Arnold, and the latter's plea for the Celt is [...] not as convincing as it was even to the most partisan. (Smith 1919: 1)

Smith attributes Scottish literature's "two moods" (Smith 1919: 27) to medieval origins instead. Ideological difficulty caused by those powerful nineteenth-century constructions, Celt and Saxon, may be the subjective source of a seeming contradiction, which Smith adduces as historical fact. Here London is Smith's target audience, since he begins his book by complaining that the English don't really "know their Scot", and generally suggests that no Scot would stoop to the populist methods whereby the neo-Kailyard "beginners" who write dialect "Abbey Theatre and 'Ulster' plays" have claimed a reputation that should rightfully be Scottish (Smith 1919: 50–51). He says:

Had the northern partner busied herself with a "Renaissance", harped on the sorrowful Deirdres and eloquent Dempseys, hoed the cabbage-patch [...] and out-tartaned Kiltartan, she might have had readier recognition of "nationality" in literature – or opera-bouffe. (Smith 1919: 278).

Sixty years later Edwin Morgan, normally the most equable of critics, echoed Smith's chagrin in "What it feels like to be a Scottish poet":

Scottish poets should not – though I dare say they do – feel envious of the greater attention paid at present by English reviewers and critics to the poets of Ireland. Irish poetry is good, but I suspect the English praise of it is not unlinked to some subconscious guilt about the Irish situation, coupled with the fact that the Irish poetry is very accessible and manageable. Poetry in Scotland seems more various and adventurous, more willing to take risks. (Morgan 1979: 72–73)

Once again, a Scot implies that the Irish have stolen unfair literary advantage through the exercise of specious charm. (And it may be true, as a sweeping proposition, that the Scots set out to impress the English whereas the Irish – more subtly – try to charm them.)

Hugh MacDiarmid was not only paradoxically enthused by Smith to write in Scots. He also constructively misread Smith's disdain for starting a "Renaissance" and ignored his literary-critical unionism, sharpened by living in Ulster. Yet just as Yeats could be inaccurate about Edinburgh and Burns, so MacDiarmid saw what he wanted to see: the more or less unified Irish Revival of 1890 rather than the fissures of 1930 – perhaps another constructive misreading, but also one that secreted problems. MacDiarmid ends his seminal essay "English Ascendancy in British Literature" (1931) by quoting Daniel Corkery's *The Hidden Ireland* (1925), which recreates (some would say "invents") the lost world of Gaelic Munster, largely in reaction against the movement sponsored by Yeats and AE (MacDiarmid 1992: 79–80). But perhaps Corkery's nativist hostility to Anglophone Irish literature spoke more deeply to the political and linguistic character of MacDiarmid's own agenda. While demurring on details, he defended the hard-line "position" later taken by Corkery in *Synge and Anglo-Irish Literature* (1931) (see Grieve et al. 2001: 44–45). It was Corkery, indeed, who first formulated the essentially (or essentialist) post-colonial notion of "getting back behind the Renaissance" on the grounds that "The antithesis of Renaissance art [...] is national art".[1] Cairns Craig has criticised this aim, as taken up

---

[1] The passage quoted by MacDiarmid from *The Hidden Ireland* in "English Ascendancy in British Literature" features Corkery on the Renaissance.

by MacDiarmid, for abolishing literary and cultural history in the name of a counter-productive scorched earth policy: "an act of historical egotism which annuls the past except as a series of precedents for himself" (Craig 1996: 108). MacDiarmid was also influenced by Aodh de Blácam's work of nationalist literary history *Gaelic Literature Surveyed* (1929). Given MacDiarmid's continuing force in Scottish literary studies, specifically as contrasted with Irish resistance to Yeats's foundational role, his pick 'n' mix use of the Irish Revival(s) as a de-Anglicising model remains relevant.

Meanwhile in Ireland, the Censorship Act (1929) was in place, Beckett would soon take the boat, and by 1935 Austin Clarke would be asking what had happened to "Home Rule in our literature". Part of Clarke's complaint, in an essay called "Irish Poetry Today", was that Yeats had "returned to the main sources of English literature", thus rendering Irish poetry "destitute". The essay amounts to a contradictory lament that Dublin has both ceased to be a literary metropolis and that Irish poetry, owing to "a critical tariff", has ceased to be noticed in London (see Clarke 1935). The case of Clarke underlines the point that, in the twentieth century, the Irish literary grass often looks greener from Scotland. There is a recurrent envious image of Irish literature, like Irish national consciousness, as having got its act together. For Muir, Irish literature in the mid-1930s was "central and homogeneous", whereas Scottish literature was "parochial and conglomerate" (Muir 1936: 179). Similarly, if in more political terms, Neil M. Gunn praised late-1930s Dublin rather as British literary communists were then praising Moscow (see Gunn 1987). But in both countries publishing lapsed between the 1920s and the 1960s, and other shared complaints were/are the inadequacy of criticism and the belatedness of Irish/Scottish literary studies. In 1936 Muir accused Scottish criticism of lacking "either sensibility or a standard" (Muir 1936: 43); in 1945 John V. Kelleher found Irish poetry suffering from an "absence of interplay and mutual criticism" (Kelleher 1945: 348); in 1992 Douglas Dunn regretted a "failure of criticism, a flaw in the [Scottish] literary atmosphere" (Dunn 1992: xxxv).[2] *Contra* Clarke, it might be argued the Irish Revival was not over by 1930: rather, it had

---

[2] See other Irish instances summarised in Longley 1999–2000.

changed its conceptual and actual ground. But, as in Brian Fallon's *The Age of Innocence: Irish Culture 1930–1960*, there are occasional attempts to improve the poor image of mid-twentieth-century Irish cultural life. Interestingly, Fallon co-opts MacDiarmid into a retro-spective justification of artistic isolationism and of necessary meas-ures against "the dominance of powerful neighbours". He says: "Scotland, as late as the 1930s, produced a literary renaissance of sorts dominated by the Anglophobe poet Hugh MacDiarmid" (Fallon 1998: 26).

Outside competitive wooing of London, twentieth-century Scot-tish poets and critics generally wooed Ireland more ardently than *vice versa*. Some of this may be due to Irish independence, some to Irish insularity, some to Ireland's greater literary success in the world. To give examples from both ends of a century: William Sharp and Willy Maley. In 1897, as William F. O'Halloran has shown (see O'Halloran 2001), there was a prelude to future problems with Sharp's secret identity as Fiona Macleod and with pan-Celticism in general – always more attractive to Scottish writers. At that time, Lady Gregory told Sharp that "Yeats's friends were of the opinion the Celtic movement wd be injured by them merging into one camp [Scottish and Irish] – that they shd rather be allies like the Unionists & Tories" (a piquant analogy). Later AE (who came to see Sharp's brand of Celticism as Unionist) wrote briskly of "Fiona": "every time she bobs her head out of the Astral Light I will whack it, at least so long as it bobs up in connection with Irish things".[3] So "keep off the grass", as well as "the grass is greener", may sometimes affect literary cartography.

Is it (paddy)whackery to criticise Willy Maley's recent essay on Joyce and Scotland for speaking so much in the tone of a spurned suitor? Maley complains:

How could an Irish author of such deep learning and possessed of a cultivated Euro-pean and world view overlook Scotland, especially given that the so-called "Irish Question" in its modern form, from plantation to partition, is posed first and foremost by Scotland? (Maley 2000: 206)

---

[3] Letter from AE to Lady Gregory (1900), cited in Foster 1997: 197.

On the one hand, Joyce is perfectly entitled to "overlook Scotland". On the other hand, when those whom Maley terms "Irish nationalist critics" also overlook Scotland, or notice it selectively, it is precisely owing to presbyterian Scotland's complicity in "plantation and partition". It is because "Scotland and Ulster" lurks in "Scotland and Ireland". Maley answers and begs his own question when he finds Joyce sadly blind to the difference between good and bad Scots – the latter being "incorrigibly Protestant, Conservative, and Unionist" (Maley 2000: 215–16). He also deplores the reluctance of another constituency – "postcolonial critics" – to "accept that Scotland has a claim to the same territory". Yet Maley may be on the right twin-track, since, for "Irish nationalist critics", the more Scotland offers itself in postcolonial or Jacobite costume, the more attractive it is likely to be.

In fact, Joyce and Yeats shared an anti-Ulster prejudice with implications for Irish-Scottish literary intercourse. This prejudice marks regional and religious (not just Catholic/Protestant but also Anglican/Presbyterian) partitions in Ireland. It surfaces, for instance, in Yeats's account of an anti-Scottish *coup* he executed in the London Rhymers' Club. Behind his particular animus against John Davidson, a charitable reader might discern a deeper aesthetic and philosophical rejection of nonconformism and all its works. Here, too, Irish-Scottish competition shows itself within the metropolitan poetic domain of the 1890s:

An infallible Church, with its Mass in Latin and its mediaeval philosophy, and our Protestant [Yeats means "Anglican"] social prejudice, have kept our ablest men from levelling passions; but Davidson, with a jealousy which may be Scottish, seeing that Carlyle had it, was quick to discover sour grapes. He saw in delicate, laborious, discriminating taste an effeminate pedantry, and would, when that mood was on him, delight in all that seemed healthy, popular, and bustling. He, indeed, was accustomed, in the most characteristic phrase of his type, to describe the Rhymers as lacking in "blood and guts", and very nearly brought us to an end by attempting to supply the deficiency by the addition of four Scotsmen [...]. He insisted upon their immediate election, and the Rhymers, through that complacency of good manners whereby educated Englishmen so often surprise me, obeyed [...] and it cost me seven hours' work to get another meeting and vote the Scotsmen out. (Yeats 1955: 317)

We may agree with Davidson that the Rhymers needed a blood transfusion, while noticing that the delicate "Celtic" Yeats could bustle in

supposedly "Saxon-Scot" style when necessary. In any case, that rel-
ished memory suggests that not only the English foment stereotype
and division. Contrariwise, in *Scottish Scene*, Lewis Grassic Gibbon
blends anti-Celticism, anti-nationalism and anti-Irishness when he
attacks

disgusting little stretches of the globe, claimed, occupied and infected by groupings of
babbling little morons – babbling militant on the subjects (unendingly) of their
exclusive cultures, their *exclusive* languages, their *national* souls, their *national* genius, their unique achievements in throat-cutting [...] they cease from their yelpings at
the passers-by only in such intervals as they devote to civil-war flea-hunts (Gibbon
and MacDiarmid 1934: 144).

The "Ulster" poet John Hewitt (1907–1987) did not overlook
Scotland: a fact itself overlooked. Hewitt's seminal essay, "The Bitter
Gourd: Some Problems of the Ulster Writer" (1945), takes its cue
from Muir's sense of the Scottish literary predicament. Among the
shared negative images of Belfast and Glasgow has been the idea that
these cities are at once unamenable to literary representation and in-
conceivable as the locus of literature itself. Clearly, it is not just a
matter of perceptions, but of cultural history and the time it takes for
an Alasdair Gray, Edwin Morgan or Ciaran Carson to appear and create their word-cities. Nonetheless, images and self-images of "Calvinism" as inimical to the arts (currently the object of some revisionism by Scottish intellectuals) may be overdone. And perhaps it would
be accepted of no other UK cities, in quite so unhistorical and unnu-
anced a way, that literary activity in the 1960s had to be kick-started
by the Hobsbaum groups. Hewitt's cultural mission both confirms (in
what it opposed) and contradicts (in what it proposed) the stereotypes.
In 1945, like Muir writing on Glasgow, Hewitt had already targeted
"externalised energies" (conditioned by Ulster Protestants' historical
recourse to "Scottish universities") as one factor that inhibited literary
culture. The Scottish renaissance was his most immediate model for
an Ulster salvation: a Scottish solution to an originally Scottish problem. But, unlike Muir, Hewitt perceived Scottish literature as enviably
coherent: "We have no such literary heritage, no such ancient language [i.e. Scots]" (Hewitt 1987b: 109). He also knew that his own
necessary term "regionalism" not only contrasted, but conflicted with

national literary emphases in both Scotland and Ireland: "Ulster's position in this island involves us in problems and cleavages for which
we can find no counterpart elsewhere in the British archipelago"
(Hewitt 1987b: 112). Hewitt's Scottish orientation included keeping
up with Scottish poetry and criticism; friendships with Muir and
Douglas Young; and his work on the Ulster weaver-poets. Young was
persuaded by Hewitt to include some Ulster Scots poetry in his anthology *Scottish Verse 1851–1951*.

Hewitt's regionalism spilled over into nine-county Ulster, and his
Scottish horizon was counterpointed by his consciousness of the Irish
Revival. In the 1920s, after some encouragement from AE, he and his
Belfast friends "began to appreciate that Dublin was our literary capital" (Hewitt 1987a: 150); in the 1940s northern writers had a Dublin
base in the *Bell* and its poetry editor Geoffrey Taylor (the *Bell* itself
had links with the Scottish journal *The New Alliance*). Recalling some
1940s Irish anthologies, Hewitt says that they "marked the appearance
of the northern poets on the national scene" (Hewitt unpub.). The
magazine *Lagan* (1943–47), part-prompted by the *Bell*, brought
together all these influences. Hewitt sums up its regional ethos as "a
moment of unity of some kind, a phase of emotional maturity" (Hewitt
unpub.). Why have Hewitt's Dublin-Edinburgh literary co-ordinates,
with their implications for Northern Ireland as a literary locus, faded
from view? In 1962 at a leaner time when, to quote Seamus Heaney's
retrospect, "Belfast had no literary publishers, no poetry readings, no
sense of literary identity", Heaney researched the history of literary
magazines in Ulster. *Lagan* presumably helped to give him what he
calls "a basis for faith in our cultural existence as northern, Irish and
essentially ourselves". In the same passage Heaney describes his
"sense of being on the outside of things, of being far away from
[Kavanagh's] 'City of Kings'" (Heaney 1988: 6–7). So motifs recur.
And my sketch of Irish-Scottish mutual literary awareness since 1845
– misreadings notwithstanding – points to a kind of Revival or Renaissance roundabout with continuing literary and literary-critical
repercussions.

Heaney is more mentioned than Hewitt by Scottish critics (although Tom Leonard has acknowledged the influence of Hewitt's

Rhyming Weavers anthology on his *Radical Renfrew*).[4] Heaney is also more mentioned as "Irish" than as "northern, Irish", with a careful comma between the words. The ways in which some Scottish critics allude to Irish poetry depend on where they want to locate Scottish poetry or literature. This, in turn, may mislocate Irish poetry. First, it usually *is* Yeats or Heaney (occasionally Tom Paulin), rarely a poet from the Republic. Thus what may be required are: (apparently) clear national-ethnic credentials or themes; a UK framework; and (apparently) clear resistance to it. The subtler intertextualities of Northern/Irish poetry are elided, as are forms, structures and traditions. Second, Irish poets are conscripted into devolutionary rhetorics that may not fit independent Ireland; or they are invoked for qualities whose dialectical context in debates centred on Northern Ireland may not be fully perceived. Witness Robert Crawford's team of so-called linguistic "Barbarians" in *Devolving English Literature*:

> Though the positions of all these writers [Heaney, Dunn, Harrison, Morgan, Leonard, Paulin etc.] are far from identical, there are sufficient similarities between them to show that there is a widespread wish in recent poetry to be seen as in some manner barbarian, as operating outside the boundaries of standard English and outside the identity that is seen as going with it. Such a wish unites postcolonial writers such as Murray and Walcott with writers working within the "Anglo-Celtic archipelago", it joins the post-colonial and the provincial. (Crawford 1992: 300)

While conceding differences of "position" (n.b. "position" not "aesthetic"), Crawford represents Ireland and Scotland as at one with regard to "issues of the provincial and barbarian versus the proprieties of the ruling centre" (Crawford 1992: 302). Here poetic "language", because of the language question in Scottish poetry, is understood in identitarian and metaphorically over-extended terms. For instance, the configuration of Scots speech in Northern Irish culture differs from the configuration of Scots in Scotland (see Kirk and Baoill: 2001, 2002). Third, the motif of "periphery" and "centre" in Scottish criticism conflicts with those Irish maps that centre on Dublin.

Yet all such cartographies become too literal – as do the challenges to them. What of the current prominence of Irish and Scottish writers and publishers in London? Is this a fresh twist on London as

---

[4] During a poetry-reading in Belfast, 2000.

Irish/Scottish literary metropolis under the union: Micks (and Jocks) "on the make", to quote Roy Foster (see Foster 1993)? Or has it more complex cultural meanings? Again, Crawford's chapter "Modernism as Provincialism" implicitly accepts as well as renovates the term "provincial". He annexes the centralising power of academic modernism without allowing each term to complicate the other. Nor are the postcolonial and provincial (as Maley is aware) so easily joined. Invocations of "-isms" by Scottish and Irish critics offer a fruitful comparative field.

Nonetheless, in their preoccupation with the union, Crawford and other Scottish critics cast useful light on a context for *Irish* literature, past and present, which is less noticed than it might be.[5] Thus Cairns Craig convincingly argues in *Outside History* that metropolitan constructions of English literature absorb Irish or Scottish writers into a supposedly integral centre and thereby make their asset-stripped local contexts appear fragmented – as Scottish literature does to Muir. An obsession with all-or-nothing literary "unity" (Craig 1996: 175) keeps surfacing among Scottish and Irish critics. In contrast, Craig favours a dialectical concept of "being between", and rightly notes that accounts of the making of modern poetry are skewed where Yeats is read according to "'cosmopolitan' and 'English' maps of the twentieth century" (Craig 1996: 202, 181). But perhaps Yeats's equally problematic "Irishness" requires more complex adjustment of the critical map to accommodate inter-national in-betweenness all round. Elsewhere, Craig anachronistically resituates the Irish Revival as filling the vacuum of English literary exhaustion after the Great War; and he oddly regards the 1916 Rising as "a revolt in English against the Imperium of the English language" inspired by Yeats (Craig 1987: 4: 5). Nor do Yeats and Chinua Achebe mean the same thing by "Things fall apart". Craig's later essay, "Constituting Scotland", presents a more complex picture (with corollaries for Ireland) in stressing the extent to which Scotland's national identity was constituted *within* the union (Craig 2001). Modern Irish and Scottish criticism have both been significantly constituted by contestation between unionist and nationalist frameworks.

---

[5] A recent exception is Stewart (ed.) 2002.

The theme of the periphery taking over an exhausted centre, of barbarians storming the Capital, recurs in American, Irish and Scottish narratives of modern poetry. It is often allied to the claim that Irish or Scottish poetry is more cosmopolitan (a.k.a. "Modernist") than that of a provincial England, although English poetry includes an internal opposition along the same lines. There have indeed been crucial engagements with poetry from abroad, exemplified by Edwin Morgan and Ian Hamilton Finlay. However, Robert Crawford may go too far when he says:

Identifying Poets has a Scottish accent, but covers an international range of writers […] An awareness of [the identifying poet] lets us see Scottish poetry (in English, Gaelic and Scots) as essential rather than peripheral to the development of poetry in [the twentieth century]. (Crawford 1993: 1)

Here "international" (one of the fuzziest words in contemporary poetry criticism) means Australia and the USA. It is as if Les Murray has become a colony of Scottish poetry to give it combined international and peripheral credibility. Do some maps that situate Irish and Scottish poetry in the Pacific or Atlantic merely export national geographies? When claiming a global presence, Crawford can sound like the imperial Scot, just as Declan Kiberd in *Inventing Ireland* can sound like the Irish Foreign Missions. Tom Leonard hits at this kind of thing in "Sourscenes from Scottish Literary Life":

The mainstream of world literature
has this moment been re-routed
to arrive at the Collected Works
of yonder two drunks.
No wonder they look happy!

To conclude: there have been productive readings and misreadings in both directions. May the revival roundabout keep spinning! But some contemporary Scottish criticism either unduly incorporates Ireland into the structures of its quarrel with itself (and with England), or presumes an Irish homogeneity that masks Scottish fissures as well as broader Britannic "problems and cleavages" (to quote Hewitt). Colin Graham and Richard Kirkland lament that "established Irish studies" seems able "to impose its strictures on those conceptual forces which come to it from the outside" (Graham and Kirkland 1999: 2). Does the same protectionist principle apply to Scottish studies? Or to encounters between the two? Comparative criticism, surely the *sine qua non*, is harder work than trading in superficial parallels or imposing prepared templates. Perhaps all our post-Ukanian whereabouts need sharper, mutually honed, contextually sensitive, theoretical tools. The truly critical argument for exposing Irish and Scottish literary studies to one another is the historical mix of similarity and difference, interpenetration and disconnection: a mix that includes many variables in relation to "English" literature and in perceptions of that relation. National protectionism also shelters writers from the harsh but bracing winds of value-judgment. To quote Douglas Dunn on the problem of criticism in small countries: "Back-slapping and other exaggerated forms of courtesy can turn the critical process into little more than flag-waving" (Dunn 1992: xxxi). Unreflective pan-Celtic back-slapping will not help matters.

There may be a warning in a recent Irish-Scottish map – a kind of literary Dalriada – the well-meaning anthology *Across the Water: Irishness in Modern Scottish Writing*. Although the editors embrace an "impure, complicated Hiberno-Scottish hybridity", what they hail as "recognisably Irish" is a Celticist "patter and pattern, a streetwise rococo, long lyric speeches, with a come all ye swagger and elegiac sombreness to contrast with this" (McGonigal et al. 2000: 20, 23). They also assign all Ulster Protestant literati to "the loyalist tradition" (McGonigal et al. 2000: 21). Edwin Muir remarks that Scottish people overdo "Englishness" when they adopt it (Muir 1935: 26–27); I hope that they are not about to overdo "Irishness" instead. Bernard MacLaverty declined to write a paragraph on the Irishness of his writing for *Across the Water*, and Tom Leonard refused to be on this map at all.

Bibliography

Clarke, Austin. 1935. "Irish Poetry Today" in *Dublin Magazine* 10(1): 26–32.
Craig, Cairns (ed.). 1987. *The History of Scottish Literature*. 4 vols. Aberdeen: Aberdeen University Press.
—. 1996. *Outside History*. Edinburgh: Polygon.
—. 2001. "Constituting Scotland" in *Irish Review* 28: 1–27.
Crawford, Robert. 1992. *Devolving English Literature*. Oxford: Clarendon Press.
—. 1993. *Identifying Poets: Self and Territory in Twentieth-Century Poetry*. Edinburgh: Edinburgh University Press.
Denman, Peter. 1990. *Samuel Ferguson: The Literary Achievement*. Gerrards Cross: Colin Smythe.
Dunn, Douglas. 1992. *Faber Book of Twentieth-Century Scottish Poetry*. London: Faber.
Fallon, Brian. 1998. *An Age of Innocence: Irish Culture 1930–1960*. Dublin: Gill and Macmillan.
Foster, R.F. 1993. "Marginal Men and Micks on the Make" in *Paddy and Mr Punch: Connections in Irish and English History*. London: Allen Lane. 281–305.
—. 1997. *W.B. Yeats: A Life. I: The Apprentice Mage*. Oxford: Oxford University.
Gibbon, Lewis Grassic and Hugh MacDiarmid. 1934. *Scottish Scene or The Intelligent Man's Guide to Albyn*. London: Jarrolds.
Graham, Colin and Richard Kirkland. 1999. "Introduction" in Graham, Colin and Richard Kirkland (eds) *Ireland and Cultural Theory: The Mechanics of Authenticity*. Houndmills: Macmillan. 1–6.
Lady Gregory. [1913] 1972. *Our Irish Theatre: A Chapter on Autobiography*. Gerrards Cross: Colin Smythe.
Grieve, Dorian, Owen Dudley Edwards and Alan Riach (eds). 2001. *Hugh MacDiarmid: New Selected Letters*. Manchester: Carcanet.
Gunn, Neil. 1987. "Eire" and "President of Eire" in McCleery, Alistair (ed.) *Landscape and Light: Essays by Neil M. Gunn*. Aberdeen: Aberdeen University Press. 181–87.
Heaney, Seamus. 1988. *The Government of the Tongue*. London: Faber.
Hewitt, John. 1987a. "No Rootless Colonist" in Clyde, Tom (ed.) *Ancestral Voices: The Selected Prose of John Hewitt*. Belfast: Blackstaff. 146–57.
—. 1987b. "The Bitter Gourd: Some Problems of the Ulster Writer" in Tom Clyde (ed.) *Ancestral Voices: The Selected Prose of John Hewitt*. Belfast: Blackstaff. 108–21.
—. unpub. *A North Light* [Unpublished autobiography]. Hewitt Archive, University of Ulster, Coleraine.
Kavanagh, Patrick. 2003. "From Monaghan to the Grand Canal" in Quinn, Antoinette (ed.) *Patrick Kavanagh: A Poet's Country: Selected Prose*. Dublin: Lilliput Press: 272–81.
Kelleher, John V. 1945. *Bell*. 10(4).
Kelly, John and Ronald Schuchard (eds). 1994. *The Collected Letters of W.B. Yeats: 1901–1904*. Oxford: Oxford University Press.

Kirk, John and Dónall P Ó Baoill (eds). 2001. *Language Links: The Languages of Scotland and Ireland*. Belfast: Cló Ollscoil na Banríona/Queen's University Belfast.

—. 2002. *Language Planning and Education: Linguistic Issues in Northern Ireland, the Republic of Ireland, and Scotland*. Belfast: Cló Ollscoil na Banríona/Queen's University Belfast.

Longley, Edna. 1999–2000. "'Catch hold of this heretic': Ireland and Literary Criticism". The Parnell Lecture 1999–2000 (Magdalene College Occasional Paper No. 27).

MacDiarmid, Hugh. 1992. *Hugh MacDiarmid: Selected Prose* (ed. Alan Riach). Manchester: Carcanet.

McGonigal, James, Donny O'Rourke and Hamish Whyte (eds). 2000. *Across the Water: Irishness in Modern Scottish Writing*. Glendaruel, Argyll: Argyll Publishing.

Maley, Willy. 2000. "'Kilt by kelt shell kithagain with kinagain': Joyce and Scotland", in Attridge, Derek and Marjorie Howes (eds) *Semicolonial Joyce*. Cambridge: Cambridge University Press. 201–18.

Morgan, Edwin. 1979. "What it feels like to be a Scottish poet" in *Aquarius* 11: 72–73.

Muir, Edwin. 1935. *Scottish Journey*. London: Heinemann/Gollancz.

—. 1936. *Scott and Scotland*. London: Routledge.

O'Halloran, William F. 2001. "W.B. Yeats, William Sharp and Fiona Macleod: A Celtic Drama, 1897" in *Yeats Annual* 14: 159–208.

Smith, G. Gregory. 1919. *Scottish Literature: Character & Influence*. London: Macmillan.

Stewart, Bruce (ed.). 2002. *Hearts and Minds: Irish Culture and Society under the Act of Union*. Gerrards Cross: Colin Smythe.

Walker, Graham. 1995. *Intimate Strangers: Political and Cultural Interaction between Scotland and Ulster in Modern Times*. Edinburgh: John Donald.

—. 2002. "The Role of Religion and the Churches" in Hassan, Gerry and Chris Warhurst (eds) *Anatomy of the New Scotland: Power, Influence and Change*. Edinburgh and London: Mainstream. 253–59.

Yeats, W.B. 1955. *Autobiographies*. London: Macmillan.

"Creation Festers in Me": Calvinism and Cosmopolitanism in Jenkins, Spark and Gray

Gerard Carruthers

The Calvinist inheritance of Scottish literature is not a parochial burden. Rather, as a survey of post-war Scottish fiction demonstrates, the Calvinist imagination is a means by which Scottish literature may obtain a broader, cosmopolitan viewpoint on human existence.
Keywords: Robin Jenkins, Muriel Spark, Alasdair Gray, Calvinism, cosmopolitanism, post-war Scottish fiction.

A dominant note in much hand-wringing Scottish criticism from 1919 to 1964 was that Scottish literature and culture had too often suffered from a time lag, clinging to old modes of expression and dwelling on "native" identity long after these things had ceased to represent useful currency. Primed by some flippant remarks made by Robert Louis Stevenson in *Weir of Hermiston*,[1] G. Gregory Smith diagnosed Scottish literary and cultural conservatism as the "historical habit" (Smith 1919: 41–70). Others followed, most notably Edwin Muir, David Craig and David Daiches, all reading Scottish literature and culture as more bound by "behind the times" native conditions and so less cutting edge than English literature (Muir 1936; Craig 1961; Daiches 1964). The paradox in the rise of the contemporary study of "Scottish Literature" emerges in the fact that all these critics cared deeply about Scotland from intensely Anglocentric positions and were important encouragers of the new discipline, as they put in place a very strong sense of Scottish literature as other than, even although also less than, English literature. Arising in opposition to this desire for the elixir of southern cultural air, a different critical tack emerged from the late 1950s, especially in the work of German critic Kurt Wittig (although the foundations had been laid for this in the bellicose,

---

[1] "For that is the mark of the Scot of all classes: that he stands in an attitude towards the past unthinkable to Englishmen, and remembers and cherishes the memory of his forbears, good or bad; and there burns alive in him a sense of identity with the dead even to the twentieth generation" (Stevenson [1894] 1979: 104).

anti-metropolitan, Modernist pronouncements of Hugh MacDiarmid from the 1920s), with the notion that it was a virtue that Scottish literature tended to be more rooted or "traditional" than elsewhere (Wittig 1958). Thus a range of stubborn characteristics slowly began to be reappraised in Scottish culture and literature: the previously much-maligned Calvinist mentality of Scotland; the strong concern with "morality", derived not only from Calvinism, but also from another derided bulwark of modern Scottish identity, the Enlightenment; and the extended currency of folklore and the supernatural in Scottish writing (incorporating also, it has sometimes been claimed, a foundational orality to Scottish literature, which ought to be read as distinct from the more "literary" English tradition as identified by Edwin Muir and others). Sidestepping suspect competing essentialist preferences for the conditions of English and Scottish literature, I wish to examine such formations of cultural "tradition" and the status of "literature" (and, to some extent, "art" more generally) in post-war Scottish fiction. In particular, I intend to focus on several texts by Robin Jenkins, Muriel Spark and Alasdair Gray where there is a tension between the idea of the Calvinist *Weltanschauung* of Scotland and a cosmopolitan sensibility. Novels by these writers show the "historical habit" of Scotland fruitfully enmeshing with modernity and even post-modernity, so that, in this period, we might at last put away notions of either derided or defended anachronistic Scottish literature, and see this literature instead as being as cosmopolitan as anywhere else, even while, at the same time, being a particular product of place.

Robin Jenkins's *The Cone-Gatherers* (1955) provides a Scottish landscape that is also, and at the same time, "elsewhere". The combination of these two textures of location, in fact, provide for a vivid or "realistic" setting, and one that is uncomfortably overloaded with significance:

It was a good tree by the sea-loch, with many cones and much sunshine; it was homely too, with rests among its topmost branches as comfortable as chairs.
     For hours the two men had worked in silence there, a hundred feet from the earth, closer, it seemed, to the blue sky round which they had watched the sun slip. Misted in the morning, the loch had gone through many shades of blue and now was mauve, like the low hills on its far side. Seals that had been playing tag in and out of

the seaweed under the surface had disappeared like children gone home for tea. A destroyer had steamed seawards, with a sailor singing cheerfully. More sudden and swifter than hawks, and roaring louder than waterfalls, aeroplanes had shot down from the sky over the wood, whose autumnal colours they seemed to have copied for camouflage. In the silence that had followed gunshots had cracked far off in the wood. (Jenkins 1987: 7)

The first sentence obviously recalls the creation of the world by the God of Judaeo-Christian tradition. At the same time, however, human presence in the world appropriates creation through acts of perception, something we see also in the labelling of the tree as "good" and in the anthropomorphism increasingly inflicted upon nature (so that, for instance, the seals are "like children"). The end of the passage, with its weapons of mass destruction, confirms our awareness of the sinister mastery of nature by humanity, the aeroplanes outdoing hawks, and the occluding movement from this Ariel frame of reference to the presence of humans in the woods with their insidious firearms. The supposed Divine creator and his manifold work, then, are gradually, and somewhat ironically, trumped or "brought down to earth" by human power. This is a very Scottish setting in mental as well as physical terms. The light and colour of the scene, especially in its observed transmutations, speak realistically of the Highland west coast of Scotland, and the scene carries also the metaphysical weight of the Calvinist mindset (the first phrase is immediately an act of moral discernment) and, implicitly, the Calvinist fear of the imagination in the deceptive (because fallen) world, mimicked by the slippery, metaphorical exuberance of the opening passage.

The Cone-Gatherers is sometimes identified as a "fable", but such labelling pays inadequate attention to the colliding, imploding mythic, fictive and realistic terrains and textures incorporated within the novel and signalled in the opening passage. The central myth of good versus evil is set up with a sardonic aplomb that is underappreciated in the response to Jenkins's novel. For a start, there is a heaviness of nuance that should place us on our guard. Calum, the hunchbacked innocent with learning difficulties put to work gathering cones in Argyllshire during World War Two, is a rather too obvious "holy fool" figure, who has a St Francis-like empathy with the birds and other dumb creatures and who ends the novel in Christ-like sacrifice. Set against him, appalled by his deformity and its presence in such a naturally beautiful setting, is Duror the gamekeeper of the estate where Calum is set to work. Duror too, has deeply inscribed cultural ancestry in his character makeup. His name points us towards Albrecht Dürer, who painted *Adam and Eve* (1507), whose work purveys a strong allegorical vision generally, and who was intensely interested in human proportion and sympathetic to the growth of Protestantism. We perhaps realise, then, that in this opening passage, with its allegorical first sentence and its painterly attention to scene, the action is actually focalised through the character of the gamekeeper; and all the more so when we later learn that he is seen to be suffering with an overwrought Calvinist view of the world. The allegorical perception of Duror is a problem in the novel, as he facilely reads deformity as inherently evil, and so should warn us against collaborating with such a vision of the world, even as we are confronted with the novel's insistent (though diffuse) allegorical resonances. Duror is a weak man, disintegrating psychologically, around whom the novel gathers a formidable cloaking of primal evil. Like Calum, he is overloaded with representational nuance. He is the serpent in the woods or the "green man" figure stalking his *demesne* with destructive intent in his desire to purge the place of Calum's imperfection.

We find deliberately heavy symbolism elsewhere in the cast of characters. Calum's brother Neil (his "brother's keeper") is at certain points a self-denying Christ figure, prompting comparison with the central duo of John Steinbeck's *Of Mice and Men*, a novel taking its title, of course, from Robert Burns's poem, "To a Mouse". Among other long fictive character-trails (which might be thought ultimately to be wild goose trails) in *The Cone-Gatherers*, there is the couching of the young boy, Roderick, the son of estate-owner Lady Runcie Campbell, who is seen by his mother as the Arthurian knight Galahad in his attempt to champion the cause of Calum and Neil, as they are unjustly persecuted by Duror. Amidst the surfeit of prefigured fictionality and story-telling, Lady Runcie Campbell's vision of Calum slaughtered by Duror ends the novel in a way that is consonant with the gamekeeper's Edenic perception with which it begins. She sees Calum shot amidst the branches of a tree: "Then she went down on her knees, near the blood and the spilt cones. She could not pray, but she could weep; and as she wept pity, and purified hope, and joy, welled up in her heart" (Jenkins 1987: 222). We have gone from the opening of the novel to its end, from *Genesis* in the Old Testament to the central act of the New Testament, with Christ's act of redeeming death and the bringing of salvation for all. This fast-forwarding of the Bible is in itself an act of mockery. The cathartic ending is no less false than the opening, as Lady Runcie Campbell, in her Christian and Aristotelian reflexes, is as prone to superimposing on her world simplistic stories as her gamekeeper has been in his belief that he is a force for good, ridding the woods of the evil imperfection of Calum (and here we might note another strong force in Duror's literary gene-pool, the Scottish "justified sinner" pioneered by Burns and James Hogg, who believes himself to be an agent of morality no matter the murderous particularity of his actions). Lady Runcie Campbell, we might realise, is merely relieved that Calum has now been removed as an encourager of what she takes to be Roderick's indiscriminatingly benign attitude towards the world, something that is unsuitable in a male who will have to fulfil certain class responsibilities (masculinity and class are other rigid structures, or human "stories" witheringly viewed in the novel). As Calum is safely and theoretically transformed in death into an ideal of innocence, Lady Runcie Campbell no longer has to deal with his actual innocence and love toward all creatures. Lady Runcie Campbell, no less than Duror, is a character hiding behind a prefabricated story so as to avoid the messy reality of the world (her perception of her son as an Arthurian knight similarly marks out her wilful hypocrisy, as she tries to reclaim a sense of Roderick's proper "nobility" within a story of "chivalry", and momentarily her misgivings about her son are wrapped in a comforting myth).

The messy reality of Duror's world is seen as his repugnance at Calum echoes the revulsion he feels towards his bed-ridden wife. In this ugly psychological situation Calum, with his beautiful face and his twisted body, is read by Duror as a kind of mockery of his de-formed marital relationship and of the supposed perfection of creation generally. Duror's murder of Calum is a vicarious act against his wife, but, to complicate matters, we are told that Duror's horror of ugliness predates his marriage and was evident even in his childhood. Cleverly,

then, we are at first led towards an explanation that might elicit a
measure of sympathy in us for Duror, only to be taken beyond this and
made aware that his malaise has deeper, more gratuitous roots, fed not
by experience, but by superstitious expectations about the separate
existence of beauty and ugliness, good and evil. We see a gradual
process in Duror whereby his own physical monstrosity mounts as his
obsession with the innocent impurity of Calum gathers pace:

> By the whins then, empty of hope, he knew there was one thing on earth he did not
> want ever again to see: the smile of the hunchback. He swung from it as a pony from
> an adder. So vivid was his horror of seeing it that he actually shut his eyes there on the
> darkening road; but there were eyes within him he could not close at will, and these
> now began to see that smile, and only that smile. (Jenkins 1987: 120)

Expecting that the world should be governed by dramatically clear
philosophic divisions, and unable to cope with the bewildering, un-
governable complexities of nature, Duror festers inwardly and becomes a rotten figure who is increasingly rendered in supernatural undertones. The narrator somewhat mocks him in the passage above at
first as "a pony" – a metaphorically pleasant, benign image – and then
plunges him almost immediately into the terms of demonic possession. The man who expects cleanly demarcated symbolism in the
world, who looks in primal subjectivity to the whins for "hope", has
visited upon him a derisively slippery, uncertain and even manic imagery.

Duror's moral state is offset by two characters of profoundly undramatic vision who stand for goodness in the world. In a qualified
way this is true, first of all, of Calum. The man possesses such a
guileless innocence that he is little aware of the existence of evil, or at
any rate pushes what dim cognisance he does have out of his mind:

> This was the terrifying mystery, why creatures he loved should kill one another. He
> had been told that all over the world in the war now being fought men, women, and
> children were being slaughtered in thousands; cities were being burnt down. He could
> not understand it, and so he tried, with success, to forget it. (Jenkins 1987: 9)

Calum is the polar opposite to Duror in this regard, but in this untor-
tured outlook he is vulnerable to others more than to himself, and
stands as an appropriately foregrounded instance of the individual per-

secuted without motive by larger forces in the contemporary wider world, such as the Nazis. Calum does little "good" in itself and, indeed, wishes to evade moral questions for which his mind has no capacity, but he might be read as "good" simply inasmuch as he harbours for the world no malice whatsoever. Duror self-pityingly realises that Calum has a "smile for every limping dog" (Jenkins 1987: 126), though none for him. Calum's behaviour here speaks not even of resentment, but of cautious avoidance: he displays no explicit emotion at all towards the gamekeeper and is in fact deeply frightened by him. Almost unnoticeably, Tulloch, the foreman to the brothers and the conscientious objectors with whom they work, is the most powerfully good character in the novel. He does what he can to make the lives of his despised charges as bearable as possible, even though he might be thought to be entitled to resentment towards the COs, since his brother has been killed on active service in the war. Tulloch is a man who refuses, however, to construct such story-like connections and maintains instead the capability to treat every individual and situation as a separate moral case. He refrains from large-scale judgements and utilises instead quiet, undramatic discernment as a strategy for living kindly in the world.

Among a number of ironic manoeuvres that *The Cone-Gatherers* carries out, the "home front" is contrasted with the large conflict of world war raging without. World War Two might well be seen as a war against the evil of Nazi ideology, but an inevitable part of the propaganda inherent in executing such a struggle is the premise that this evil can be definitively defeated. In foregrounding a "fabulistic" tale in the woods, the novel at once enters into a situation that looks as though it will have clear moral resonance in a way that echoes the supposedly definitive struggle outside. In fact, in the surfeit of received literary and cultural resonances that the book purveys, we find instead a decaying effect where echoes interfere with one another and we are denied easy access to a clear-sounding story. We also find, of course, that the struggle with evil, however this is defined, is not external or beyond the idyllic home-front, but rather internal, inherent in human nature, and visible indeed in Duror's persecution of Calum. We must not make the mistake of Duror and think that the struggle with imperfection can be definitively won, either through epochal conflict or by more "local" action.

The Cone-Gatherers could not be called a Christian novel; indeed, as I have shown, it replays the central Christian myth most sardonically. And it tends, perhaps, towards Manichean heresy in positing the almost equal and endless combat between the forces of good and evil. The book is even somewhat demonic in its multi-voiced rendering of various received stories, motifs and symbols, and mocks the unaware reader who looks to read the novel as simply analogous with any of these familiar narratives. In performing in this way, however, the novel can also be seen to replay the Scottish interest in demonic disorientation, most famously found in Hogg's *Private Memoirs and Confessions of a Justified Sinner* (1824). Jenkins's novel shares this interest in its rendition of the Calvinist pursuit of clear categories that gradually become less clear, precisely because they are so relentlessly pursued – by Duror and potentially also by the reader. It is a novel that conforms to recent revisionism, most especially in the work of Cairns Craig, where we find the idea that the Calvinist culture of Scotland makes for a crucial counterpoint to the imagination (Craig 1999). In this dialogue between moral, theological certainty and rampant uncertainty engendered by the overwrought sureness of the Calvinist starting point, we find a very "modern" mentality deep within Scottish historical experience. In its louche replaying of narrative and moral terms that are so clearly recognizable on the surface, *The Cone-Gatherers* – within both Scottish and broader terms of reference – is a powerful site of the modern, even post-modern, alienation from the idea of easily accessible absolute truth.

Like *The Cone-Gatherers*, Muriel Spark's *The Prime of Miss Jean Brodie* (1961) deals with confused identity, explicitly cultural as well as moral, but also peddles traditional Scottish materials in an intertextual package even more riotously configured than in Jenkins's novel. As with *The Cone-Gatherers*, critics have been slow to notice a highly "supernatural" texture, where once again this traditionally strong "Scottish" interest is rendered in widely resonant fictive fashion. For instance, Jean Brodie is something of a "Frankenstein's Monster" (Spark, notably, is intensely interested in the work of Mary Shelley), as she is constructed from dead parts of the Scottish body cultural, most obviously those archetypal, competing character-elements John Knox and Mary, Queen of Scots. On top of this we have Brodie's own attempt to create life from pre-existing parts; thus her lover fallen in World War One, Hugh Carruthers, is a combination of a Robert Burns figure, with his country ways and couthy turn of phrase, and the two lovers – art master and singing master respectively – she has now taken at Marcia Blane's school. Poignantly, Hugh, about whom we learn only in Brodie's vividly unreliable reports of his life to her girls, may never have existed at all. We find Jean Brodie also attempting to fabricate, almost as zombie-like automatons, the future roles of her girls, as for instance when, for reasons of creating a resonant and vicarious romance, she decides that Rose Stanley should take her own place in the bed of the art master, Teddy Lloyd; or when, more successfully, she encourages Joyce Emily Hammond to go off to fight in the Spanish Civil War in the service of Franco, whom Brodie so admires. The most extensive supernatural thread, however, has to do with the notion of the demonic possession. A crucial subterranean text for the novel is the Gospel of Mark 5.9: "My name is Legion: for we are many". We might notice that Jean Brodie, at one point, is described as being among "legions of her kind" of newly, partially liberated women in the western world of the 1930s (Spark 1965: 42). Related to the Gospel text also is the fact that Brodie's most intelligent pupil, Sandy Stranger, has "little pig-like eyes" (Spark 1965: 66), which squint in sinister fashion throughout the novel. When Christ exorcises the demon from the man in the land of the Gadarenes, he drives it into a herd of swine and over the cliff. The outcast status of swine in Jewish society can be related to Sandy Stranger (the name itself denoting something of this) and, humorously, to her status as half-English and half-Scottish, so that she is weirdly resonant with Jean Brodie herself in her somewhat heterogeneous identity. Acting with a rather skewed moral sense, Sandy seeks to defeat Brodie's purpose of putting Rose in the bed of her lover, Teddy Lloyd, by becoming herself the art teacher's lover. Eventually, she becomes bored with the man, but only after she had "extracted […] his religion as a pith from a husk" (Spark 1965: 123). Sandy adopts his Catholic faith and eventually becomes a nun. What we have, then, is another rather fictive supernatural undertone in Sandy's "consumption" of the man's

brain, as well as, in the porcine metaphor, the extension of the demonic comparison. The demonic logic of Sandy's character can be
read as one of transference, where Jean Brodie's devilish, shape-
changing, identity-bending propensity has "jumped" into Sandy. This
scenario, then, both encompasses the idea of poetic justice, that Jean
Brodie should, like Deacon Brodie, the forbear she claims from Edinburgh history, be "hanged on a gibbet of [her] own Devising" (Spark
1965: 88), as well as providing a warning to the reader not to dis-
criminate too easily between Miss Brodie and Sandy over which is
morally good and which is bad.

   Like Jenkins, Spark explicitly replays the scenario of Scottish
Calvinism's supposed hubristic initial certainty leading to mental con-
fusion and personal destruction. Yet, unlike the case of *The Cone-
Gatherers*, this world-view is not simply cast in a negative light. In
The Prime of Miss Jean Brodie, Calvinism becomes strangely "desir-
able" to Sandy Stranger:

Fully to savour her position, Sandy would go and stand outside St Giles Cathedral or
the Tolbooth, and contemplate these emblems of a dark and terrible salvation which
made the fires of the damned seem very merry to the imagination by contrast, and
much preferable. Nobody in her life, at home or at school, had ever spoken of Calvinism except as a joke that had once been taken seriously. She did not at the time
understand that her environment had not been on the surface peculiar to the place, as
was the environment of the Edinburgh social classes just above or, even more, just
below her own. She had no experience of social class at all. In its outward forms her
fifteen years might have been spent in any suburb of any city in the British Isles; her
school, with its alien house system, might have been in Ealing. All she was conscious
of now was that some quality of life peculiar to Edinburgh and nowhere else had been
going on unbeknown to her all the time, and, however undesirable it might be, she felt
deprived of it; however undesirable, she desired to know what it was, and to cease to
be protected from it by enlightened people. (Spark 1965: 108)

Scottish Calvinism here for Sandy is "other", and it is so not only because of her partly English background, but because it represents an
outlook that takes seriously a now discarded notion of theocentric human destiny that increasingly makes sense to her. With its belief in
election and predestination, it helps Sandy to understand the control-
ling actions of Jean Brodie. Brodie is the "emblem" of Calvinism that
Sandy eventually rejects by reporting her apparent Fascist leanings to
the head teacher. Calvinism provides Sandy with a moral template

against which to judge her teacher and to realise how grave her be-haviour is. Paradoxically (as in the case of Duror in *The Cone-Gatherers*), Calvinism, supposedly so hostile to the imagination, speaks to her imagination. All of this is not without irony, as Sandy "elects" Edinburgh to a somewhat special place among other, blander British cities. Sandy the bright schoolgirl is earlier drawn to fictional fabrication, as she imagines herself as a character in *Kidnapped*, or being the ballerina, Anna Pavlova. She does not simply outgrow such fantasies as she becomes older, but, perhaps as we all do, the novel implies, merely creates more serious fantasies. Her extreme empathy with both Miss Brodie and Edinburgh lead her to magnify melodram-atically their Calvinist inheritance, when there are other frames of ref-erence that might be applied. Miss Brodie is wilfully sure enough in her behaviour to resemble a "justified sinner" type, but, in her love of Romantic poetry, her chaotic love life, and also in her historical loca-tion of "war-bereaved spinsterhood" (Spark 1965: 42), or as a woman enjoying and experimenting with more freedom than she might other-wise have enjoyed had it not been for the Great War, she is other things too. She is as much a contemporary women as she is any kind of older cultural type and, in her love of poetry and painting, she stands in complete opposition to Calvinism's basic hostility to the aesthetic sphere. Later on Sandy realises something of the more uni-versal multiplicity that has surrounded her:

And many times throughout her life Sandy knew with a shock, when speaking to peo-ple whose childhood had been in Edinburgh, that there were other people's Edin-burghs quite different from hers, and with which she held only the names of districts and streets and monuments in common. (Spark 1965: 33)

Just as each individual is comprised of many, sometimes contradic-tory, facets, the human race as a whole is a rather mysterious agglom-eration of individual lives and perceptions. The Scottish "split person-ality", attributed variously in Scottish criticism to Anglo-Scottish con-fusion or to Calvinism's psychological tensions, becomes in *The Prime of Miss Jean Brodie* something much more general, normative even. Sandy Stranger, an Anglo-Scot who becomes fascinated by the Calvinist mental condition of her city and of her teacher, speaks to Scottish criticism's profusion of national identities and, indeed, potentially mocks its despair in the face of such profligacy. We find wry conflation too in Jean Brodie, who is both the "justified sinner" and alternatively exotic in her free-loving, romantic poetry-loving ways. All identities are fluid, and Sandy, at times, has a powerful apprehension of this:

Sandy felt warmly towards Miss Brodie at those times when she saw how she was misled in her idea of Rose. It was then that Miss Brodie looked beautiful and fragile, just as dark heavy Edinburgh itself could suddenly be changed into a floating city when the light was a special pearly white and fell upon one of the gracefully fashioned streets. In the same way Miss Brodie's masterful features became clear and sweet to Sandy when viewed in the curious light of the woman's folly, and she never felt more affection for her in her later years than when she thought upon Miss Brodie as silly. (Spark 1965: 111)

Here the seemingly solid Calvinism of the Scottish capital has melted away. As in other parts of the novel we find a kind of transformed, almost supernatural texture, both to the city and to Miss Brodie herself (although this contrasts starkly with supernatural elements elsewhere in the novel). Use of expressions such as the "gracefully fashioned streets" is a typically conflating manoeuvre on the part of Spark, referring as it does both to Edinburgh's Georgian elegance and, at the same time, to the theology of "grace". At this point Sandy's perception is transformed as she is given the ability to see things differently, a touchstone for Spark of the possibilities that God allows always to human beings. This is not necessarily always an entirely comfortable capacity, as, for example, when we learn of the future life of one of the Brodie set:

It happened she was standing with a man whom she did not know very well outside a famous building in Rome, waiting for the rain to stop [...] She supposed herself to have fallen in love with the man [...] There was nothing whatever to be done about it, for Jenny had been contentedly married for sixteen years past; but the concise happening filled her with astonishment whenever it came to mind in later days, and with a sense of the hidden possibilities in all things. (Spark 1965: 80–81)

The Prime of Miss Jean Brodie is about the mystery of life, or "the hidden possibilities in all things". What we think we know to be true, how we categorise people, is ultimately a deceptive thing. At any moment we might find, in the words of a treatise by Sister Helena, after Sandy becomes a nun, "The Transfiguration of the Common-place". Spark's basic premise is that we are not in control, a moral precept that Jean Brodie breaches; but so too, to some extent, does Sandy Stranger. The ultimate truth is that Jean Brodie is not a particu-larly special sinner, and neither is she possessed of a special imagi-nation. She is a somewhat "silly" creature, as all humans are from a God's-eye view. We should not feel that such confusion and contra-diction is especially a part of the Scottish (Calvinist) experience; it is something more universally human. The logic of Spark's premise is that we should delight to some extent in the flux of life, with its possi-bilities of grace, and cling to no solid ideas about the people and places with whom we come in contact: this is the ultimate belief in predestination that the world, under God's grace, will prove time and again to be wrong.

Alasdair Gray's *Lanark* (1981) also makes much of the seeming fragmentation of Scottish experience and its Calvinist cultural climate. Just as *The Prime of Miss Jean Brodie* is a bold imaginative reclama-tion of Edinburgh, Gray's novel is explicitly a reclamation of Glasgow for the fictional terrain, which, in Gray's (or Duncan Thaw's) estima-tion, has been lost to the imagination:

"Glasgow is a magnificent city," said McAlpin. "Why do we hardly ever notice that?" "Because nobody imagines living here," said Thaw. McAlpin lit a cigarette and said, "If you want to explain I'll certainly listen."
"Then think of Florence, Paris, London, New York. Nobody visiting them for the first time is a stranger because he's already visited them in paintings, novels, history books and films. But if a city hasn't been used by an artist not even the inhabitants live there imaginatively. What is Glasgow to most of us? A house, the place we work, a football park or golf course, some pubs and connecting streets. That's all. No, I'm wrong, there's also the cinema and the library. And when our imagination needs exercise we use these to visit London, Paris, Rome under the Caesars, the American West at the turn of the century, anywhere but here and now. Imaginatively, Glasgow exists as a music-hall song and a few bad novels. That's all we've given to the world outside. It's all we've given to ourselves." (Gray 1987: 243)

All of the examples that Thaw cites are actually metropolitan, colo-nising ones, somewhat outside the control of Glaswegians to resist. At the other extreme, Thaw is alluding, obviously enough, to largely in-ternally created melodramatic renditions of Glasgow as a tough place,

both in sensationalistic fiction and in its reputation as second city of
the empire: as a place of shipbuilding and heavy industry. Caught
between these two extremes of a colonising imagination and a de-
nuded local aesthetic, Thaw sets to work on his mural of Genesis on a
structurally condemned Presbyterian church. This is both defiantly
comical, as Thaw mimics Michelangelo in a supposedly inimical
Scottish context, and also poignant. Mr Rennie the minister has kindly
extended this opportunity to Thaw as the young artist recuperates from
a debilitating illness, partly physical, partly psychosomatic. Thaw's
response is to comment on his project in seemingly precious fashion
and in a way that suggests to Mr Rennie that he continues to be over-
sensitive in his mental constitution:

I believe this church will be knocked down, but first the mural must be made perfect.
When a thing is perfect it is eternal. It can be destroyed afterward, or slowly decay,
but its perfection is safe in the past, which is the only inevitable part of the universe.
(Gray 1987: 337)

Thaw has earnestly entered into the idea of the transcendence of art, in
defiance of his national context as a place of philistine practicality. He
is partly correct in his diagnosis of the absence of art from Glasgow
(though whether this is a question of art's actual existence in the city
at that time or of its accessibility is another question), but he is also, as
the extremism of his remark shows, somewhat unrealistic in his attitude: signalling even his desire to escape into solipsistic fantasy
(usurping even and appropriating to himself, in quasi-Calvinistic
fashion, the role of God).

   Lanark, in general, might be read as an indulgence of Thaw's desire to enter into the imagination. The title itself, of course, refers
obliquely to Glasgow in being the small market town that gives its
name to the county in which Glasgow stands. In this manoeuvre, we
have a gesturing toward the desire for Glasgow to be more like its
originally Gaelic-derived name meaning "dear green place". No less
than in *The Prime of Miss Jean Brodie*, we are to be shown a city un-
derneath the seemingly everyday or surface reality. In *Lanark*, however, in an ironic counterpoint to the idea of the dear green place,
Glasgow is transformed into its nightmarish, dystopian double "Unthank" (a name that is both a real place in the south of Scotland and

one that allegorically refers to what Thaw takes to be the ungrateful – again the proximity of the word "grace" should be noted here – character of Glasgow).[2] Thaw disappears, only to be transmogrified as "Lanark", re-appearing in Unthank, where he is exposed to the machinations of the Institute (an obvious enough metaphor for the cold capitalist-powered transactions of the world).

In *Lanark*, as in the case of the novels by Jenkins and Spark, we may diagnose a deliberately overloaded weight of meaningfulness. Thaw is an over-sensitive individual, not unlike Duror or Sandy Stranger, who makes more of his own suffering and its of relationship to an overarching pattern than ought to be taken seriously. He exemplifies the paradox of the artist who wishes life to be redolent of aesthetic pattern. Thaw's critique of Scotland's relationship to art is also somewhat precious, even as he ironically castigates the principle of division of labour (the invention, supposedly, of that great practical Scot, Adam Smith): "People in Scotland have a queer idea of the arts. They think you can be an artist in your *spare* time, though nobody expects you to be a spare-time dustman, engineer, lawyer or brain surgeon" (Gray 1987: 211). This may reflect Gray's own belief that art is something useful and valuable, but are we to take Thaw's descent into a full-time, ultra-aesthetic world of surrealism and Dantean dystopia as entirely healthy? Obviously, this world in which Thaw becomes Lanark (ironically, a name that might be seen on the surface as tending towards pleasant pastoral label) is not healthy. It would seem to suggest an extreme opposite reaction to the suppression of art diagnosed by Thaw. And this is verified as Thaw continues his critique of a disenfranchised, disembodied art, so unlike that of the Venetian republic: "As nobody employs us nowadays we've had to invent our own reasons for painting" (Gray 1987: 306). Thaw is hung up on utility to the extent that he becomes more and more dysfunctional as he pursues his artistic career, actually guilty that he has his "own reasons for painting". Thaw is someone desperate to relate his personal situation to a wider cultural context, both Scottish Calvinist iconoclasm and the supposed decline of the stature of art in

---

[2] Unthank is, perhaps significantly, located near Langholm in the Scottish borders, the birthplace of Hugh MacDiarmid. I would like to thank Alexander Mackay for pointing this out.

the west since the Renaissance; on the other hand, however, he may just be a constitutionally maladjusted individual, struggling hopelessly to fit in with everyday life. Ironically enough, even as Thaw/Lanark manifests his artistic alienation by plunging into deep fantasy, he takes possession of the very "higher aesthetic sphere" that he seems at times to be claiming is shut off to him in his unamenable cultural location. This circularity culminates in one of the sequences that have earned the novel the description "postmodern", as Lanark's disconnection from himself and society, or Thaw's fantasy life, becomes so extreme that eventually he meets his "author":

"I am your author."
Lanark stared at him. The author said, "Please don't feel embarrassed. This isn't an unprecedented situation. Vonnegut has it in *Breakfast of Champions* and Jehovah in the books of Job and Jonah."
"Are you pretending to be God?"
"Not nowadays. I used to be part of him, though. Yes, I am part of a part which was once the whole. But I went bad and was excreted. If I can get well I may be allowed home before I die, so I continually plunge my beak into my rotten liver and swallow and excrete it. But it grows again. Creation festers in me. I am excreting you and your world at the present moment. This arse-wipe" – he stirred the papers on the bed – "is part of the process."
"I'm not religious," said Lanark, "but I don't like you mixing religion with excrement." (Gray 1987: 481)

On one level we have the jumble of Lanark's/Thaw's mind, reaching out to American literature, the Bible and Greek mythology, his own sense of worthlessness (as excrement) and his deep-seated Calvinism, both in his apprehension of being a creation as well as his prudish dislike of his "author's" seeming profanity. At the same time these elements represent an intertextuality, through which Gray's central protagonist is joyously purged of his limitations of cultural location. "Creation festers in me" may be a dark expression of "Calvinist guilt", but it also contains an irrepressible force of imagination, which brings not necessarily comfort, but the ability to engage humorously, at least, with the diffuse (and by no means uniquely Scottish) hopeless state of human existence. This "process" is a constant in the novel, with the result that the "authorial" perspective becomes wantonly claustrophobic: Thaw imagines himself, for example, on Ben Rua as "starting across the moor like a louse up a quilt" (Gray 1987: 140). Thaw's self-loathing increases as his stature as an artist grows, and so art offers no specific hope or salvation; all it can offer, in an effective antidote to the self-importance of the Calvinist vision, is the realisation that we are creatures who do not stand at the centre of any divine pattern, and who do not in fact posses the subjective powers that might bring God down to earth, or the author into the text. Lanark's meeting with his (and Thaw's) author is confirmation that he is not personally constrained by some overwhelming *cultural context*; it is also confirmation of an *intertextual* space, in which is inscribed an intensely subjective matter for the artist (both Gray himself and his central character). Art triumphs in *Lanark* even as it seems to be the index of a maladjusted personality; it is not, however, as the Scottish sensitivity to its own cultural dearth might suggest, the index of wholeness of culture or personal individuality, but of the ability to imagine oneself imperfectly (in one sense, ironically enough, akin to the theological meaning of this word). In the fantastic, anti-*bildungsroman* case of Thaw/Lanark, art might even be an index of the most indulgent self-pity, warning us against and undermining the over-blown objective claims that art so often makes for itself. "Lanark" represents both an individual (or a part of an individual), but also a wider identity (as the name of a county town); but the former is sardonically derived from the latter, and need not necessarily be read as symbolic or representative of anything beyond the tortured psyche of one individual.

The three novels examined above all begin by viewing the condition of Scotland as historically problematic and all engage with the idea of Scotland as a place of diseased imagination. They all make capital from the perceived fragmentary nature of Scottish experience, but, equally, they all go beyond it, and end by casting doubt on the existence of any ingrained "co-ordinates of debilitation" within Scottish culture at large. These fictions simultaneously conjugate local (Scottish) culture through cosmopolitan experience and, in so doing, liberate it from its myths of entrenchment. In late twentieth-century fiction, the Scottish "experience" has become as creative as anywhere else.

Bibliography

Craig, David. 1961. *Scottish Literature and the Scottish People 1680–1830*. London: Chatto & Windus.

Craig, Cairns. 1999. *The Modern Scottish Novel*. Edinburgh: Edinburgh University Press.

Daiches, David. 1964. *The Paradox of Scottish Culture*. London and New York: Oxford University Press.

Gray, Alasdair. 1987. *Lanark: A Life in Four Books*. London: Paladin.

Jenkins, Robin. 1987. *The Cone-Gatherers*. Harmondsworth: Penguin.

Muir, Edwin. 1936. *Scott and Scotland*. London: Routledge.

Smith, G. Gregory. 1919. *Scottish Literature: Character and Influence*. London: Macmillan.

Spark, Muriel. 1965. *The Prime of Miss Jean Brodie*. London: Penguin.

Stevenson, Robert Louis. [1894] 1979. *Weir of Hermiston and Other Stories* (ed. by Paul Binding). Harmondsworth: Penguin.

Wittig, Kurt. 1958. *The Scottish Tradition in Literature*. Edinburgh: Oliver & Boyd.

La Grille: Contemporary Scottish Poetry and France

Richard Price

In general, there has been little reciprocal influence between contemporary Scottish and French literature. However, a number of Scottish poets have defied this trend, and found a fruitful relation to both France and French literature.
Keywords: Iain Bamforth, David Kinloch, Peter McCarey, Donny O'Rourke, contemporary Scottish poetry, French influence.

There is an episode of the TV cartoon show *The Simpsons* that, with a little reflection, encapsulates Scotland's recent relationship with France. Homer Simpson, the overweight, feckless father figure decides to build a brick barbecue in his back garden. His hardworking and intellectual daughter Lisa has already laid the concrete base for the new structure. All Homer has to do is build the self-assembly barbecue into the concrete. As loyal viewers will have expected, the plan quickly goes awry. Homer's structure slips and then topples into the grey porridge of Lisa's carefully designed foundations.

Homer is not deterred. The series is testament, after all, to his overcoming greater problems than a subsiding barbecue, even if the problems are often self-imposed (see the recurring nuclear meltdown theme) and a "triumph" means that he goes right back to where he started. This time, he manages to rescue the instructions and although the English text has been obliterated by wet concrete the French version is still intact. Finally, it is time to despair: "*La grille*?!" he shouts, angrily, only to add, with a whimper, "Oh, why are foreign languages so hard to understand?"

That is not the end of the story, though. The next time we see him, his barbecue has been completed. It is utterly unusable – bricks and tools and "la grille" stick out from a concrete composite. With the luck inherent in the glorious fiction that is *The Simpsons*, an art collector happens to see it. She loves it for its "raw energy" and persuades Homer to have it installed in the most fashionable art gallery in town. It is a great success, particularly with the critics. In one of the many instances in *The Simpsons* where American anti-intellectualism is pitted against European pretentiousness, the adoring reviewers speak with snobbish mittel-European accents. Homer Simpson's art, an object built through his faulty but energetic misunderstanding of French, has, briefly, found validation.

1.

In *La Nouvelle Alliance*, David Kinloch and I assembled a number of studies of French influence on modern Scottish literature (Kinloch and Price eds 2000). There has been limited but real engagement with French literature in Scotland in the last hundred years or so, and the essays each showed very specific connections. Perhaps of all the authors covered in the book – including Hugh MacDiarmid, Neil Gunn, Sidney Goodsir Smith, James Kelman, Frank Kuppner, Alasdair Gray, Ronald Frame, Janice Galloway, A.L. Kennedy, and even Kenneth White – only Ian Hamilton Finlay could be said to have made a connection to French culture as a directing force in a large swathe of his work. This essentially confirms the findings of Kenneth White's essay "The Franco-Scottish Connection": after centuries of cross-cultural influence, White can gather very few significant links in the twentieth century (White 1998).

A few other names could be added. An essay on Veronica Forrest-Thompson might have explored whether there was a similar connection to quite different nodes in the French cultural infrastructure: to Barthes, Derrida, and Kristeva; and to Marcelin Pleynet, Denis Roche, and the poetry of *Tel Quel*. Such a study could also have investigated, however, how much Forrest-Thompson's acknowledged debt to William Empson modified or complemented her relationship with French literature and theory. Indeed the English avant-garde context in which Forrest-Thompson can also be placed, "The Cambridge School", was probably as much a conduit for French translation as any in Scotland at the time (see, for example, Peter Riley's magazine *Collection*, published in the late 1960s, with its translations of Cendrars, Apollinaire, Soupault and Francis Ponge; Forrest-Thompson was herself a translator of Pleynet and Roche).

We excluded the figures of Alexander Trocchi, Douglas Dunn, and Edwin Morgan on the basis that books already existed that looked at their work, including aspects of French influence. Morgan's extremely early contact with French – a poem of Verlaine's being the first poem he translated, in 1937, and the appropriately different modes of translation he has employed in *Cyrano de Bergerac* and *Phaedra* – suggest that, here, in particular, is another of the few modern Scottish writers whose relationship with France has been profound. Yet this is true at the level of Morgan's *respect* for French literature: unlike his enthusiasm for Anglo-Saxon literature, Elizabethan drama, and modern American literature, it is difficult, I think, to see either a stylistic or thematic influence from French literature affecting Morgan's work.

Other Francophile writers warrant further study, of course – Sean Rafferty, Gael Turnbull, and Stephen Mulrine, come immediately to mind, and among younger writers it might be rewarding to examine Guillevic's and Houellebecq's influence on Gavin Bowd, or James Robertson's use of Scots in his translations of Baudelaire. Nevertheless, considered as a phenomenon that would affect writer after writer, not just as writing which they enjoyed or even translated, there is little of substance to be said here. Or rather, there is nothing of the order of influence that one finds in, say, the Francophile "Castalian" poetry of James VI, where almost the entire frame of expression is derived from French models (see, for example, Jack 1989). These exceptions are just that and, given the changed cultural and political times, it would be a great surprise if Scotland did come within France's gravitational pull.

2.

It would be even more surprising if France was much affected by modern Scottish writing. Lack of interest does turn out to be the rule, at least if translations are an indicator of engagement (a questionable assumption). In *La Nouvelle Alliance* one of the conclusions of Paul Barnaby's chapter on French translations of Scottish texts was that "Peu d'auteurs écossais importants ont été traduits entre Stevenson et

Muriel Spark" [Few of the important Scottish authors between Stevenson and Muriel Spark have been translated (into French)] (Barnaby 2000: 261). A handful of texts by some younger writers, for example, James Kelman, Irvine Welsh, and Alan Warner, have been translated, but even these authors have generally received less attention from translators in France as compared to elsewhere in Europe. In other words, France has taken a *particularly* dim view of Scottish literature over the last hundred years. The aspiration of some Scots to be seen as cultural equals by the French, a hope whose nature introduces a self-defeating inequality from the start, is lampooned in a number of issues of the anonymously edited satirical magazine *Depression News*. Although normally an English-language magazine, two issues from 1999 were published in French (as well as being anonymous, the magazine is always undated and unnumbered, no doubt because of its often scurrilous nature).[1]

One of these numbers, entitled *Le Saviez Vous Les "Boozy Sportsmen"?*, imagines a visit to Edinburgh, where the author gleefully mixes English and French to describe the treats in store:

Le tour des pub commence dans une des cruddy-auberges du vieil Edinbourg où tossers et prostituées, football players et avocats, se retrovaiaient le World Cup de 1974 autor d'une bouteille de Merrydown, ou une bouteille peut-etre de Diamond White and Black.

As well as squalor-chic neologisms such as "cruddy-auberges" and, earlier, "anecdotes des grands pish écossais", further bathos is achieved by the easy association of prostitutes with advocates and "les football players" (the latter surely foregrounded here as an entertaining English loan phrase in French). Much fun is also had at the expense of the banal "local" drinks Merrydown and Diamond White and Black, with the implicit contrast – especially pointed up by that convivial "peut-etre" – to the sophisticated and romantic world of French wine.

Another issue of *Depression News*, devoted to "LE CLOOTIE DUMPLING et les autres plats chauds fabuleux", also seems confused

---

[1] All of these issues are now deposited with the British Library, shelfmark: RH.9.x.1309.

– orthographically, syntactically and factually – when it suggests that "ECOSSE EST NE SEULEMENT PAS POUR LE CLOOTIE – C'EST L'ORIGINE FANTASTIQUE DES EURYTHMICS, LE GERRY RAFFERTY [...] ET LE LLYOD [*sic*] COLE". Aside from the amusement of the names from middle of the road Scottish pop culture, in which the less than epoch-making Le Wet Wet Wet and Le Runrig also feature, Lloyd Cole, of course, is English (although he was based in Glasgow and his band the Commotions were, truly, Scottish). With the deliberate mistake *Depression News* seems to force the reader into making a correcting act of identification, based on cultural shibboleths, while simultaneously satirising the narrowly ethnic pedantry of such an act. In this there is the boorishness of a newspaper diary, of course – satire is often more puerile than its target – but *Depression News* is at least sensitive to a relationship in which, in fact, neither "Scotland" nor "France" are all that they might be. That these texts are written in grammatically terrible French adds one further layer of instability to the text.

3.

Despite all of the above, there are several more recent poets who buck the trend of negligible French influence on Scottish literature. Their number includes Donny O'Rourke, David Kinloch, Iain Bamforth and Peter McCarey.

Donny O'Rourke's song "Like Simone Signoret", collected in *The Waistband*, is a particularly good example of the way in which French influence is transformed in Scottish literature (O'Rourke 1997: 68–69). This beguilingly simple song is in fact a subtle expression of hopes for a sophisticated intellectual and artistic culture within Scotland, even if those hopes are to be dashed by the time the song is over. The first stanza in "Like Simone Signoret" sees the speaker watching a woman buying a collection of poems by Prévert, and likening her to the French actress of the title:

Perhaps it was the weather
Wet and hot
Or the poems of Prévert

She'd just bought
Watching her browse
I decided now's
the time to make a play
But I just let it pelt
while she knotted her belt
just like Simone Signoret

The hesitation here changes in the second stanza and the voice becomes more confident in attributing a specifically French kind of experience to the encounter:

When she asked the quickest way
To Buchanan Street
I suggested coffee
If she'd no-one to meet
Sharing her umbrella
I was that Montand fella
Trés distingué
A boulevard romance
A Glasgow Saturday in France
with Simone Signoret

"If she'd no-one to meet" is a gentle nosiness: the speaker is asking shyly if she's single. There is a charm and delicacy to the whole song, in fact, and this is complemented in both versions of the music where the hesitancies are beautifully captured, whether it's Dave Whyte's composition on the music album *Still Waiting to Be Wise* (Whyte and O'Rourke 1999) or the poet's own version in his remarkable solo performances. This and the next stanza form a sweet fantasia about Glasgow-as-Paris, where it is even possible to imagine "Sartre's making speeches / in George's Square." But the final stanza returns the singer to the cold light of day:

She'd bought the poems for a friend
Didn't read that much
Though in the café our heads were close,
They didn't touch.
Waving her goodbye
I wonder why
I'm still a fool this way
A look over her shoulder

That self-sufficient smoulder
Simone Signoret.

The turnaround and economy of those first two lines is especially dev-astating: "Didn't read that much" is as crushing as it is beautifully ob-served. The singer's new acquaintance clearly regards reading as sim-ply another leisure pursuit that you might or might not like to do. For the poetry-reading Francophile persona such an admission announces the closing down of romantic possibility, certainly, but it also brings the realisation that a whole other world exists, largely without books and largely without engagement with other cultures, a world that in-deed appears "self-sufficient". The world is, in fact, a world so foreign to him that it is outside his means of understanding. The allusion, all the evidence suggests, would be lost on the woman it is meant to de-scribe. In O'Rourke's text, "Didn't read that much" is a fragment of a sentence both because the singer is choked – gulp, he can hardly bring himself to tell us – but perhaps also because the woman is a mumbler, perhaps even an apologetic one, representing a semi-articulacy which contrasts with the extraordinary fluency and confidence of O'Rourke's poem.[2]

The ambiguity of why the singer is a "fool" is balanced between his romantic love of French culture, and just a hint of disgust about the Glasgow (and Scottish, and British?) way of life: he is a "fool", largely, for being excitably sentimental about France, but also for thinking anyone he is likely to meet at home would actually be inter-ested in foreign cinema, philosophy or poetry. Perhaps there are gentle shades of Apollinaire's "La Jolie Rousse" here: "Mais riez riez de moi / Hommes de partout surtout gens d'ici" [But laugh at me laugh / Men from everywhere especially folk from here]. The song is an unrequited love song, but not many love songs are able to evoke such cultural longing. France elsewhere in *The Waistband* represents not only philosophical and political engagement, love of cinema and love of poetry, but also aspirations towards a food and street culture, and a

---

[2] Philip Larkin uses a similar abbreviated phrase, "Don't read much now", in the poem "A Study of Reading Habits" to slightly different effect: the speaker has turned away from reading, after finding that books do not offer the self-protection and satisfying fantasy that they once seemed to promise (Larkin 1988: 131).

sultry but tender relationship to the body. It shows what Scotland might be, but is not.

One poem actually imagines the word "La Poesie" as failing to translate into "Poetry", so different is French poetry from the poetry of the poet's own language (O'Rourke 1997: 50). It is as if the central ambiguity I've described in "Like Simone Signoret" becomes settled in its bittersweet nature as difference. The first stanza of "La Poesie / Poetry" offers a tribute to surrealism:

La poesie, is
abstract as clams
in a cloudburst
or the width of wine
in a tight corner

The second stanza asserts:

    Poetry
Is sour skinned,
just so, so just,
ample as the cusp
we're beckoned by
    and love.

The Waistband uses references to France in similar ways in several other pieces, too. It is fair to say that there is a French atmosphere permeating the entire book. O'Rourke's translations of Soupault, Larbaud, Desnos and Cendrars into Scots from the collection *Eftirs/Afters* are included too (O'Rourke and Price 1995). We find an epigraph from Camus, and even the other strong flavour of the collection – tributes to and reflections on the New York School poets James Schuyler and Frank O'Hara – are refractions from poets whose work after all owes so much to French predecessors.[3] A sense of a living boulevard where there are independent cafés, restaurants, old-fashioned shops like butchers and fishmongers, galleries and book-shops is important to O'Rourke. Many of his poems are about walking

---

[3] Interestingly, as Robin Purves shows in his essay in "La Nouvelle Alliance", the New York School can also be seen as "intermediaries" in a quite different way between the poetry of Ducasse and the poetry of Frank Kuppner (Purves 2000).

in the city – alone, with friends, with lovers – and the improvisatory, hand-held quality of the prosody, with its underlying assurance, matches the theme beautifully. The rich intermingling of themes in and across poems – friendship, love, family, what constitutes "culture" – is again entirely appropriate to the *flâneur* persona. The most extensive of these Scottish boulevard poems is "Great Western Road", which opens:

Glasgow, you look beatific in blue
and I've a Saturday before me
for galleries and poems,
a house full of Haydn,
and beneath my kitchen window,
tennis stars in saris
lobbing backhands at the bins.
French coffee, and who knows maybe
Allen Ginsberg in my bath! (O'Rourke 1997: 55–56)

The poem then imagines the whole day enjoying Great Western Road and its environs, "where, today, everything is redeemable / because tonight there'll be guitar poets / from Russia [...] playing at the Third Eye Centre". Like so many O'Rourke poems, this is poetry about how one might live one's life: the *flâneur* persona is used to express a sensibility that is discriminating but open to all manner of the arts; it is a very human poetry, but it is sensitive to the varying degrees of seriousness within the art and other cultural matter it encounters, joking and delicately elegising within lines of each other. It *almost* goes without saying that O'Rourke's Francophilia is matched by a very keen concern to shift sensibility in Scotland, so that although there are poems and songs that bring France to Scotland, there is also work which pointedly, programmatically even, addresses itself to Scottish material, such as the anthemic bid to resurrect a Scottish festival in February in "St Brigid's Day", or the song to celebrate the Edinburgh Book Festival, "Charlotte Square". That O'Rourke is able to dissolve "high-", "middle-", and "low-brow" concepts in the space of a single poem is perhaps reflected in the popularity of "Great Western Road", which, as well as being an anthology favourite, has been pirated. O'Rourke, sitting in a café on the eponymous street, found himself being offered a free photocopy of his own poem by a liberator of the

text who wanted as many people as possible to enjoy it. Charges were
not pressed.

4.

With its title *Un Tour d'Ecosse*, David Kinloch's second full-length
volume of poetry announces a Franco-Scottish link with style
(Kinloch 2001).[4] The engagement is not merely title-deep: quite apart
from the fact of Kinloch having taught French at the University of
Strathclyde, his interest in Mallarmé, and his work on Joseph Joubert
(the author of the textually-idiosyncratic *Carnets*), his poetry is obviously informed by an in-depth reading of French literature. Among
other work, his remarkable prose-poems openly owe a debt to Rimbaud, not only in their form, but also for their often exclamatory, ec-
static nature. Kinloch also attributes his interest in the prose poem's
ability to work as a theoretical text to the personal encouragement of
the poet Michel Deguy, who Kinloch knew in the 1980s (at this time
Kinloch was a *lecteur d'anglais* at the Ecole Normale Supériere in
Paris). His poems emerge from a spirit of creative philosophy more
common in France than in the British Isles, to say the least. Yet, for all
that, a good deal of the poems' power derives from Kinloch's inspired
use of barely recoverable Scots:

> When I opened the window and reached for the yoghurt cooling on the outside ledge,
> it had gone. All that remained was a single Scottish word bewildered by the Paris
> winter frost and the lights of the riverbank motorway. What can *dustie-fute* say to a
> night like this? (Kinloch 1994: 30)

There is the gentleness of genuine enquiry in these poems, as well as a
mixing of many different kinds of text, a reaching out to theory-by-
poetry, an extension exemplified by the comic-melancholic figure of
the student reaching for that transformed yoghurt ("dustie-fute" is a
traveller-figure, a stranger, a juggler, an acrobat).

---

[4] Kinloch's previous volume, *Paris-Forfar* (Kinloch 1994), announced the same
cultural connection

The relationship between France and Scotland is itself one of the risk-taking metaphors in *Paris-Forfar* where "the auld alliance" is between "words and things" (Kinloch 1994: 30). In an interview I conducted with him for *PN Review* and in subsequent correspondence, I asked Kinloch about the French aspects in his work. It was clearly important to him to emphasise the particular human moments of his coming to terms with France (in the same way that the poems that engage with French life and culture are also, tenderly, about and *through* actual people, the poet-as-student, the speaker's aunt and so on):

Well, France for me has always been about people and places first and foremost. I first spent a year in Paris in 1979 and the first man I fell in love with, who was about five years my senior and heavily into most kinds of literature, more or less gave me a crash course in "the books you ought to read" or rather the ones he thought I ought to read. I can remember achingly romantic walks to visit Chateaubriand's tomb at St Malo and lazy picnics reading passages of Flaubert and Proust to each other. Sadly the romance was all on my side but he put me onto Joubert so I suppose he had quite a long term effect! In this sense books have usually come to confirm things I've already felt or experienced and that has been a pattern in my life. ("Interview" 2001: 23)

This is an important element of Kinloch's self-classification, and one that is palpable in his poetry: the mediation of literature through human contact, usually through love, and occasionally through the lack of it. In the poem, the word "dustie-fute", like an old forgotten luggage label that has temporarily been given animation in an art-house cartoon, is created as part of the poet's sense of isolation in Paris: it is both a delightful literary conceit and a tentative answer to a real human need (the need to *place* oneself, knowing that this may be an act of will as much as a realisation of what already *is*). The word, as a Scots word, connects Kinloch to the Scotland he misses, to a Scotland that probably cannot exist except in the imagination (it is a word from an obsolete kind of Scots), and, paradoxically, it connects him to his sense of alienation in Paris, since the word means a foreigner. Aspirationally, however, the word eventually answers itself, as the poem explains, "triumphantly": it is "the dustie-fute of revelry, the acrobat, the juggler who accompanies the toe-belled *jongleur* with his merchant's comic fairground face" (here I think of Edwin Morgan's "Cinquevalli"). As Kinloch goes on to say:

I don't feel that I'm a bookish poet in spirit although obviously my profession informs how I approach my work. Perhaps it's this rather "unacademic" approach to literature that has led me in the directions I've taken as an academic: Joubert was a real eccentric who wasn't really interested in publishing a regular book and far more in the mental and creative processes of writing itself. In this respect he was streets ahead of his time. Rimbaud, who is another of my great passions, was not a conventional "author" either, someone who was able or perhaps compelled to give up writing when he felt it no longer served any purpose. ("Interview" 2001: 23–24)

Nevertheless, Kinloch's relationship to Francophone literature, notwithstanding his interest in those traditionally seen in particular and different ways as "outsiders", Joubert and Rimbaud, is far from straightforward:

Latterly, I have experienced a certain fatigue with metropolitan French culture and literature and I've struck out in the directions you've mentioned [other Francophone territories] although my interest in Quebec and the Caribbean has as much to do with Scotland and Scottish literature as with France. [...] Where I differ from other writers perhaps, is that for me France is also French, and the foreignness is also a linguistic foreignness and although I have come to speak and write that language quite well it remains tantalisingly foreign for me. I like the feeling of simultaneous nearness and distance partly because it echoes how I feel about the Scots language – and indeed about Québécois – and also on a much more general level because it speaks to what it feels like to live in "straight" society as a gay man. In my poetry I've tried to remain faithful to these senses of linguistic foreignness and difference, to point up connections but also to mark the differences, the "apartness". It's in this context that my poems are sometimes "about" language. I don't always feel able to "speak through" it as if it were a transparent medium. ("Interview" 2001: 24)

The concern with apparently anomalous states of being, as fundamental as the "wrong" kind of sexuality, is central to *Paris-Forfar* and is surely linked to a kind of synaesthetic existentialism, in which "to be" can only be understood through analogy, and analogy itself can only be understood through the exercising of unfamiliar and conventionally inappropriate senses. Of course, *Paris-Forfar* represents a startling and, to some, provocative use of the traditionally macho, hide-bound Scots language, now re-written within a gay discourse, but that is surely of a piece with the rich text that it is: as with the affectionate relocation of Whitman and Hervé Guibert and their techniques in *Un Tour d'Ecosse* (and, in a single poem, a homage to O'Hara and

Apollinaire – that American-French matrix again), it is a poetry available to, but not circumscribed by, meta-poetry.

An important part of *Paris-Forfar* is Kinloch's elegiac poetry for victims of AIDS and for victims of anti-gay prejudice. This includes moving poems centred on the experience of an AIDS sufferer in hospital, as well as "Warmer Bruder", which reminds the world of the Nazi treatment of gays who were were killed in concentration camps *en masse* during the Second World War. At the same time it very clearly connects that genocide to the AIDS crisis, through the at-first-mysterious recurrence of the word "Grangemouth": only later does the reader realise Kinloch is talking about a modern-day hospice, a link made through the conceptual hinge of "snow", snow being moved by forced gay labour in the concentration camps, snow being moved by hospice employees (or perhaps council workers) in Grangemouth to keep the hospice open to visitors.

There is no rivalry among the dead, but "Warmer Bruder" is surely an intervention in the politics of interpreting the Second World War and contemporary life through each other. Again, the poet relates such involvement in gay politics to a specific French experience. In correspondence, he speaks of becoming politicised through the unexpected route of co-editing Joubert's *Carnets* with Philippe Mangeot:

Philippe was one of the founder members of the Paris Act-Up coalition of AIDS activists. I was collaborating with him on our edition of Joubert's *Carnets* while he was busy organising and taking part in some of the AIDS direct action campaigns. [...] There was a recognition that AIDS posed society some very real ethical dilemmas in France and gay men and women were vociferous in trying to force these issues into the public arena and stimulate debate. I was very aware when I was living in France that I was taking part in an unfolding drama whereas here so much was just not mentioned, swept under the carpet or treated as of marginal interest. (Kinloch pers. comm.)

This also forms the background to *Un Tour d'Ecosse*, a book nevertheless characterised by a greater formal range and, frankly, levity. The greater number of comic poems – satirical, affectionate, and marked sometimes by a quite broad sense of humour – might be perplexing at first, given the seriousness of Kinloch's recurring theme, but the effect is to assert "the love that dare not speak its name" within all areas of discourse, not just the elegiac mode. As Kinloch told me:

In his introduction to his collection of short stories *Monopolies of Love*, Adam Mars-Jones suggests that when confronted by AIDS writers have to make a choice between "denial and apocalyptic brooding". I don't accept that, and neither does Christopher Robinson in his study of male and female homosexuality in 20th century French literature, *Scandal in the Ink*. He's pointed out that the choice presents itself in more complex terms than this and that it offers the novelists (and poets too I think) the opportunity to stretch the boundaries of fiction in so far as AIDS fiction is obliged to accommodate a significant documentary element – medical narrative – which in Mars-Jones's view can simply swamp the fictional element. (Kinloch pers. comm.)

In this way, *Un Tour d'Ecosse*, as the title suggests, is a deliberate and self-conscious import into Scotland, in which France's versatile treatment of homosexuality in literature can now be adapted for Scottish concerns. The humour of Kinloch's "Des Lits de Guibert" has serious intent, though it again returns the reader, at the level of commanding structure, to the careful mixing of kinds of text that is present in *Paris-Forfar*. Kinloch glosses Guibert's novels in terms of intertextual innovation:

Hervé Guibert in particular was never put off by this danger [inherent in medical narrative], deliberately blurring the distinction between fiction and documentary, autobiography and biography in order, as Robinson puts it, "to explore the psychological and metaphorical implications of a take-over by the virus". Guibert's fiction is essentially about the relationship between reality and fiction and "the necessary and near-impossibility for the AIDS-struck artist of conquering life in art". In this context you can see, perhaps, why the "fake" in art and life is important. This is the matter of Guibert's *L'Homme au chapeau rouge* and it's this novel that is behind the first few sections of my own "Des Lits de Guibert". (Kinloch pers. comm.)

He adds, "There is a pun in the title by the way, in case you hadn't spotted it. The beds in question are the beds of love and death but "un délit" is French for an offence or misdemeanour", before continuing to expound on the idea of the inauthentic in *Un Tour d'Ecosse*:

[This is] why the character "Guibert" is so pleased when he discovers that Alastair Crotach's sarcophagus is in fact empty, a fake. (It's also shaped like so many of the pills or placebos (i.e. fake medicine) AIDS sufferers have to swallow). So AIDS allows writers to re-examine some fundamental aesthetic issues but within a deeply ethical context where the matter is literally that of life and death. The French, not the Americans or the British, do that in the most sophisticated and intelligent manner in my view. (Kinloch pers. comm.)

5.

Like David Kinloch, Iain Bamforth also has a France-orientated poem that is key to his work overall, and which involves a stylised autobiographical episode in Paris: "Alibis", collected in *Sons and Pioneers* (1992). As in "Dustie-fute", the idea of the individual before a window is important. The beginning of the poem introduces the hopes of Enlightenment France, represented by one side of the Pont Neuf. Bamforth tells the reader the bridge was unpopular for centuries. On one side of it we find "those bourgeois sins, complacency and self-regard, / strode out of their century, asking why we needed this". On the other side we find

a tour through the skin trade: fast food, fast sex
and a gallic Punch giving Judy the once-over;
little secrets Maigret might have kept from his wife
and the big-time vendors of the naked truth. (Bamforth 1992: 59)

The window therefore partitions rational idealism from the physical "limitations" the Enlightenment spirit can't quite escape, and the poem seems to understand each as socially-mediated phenomena. Such an analytical process, its reversibility, and its interstices, are critical to Bamforth's poetry in general. This is no doubt in part to do with his profession, a doctor and scientific translator, but Bamforth has also long been engaged in the reading and re-interpretation of the history of philosophy, a subject which surely feeds his convincing abstractions (and his satire) – "Those bourgeois sins, complacency and self-regard" – and which, in other poems, are foregrounded much more.

In fact, a willingness to use abstract nouns, to generalise without need of a Movement-style observing persona, and to change metaphor and simile again and again in the same poem, places Bamforth closer to a French (and a much wider European) tradition than to any other British poet I know. This can make some of Bamforth's poems seem difficult because they appear so obtuse (especially when there is a suggestion that something very specific is actually meant), but it can also to lead to stunning effects: a sense of lyric authority and therefore propulsion, exhilaration; a match of a series of different analogies to the theme of mutability itself – as in the appropriately shape-changing qualities of the nation-state of "Men of Fire"; and a suddenly burning, mordant, use of colloquialism, renewed because contrasted within the abstract frame. (Bamforth 1992: 11)

If there is a stylistic affinity with French poetry, however, Bamforth's relationship with French culture is far from simple, as his comments on French philosophy will have indicated. He certainly expresses an interest in French poetry, and, like the other poets discussed here, is especially interested in Baudelaire:

French poetry: yes, I've always been interested in it, although like most people my appreciation of it halts somewhere around Jacottet, Bonnefoy. My first book in 1984 [*The Modern Copernicus*] had a version of Baudelaire's "spleen" poems and, as you know, I've been translating him throughout my career. I even tried to write a kind of Racine-like dialogue into my first book (not very successfully!). There's a Rimbaud poem "Movement" slotted for my next collection. [...] All in all, I think Baudelaire's poetry has been most important for me, principally because he never completely renounced his very classical feeling for form while remaining absolutely up to date in his ideas, his belief in freedom, and his despair at its being trampled on; his dandyism has always appealed to me. [...] [O]ne of the most important books for me was Michael Hamburger's *The Truth of Poetry* which I read early on, and which really gave me a sense of direction. One of the points he makes is that before 1900 even, the French poets had gone the full modernist cycle from self-absorbed aestheticism to the book as grail to the poet as bloke-in-the-street. (Bamforth pers. comm.)

In a way, it is France's past glories that are the problem for Bamforth, especially France's memorialisation of itself. In "Alibis", Paris is seen as a meeting point of very different ways of viewing the world; very different, but unified by the fact that each is simply out-dated; each trades on ways of perception that may once have meant a great deal, but which can no longer have such purchase; they are merely the alibis of the title. The city is "a place my grandpa called Babylon, the Antichrist *chez lui*", but, to the poet, it doesn't even have the vitality of the Devil. It is on its uppers, resorting to various kinds of myth-peddling, a "storyline [...] scraping by on Piaf-naïf dreams of glory".

Whereas in "Dustie-fute", the magical, iconic, yoghurt cools refreshingly on the windowsill, and Kinloch's persona is able to use the complex experience of being in Paris as a liberator of self and of text, Bamforth's vision of Paris is one of disenchantment, of disgust. Paris's history is seen as typical of Europe's, "the snore of the old world outliving itself", and the sentence "Curdled leftovers occluded the windowsill" both observes, with some humour, a detail of student life, while at the same time symbolising a history whose own decay prevents perspective. This is capped, in the final stanza, by the behaviour of one of the poet's neighbours. Winning through to a clarity of a kind, "the ultimate collector" surely embodies Bamforth's anger and disappointment at "progress" since the Revolution. As the satire draws down to its final lines, the neighbour is revealed to have devoted years to amassing a museum of excrement:

Beside me, in the next block, lived the ultimate collector.
I never saw him, only heard the poisoned whisperings:
one day they called the *pompiers* in to clean him out,
houseproud among a decade's scatological relics,
each one labelled, wrapped and catalogued.

The presence of the first person singular here is untypical of Bamforth's work – "Alibis" is a revealing exception. This – again despite the regretful tone of "Alibis" – must surely come from an almost wholesale rejection of introspection, both as a worthwhile philosophical practice and as a mode of writing poetry. As Bamforth says in his note to the poems collected in *Dream State: The New Scottish Poets* (1994),

I [...] find myself impatient to pen my poetry to the conventionally "non-poetic", to indeterminacy and process, since poetry seems to me, not least in its attitude to the self, still assiduously Romantic. (O'Rourke ed. 1994: 94)

Perhaps the "impersonality" of a French-like poetic diction is attractive to Bamforth for this reason. More specifically, the experimentation of the Oulipo author George Perec (and perhaps Max Jacob) made an impact on his sequence of one hundred and one short prose poems, "Impediments". He told me:

I wrote "Impediments" under the influence of Perec, and what I tried to do was produce a cognitive self-portrait sitting one fine August day in the office of the translating agency in Paris that used to send me work. In other words I should have been working instead of playing when I wrote the sequence. I co-opted the word "Impediment" in at least two ways. You have it as a homophonic building block in 101 – "un pays de menthe", "démente", "de monts", etc., and a kind of exchange system, in the sense that what attracts is what resists, a kind of mimetic stumbling block. 101 aphorisms seemed arbitrary, but just after I'd published the book I found a sentence in the *Upanishads* which suggests it perhaps wasn't. It's even more suggestive than the Calvino quote ["Nobody excluded the possibility that things could proceed in other, entirely different ways. You would have said that each individual was ashamed of being the way he was expected to be" – from *Time and The Hunter*, quoted at the beginning of the poem]: "There are 101 arteries of the heart, one of which penetrates the crown of the head. Moving upwards by it, a man at his death reaches the immortal: the other arteries serve for departing in different directions". (Bamforth pers. comm.)

"Impediments" begins as a kind of 3-D mapping exercise, with chance as one of the vectors. Bamforth's phrase "cognitive self-portrait" captures objectivity's meeting with the subject, and again in "Impediments" there is his ambivalence towards the Romantic, as the opening section suggests: "Capture, recapture and maximum likelihood: those are my guiding principles on each excursion across the salty pavements of Paris to a room where I plot my three *points de repère:* M1, M2 and M3". However, it soon becomes a project of very different kinds of text; a miscellany, certainly, but one in which the preoccupations about the body, about substance itself, and about knowledge-organising structures recur. In this way, there are, for example, tightly-focussed images where the individual meets generalising science ("a wax model of a woman with her spine arched like an exocet. Her hand is draped across her body to the supernumerary rib indicated with a pointer"); reflections on even the reflective sense as an off-the-shelf genre ("Dissatisfaction follows me home, a fictive lack deliberating what it might have done before remorse charged the air of a bare room"); and a sustained flickering of ambiguities, in which Paris itself is an exemplar ("To take a leaf from Rabelais' book. Paris' marriage of architecture and amnesia takes two names: *Lutetia*, meaning city of mud (*lutum*) and Parisis, city of Iris, mysterious sidelong goddess of truth").

Yet Oulipo need not be a hard-edged tool. Bamforth remarked to me that he considered "Between the Rhins and the Machars" to be as much in the spirit of Oulipo as "Impediments," although its homage to Galloway life (where Bamforth was briefly a G.P.), and its incantations and brief meditations create an elegiac quality far removed in spirit from Bamforth's Parisian poem (Bamforth 1996: 20–23).

6.

Oulipo, with its characteristic play between rule, accident, and individual determination, is one of many links Bamforth shares with Peter McCarey. These include post-religious sensibilities after a devout religious upbringing, Bamforth by Plymouth Brethren parents, McCarey by Catholics; day-to-day work as professional translators; day-to-day work within the medical world, Bamforth as a G.P., McCarey as Head of Translation at the World Health Organisation; location within anomalous French-speaking regions (to Bamforth's Alsace, McCarey may reply with his many years in Geneva); and first-hand experience of international organisations (Bamforth, UNESCO in Paris and his experience of Strasbourg; McCarey, the many international bodies on his doorstep, one of which employs him). If Bamforth is interested in philosophy of the Romantics and of the Enlightenment, McCarey is especially interested in the Nietzsche-influenced Lev Shestov, Berkeley and Hume, and George Davie and the Thomist, Alasdair McIntyre. Although there may be so much nuance of difference between these similarities (and something much more obvious than nuance) that would disqualify treating them as like cases, I would argue that their poetry does share at times a prosodic quality, the broad, world-analysing gestural quality that comes down to short, pithy sayings, before swooping back up to the heights of a cooler rationality.

McCarey's early poem, "Sous le pavés – la plage," what we may now take as one in the genre, "the young male Scottish émigré at Paris window poem", is one such example:

The urban sunlight comes in the window
staggering up to its knees in sand
banknotes blowing out of its seams
like scarious leaves and carious buildings
shaking dust from my shoes but it cloys,
it clogs for I'm paid to be here.

Frontiers, harbours, roads, currencies
crowd control and corpse disposal.

Money is busy buying itself up
using what there is for collateral.

Light is said to be sculpting itself
with its only sense
of touch. (McCarey n.d.: 36)

It's worth noting in passing, the Rimbaud-like synaesthesia of light's
"sense of touch". More importantly, look here at the very characteristic presentation of McCarey's individuals as caught within a net of
capital and its enforcement systems. The apocryphal chant of the students of 1968, "Under the pavings, the beach!", is examined more
coolly – the image becomes closer to quicksand, to the desert, than to
a summer holiday – and in any case, the speaker feels himself caught
up within the job-of-work he feels compelled to do. He is satisfied
neither with utopian languor nor the grind of making a living. The
enigmatic, slowed-down, last stanza is offered, it seems to me, as a
mystical and carefully paced answer to the faster but equally ab-
stracted concept of "money buying itself up".

   If Bamforth's at times similar prosodic dynamic is founded on
body / rationality and pre-modern / post-enlightenment divisions,
McCarey's seems to emerge from somewhere else: a sensitivity to
overbearing power structures and their warping of individual will.
Both Bamforth and McCarey, of course, are attentive to materiality –
both, for example include medical and chemical data in their work –
but whereas Bamforth may be said to have been affected by Oulipo in
texts such as "Impediments," which is in part about the anthropology
of science, McCarey's Oulipoean use of, say, the English spell-
checker that "corrects" the great Scots poem "The Flyting of Dunbar
and Kennedy" ("Dhow", in *Town Shanties*) is less about technology
than the power relationships between speech-delineated groups (and,
implicitly, between unequally matched nation states) (McCarey n.d.:
68).

   McCarey repeats this in other re-appropriations of text, "Intellectual Property" being a good example from *In the Metaforest*
(2000). Here the re-use of the words of a standard copyright statement, after emerging from an almost nonsensical (and so interestingly
phonic) reconfiguration in the first half of the text, becomes in the last
few lines a poem concerned with the possibility of poetry and the

possibility of a different kind of "civil system", other than that associated with and enforced by copyright law:

> in this civil system
> the poem means
> whether otherwise or without
> any may any may may be. (McCarey 2000: 12)

Like Bamforth, McCarey is candid about his connection with Oulipo. Responding to a question about French influences, he traces his connection to this world to a chance acquaintance with the creative partnership of poet-printer John Crombie and artist Sheila Bourne (together, Kickshaws Press):[5]

So: place Fontenoy, then, in 1983. I shared an office with John Crombie on my first contract in Unesco. A big guy with a walrus moustache and a mid-Atlantic accent influenced, I guess, by his partner Sheila Bourne. John would get in at nine and whack out a tirade of translation on his mechanical typewriter. He loathed and despised the stuff he had to translate, but the occasional contract gave him just enough money with which to keep writing, printing and publishing books in Kickshaws Press, which he and Sheila ran from a small flat in Montparnasse. A very small flat, in rue de la Grande Chaumière. He showed me the press: a thing of beam-bending weight, half steam engine, half bicycle, that squatted in one of the rooms. And the book: evolving from Edward Gorey meets Alphonse Allais towards a convergence of typography, Beckett, Queneau and OULIPO. There's much more to Kickshaws than what I've learned from it, which is this: random rules, and don't let that stop you. (McCarey pers. comm.)

From here, McCarey then makes the leap that is implicit in "Intellectual Property", suggesting that the idealistic elements of Oulipo, however playful the actual texts, are still not immune to an aggressive legal system:

One of the random rules is that the law protects property, not producers. Crombie was once so enthused by an unpublished text by Raymond Queneau that he printed it – really beautifully, in a way that brought out the value of the piece. Rashly, he let a dealer have a copy, and next thing he knew he was being sued for everything he had by the heir to that author's rights. Even prior to that, Crombie had been getting fed up at the thought that only a few deranged bibliophiles were buying his work (I say his,

---

[5] For further Kickshaws information, see Chambers 1999: 17–35, as well as the numerous Kickshaws items held by the British Library.

though much of it was Sheila's too, he's the more visible partner). (McCarey pers. comm.)

Finally, McCarey sees the work of Kickshaws Press as one of the key inspirations for his long-standing *Syllabary* project, in which it is intended there will be a poem built around every syllable within the contemporary Scottish-English lexicon:

As I look through the books, I find the level of presentation and invention I'd love to see in my syllabary, and I find the push away from linear narrative that's been running my own work of quite some time. It was John that put me onto OULIPO, for which I remain grateful. (McCarey pers. comm.)

As far as Oulipo is concerned, Roubaud is more important to McCarey than either Queneau or Perec:

Not that I'm an OULIPO expert: I've attended one of their events, and I dip into their books. Of the great writers in the group, I don't know Queneau, I regard Calvino as incidentally oulipien, and I've managed to finish only one book by Perec, though his ideas are useful. The central writer of the group, for my purposes, is Jacques Roubaud. I first came across him in *Verse*, where David Kinloch (I think) translated extracts from *Quelque Chose Noir* [in fact, translated and introduced by Rosmarie Waldrop] – that powerful book of elegies to his wife, Alix Cléo Roubaud. I then read – on Peter France's advice – his *La vieillesse d'Alexandre*, which is *the* book on French prosody; it unlocked French verse to me twenty years after I'd read the stuff. Then I read *La Fleur Inverse*, an inspirational work on Provençal poetry, and anything else of his I could find on verse and the writing of it, since the man thinks hard and well on the matter. He's written on Petrarch, he's worked with Douglas Oliver; with Sorley Maclean... (McCarey pers. comm.)

It is, I think, significant, that the *sound* of French poetry – its prosody and, for speakers of Scots and Scottish English, the seeming lack of phonic vigour in French's vocabulary – should be one of the barriers to its appreciation within Scotland. This is surely why Bamforth (again, in correspondence) stresses the fascinating exception of Rabelais, and why McCarey, despite having a degree in French, sees Roubaud and his work on the alexandrine as a turning point in his previous underestimation of French poetry. Without wishing to yoke very different poets like O'Rourke, Kinloch, Bamforth and McCarey together, I think they would all agree with a significant amount of what

McCarey says when he talks about his natural disinclination towards French poetry. Perhaps this would also be the case for many others, too:

> I was never much taken by French poetry. It's rhotic languages that resonate most in me: Russian, Italian, Scottish English, some Provençal. French Gothic *architecture*, yes, and Romanesque; cosmopolitan Paris in its existential void – all of those have moved me. But not much of the poetry, magnetised as it was between a sinister religion and secular imperialism, poetry that was cerebral and measured, manipulative and nostalgic. (McCarey pers. comm.)

Of course, the important thing for all these poets is that they did overcome such distrust, reading French literature with an approach that is some distance from the *Depression News* tourist version of Francophilia, but, thankfully, is also light years from Homer Simpson's construction of *la grille*.

Bibliography

Bamforth, Iain. 1992. *Sons and Pioneers*. Carcanet: Manchester.
—. 1996. *Open Workings*. Manchester: Carcanet.
Barnaby, Paul. 2000. "Traductions en français d'auteurs écossais du XXe siecle" in Kinloch, David and Richard Price (eds) *La Nouvelle Alliance: influences francophones sur la littérature écossaise moderne*. Ellug: Grenoble. 241–62.
Chambers, David. 1999. "Kickshaws, Paris" in *The Private Library* Fifth series. 2(1): 17–35.
"Interview with David Kinloch". 2001. *PN Review* 27(3): 23–25.
Jack, R.D.S. 1989. "The French Connection: Scottish and French Literature in the Renaissance" in *Scotia: American-Canadian Journal of Scottish Studies*. 13:1–16.
Kinloch, David. 1994. *Paris-Forfar*. Polygon: Edinburgh.
—. 2001. *Un Tour d'Ecosse*. Carcanet: Manchester.
Kinloch, David and Richard Price (eds). 2000. *La Nouvelle Alliance: influences francophones sur la littérature écossaise moderne*. Ellug: Grenoble.
Larkin, Philip. 1988. *Collected Poems*. London: Faber.
McCarey, Peter. 2000. *In the Metaforest*. London: Vennel Press.
—. n.d. *Town Shanties*. Glasgow: Broch Books.
O'Rourke, Donny. 1997. *The Waistband*. Edinburgh: Polygon.
O'Rourke, Donny (ed.). 1994. *Dream State: the New Scottish Poets*. Polygon: Edinburgh.
O'Rourke, Donny and Richard Price. 1995. *Eftirs/Afters: in Scots and English*. Glasgow: Au Quai.
Purves, Robin. 2000. "L'énigme d'Isodore Ducasse" in Kinloch, David and Richard Price (eds). *La Nouvelle Alliance: influences francophones sur la littérature écossaise moderne*. Ellug: Grenoble. 193–209.
White, Kenneth. 1998. "The Franco-Scottish Connection" in *On Scottish Ground*. Polygon: Edinburgh. 115–128.
Whyte, Dave and Donny O'Rourke. 1999. *Still Waiting to be Wise* (audio recording). Last Track Records.

A Postmodern Scotland?

Randall Stevenson

Although Scottish criticism has come late to postmodern ideas, Scottish writers such as Alasdair Gray, Muriel Spark, Edwin Morgan, and others, can be seen as postmodern. Their postmodernity is due to international influences and also to Scottish culture itself – the latter having been formed by both modern rationalisation and by a degree of colonial experience.
Keywords: Alasdair Gray, Muriel Spark, postcolonialism, postmodernism.

Concepts of postmodernism and postmodernity have been discussed thoroughly, even excessively, in recent decades, and critics working outwith Scotland have regularly applied them to Scottish writing.[1] Yet in criticism and literary history recently produced within Scotland, "postmodern" is a term conspicuous by its absence, or the scarcity of its use.[2] And so much the better, you might say, given the bad press it has often received. Christopher Norris's lengthy study *What's Wrong with Postmodernism* (Norris 1990) hardly exhausts accusations levelled at postmodern concepts, sometimes even by critics most involved in disseminating them. Like Norris, Terry Eagleton warns that postmodern ideas have "produced in the same breath an invigorating and a paralysing scepticism [...] a full-blooded cultural relativism" (Eagleton 1996: 27), leaving no means of validating political convictions, or indeed any others. Patricia Waugh suggests that, in extending Jean-François Lyotard's scepticism of "grand narratives" (see Lyotard [1979] 1984) so comprehensively over contemporary literature and

---

[1] Alison Lee, for example, has sections on Alasdair Gray in Lee 1990, and Brian McHale discusses Gray's *Lanark*, *1982 Janine*, and *Unlikely Stories, Mostly* in McHale 1987 and 1992.

[2] It doesn't appear in the index of Whyte (ed.) 1995, for example, nor in otherwise very detailed chapters on "Contemporary Fiction" which conclude Gifford and McMillan (eds) 1997. In Walker 1996, Craig 1999, and Christianson and Lumsden (eds) 2000, the term is usually used only for periodisation, rather than for any of its analytic potential, though Walker does include it in a list of "contemporary issues" (Walker 1996: 392). Fuller considerations appear in essays by Cairns Craig and Alex Thomson in Bell and Miller (eds) 2004.

thinking, the postmodern has become another grand narrative itself –
an omnivorous intellectual virus, able to infect any field of enquiry
with the scepticism and relativism Eagleton disparages (Waugh 1992:
12). The ease of this process and the trendiness of the terms it employs
nevertheless encourage inexhaustible profligacy in publishing and
intellectual endeavour. As Stephen Connor suggests, the postmodern
functions for academics as a "generative machine" (Connor 1989: 18),
churning on interminably through conferences, seminars, university
courses, publishers' catalogues, essays, bookshop and library shelves.
Given the range of disciplines now involved, sheer volume has
inevitably added to vagueness, making the postmodern, for Paul
Maltby, "an overloaded and remarkably diffuse concept" (Maltby
1991: 22), and, for David Harvey, "a minefield of conflicting notions"
(Harvey 1989: viii).

  Yet the commentators quoted are usually equivocal in their criticisms: ready to envisage postmodern hot air as the exhaust produced –
maybe in disproportionate amounts – by what remains a powerful,
long-running intellectual engine: one fuelled more often by sane, sen-
sible critics than by vague or trendy ones. In any case, as Patricia
Waugh emphasises, despite her reservations, no amount of criticism
seems much to reduce the role of the postmodern as a "key term [...]
in the vocabularies of literary theorists" (Waugh ed. 1992: 1), or to
prevent its use in analysing writing as otherwise diverse as the work of
Gabriel García Márquez and Thomas Pynchon, Angela Carter and
Milorad Pavic, the *nouveau roman* and magic realism. Commentators
working later in the twenty-first century will probably continue to
consider the last decades of the twentieth as a period still digesting the
artistic innovations of modernism, and still absorbing the Second
World War's impact on Western thought and morality; they may well
find more congenial terms to define what they see. In the meantime, it
would be improvident of Scottish critics to consider postmodern
thinking so suspect as to be condemned out of hand, or remote enough
from the Scottish scene to be eliminated from their enquiries almost
before these have begun.

  How might such enquiries be conducted? What pathways can be
found through Harvey's "minefield" that might also extend across recent Scottish culture? Two fairly firm lines of enquiry, at least, can be

seen to run through the postmodern debate. One of these concentrates on the literary and artistic consequences of modernism – on the emphases of critics such as Ihab Hassan, or Brian McHale, that "postmodernism follows *from* modernism [...] more than it follows *after* modernism" (McHale 1987: 5). The other pathway explores wider evolutions of thought in the twentieth century and earlier, following the conclusion expressed by commentators such as Thomas Docherty – that to "address the postmodern, one has also to address an entire trajectory of European philosophy dating from the Enlightenment" (Docherty 1993: 36).

The first of these pathways offers the more obvious direction for literary critics. Any enquiry about legacies of modernism in recent Scottish writing need look no further than Alasdair Gray's fiction.[3] Gray's portrait of the artist as a young Glaswegian in *Lanark* (1981) – which includes regular discussion of painting, as well as examples of Gray's own graphic art – shares clearly in a tradition of interest in art and artist-figures established by modernism and widely influential on later, postmodernist writing. As Gray's "Index of Plagiarisms" sometimes confirms, this tradition can be retraced through Joyce Cary's work to modernist novels such as Virginia Woolf's *To the Lighthouse* (1927), or Wyndham Lewis's *Tarr* (1918), as well as those of James Joyce. Artist-figures in these novels were often used self-consciously, as in Gray's work, to discuss authors' interests, or to provide figural analogues for the fiction in which they appear. Lily Briscoe's painting in *To the Lighthouse*, for example, coincides with the tripartite structure of Woolf's novel itself: "a line there, in the centre" establishes "unity of the whole" for both painting and fiction, allowing satisfactory, concurrent completion of the vision of each (Woolf [1927] 1973: 63, 237). In James Joyce's work, self-consciousness and self-reflexiveness of this kind focussed, increasingly, on the literary medium, language, rather than on the figural one of paint. Stephen Dedalus begins to question how adequately words "harmonized" with the world during "a day of dappled seaborne clouds" in *A Portrait of the Artist as a Young Man* (Joyce [1916] 1973: 166); his reflections

---

[3] I have already discussed Gray's fiction in this context in "Alasdair Gray and the Postmodern" (Stevenson 1991), and reproduce the ideas involved as briefly as possible in what follows here.

later expand into the parody and linguistic inventiveness of *Ulysses* (1922) and, in the "Work in Progress" which followed, into a language scarcely seeking harmony with the world, or representation of it, but providing a self-contained music of its own instead. As critics such as Ihab Hassan have suggested, the eventual publication of this work as *Finnegans Wake* in 1939 offered – more than any other modernist writing – "prophecy of our postmodernity", being "both augur and theory of a certain kind of literature" (Hassan 1987: xiii–xiv). Following Joyce's wake, other Irish authors contributed to this self-reflexive, innovative, post-modernist form of writing: Samuel Beckett, in exploring the fragility of language and imagination in the face of life's desolation in his trilogy, *Molloy, Malone Meurt, L'Innommable* (1950–52; tr. 1955–59); Flann O'Brien, in more comic vein, in one of the first of many novels about novelists writing novels about novel-writing, *At Swim-Two-Birds* (1939).

Postmodernist "prophecy" was probably first clearly fulfilled in Scottish writing in the work of Muriel Spark. Influenced less directly by Irish than by French authors, though ones who emphasised their own descent from modernism, Spark was particularly indebted to the *nouveau roman* of the 1950s, whose self-reflexive interests in "the problems of writing" and the nature of narrative imagination followed, as its leading author Alain Robbe-Grillet explained, "after Joyce" and the work of his modernist contemporaries (Robbe-Grillet 1965: 46–47). Spark also gave early evidence of a pattern further discussed below: of Scottish writing developing not only in direct consequence of postmodern influences, but through their coincidence, or coalescence, with traditions already strongly established within Scottish imagination itself. The central figure of *The Prime of Miss Jean Brodie* (1961), for example, clearly belongs to a context of specifically Scottish education, and Scottish religion – tyrannical control of her pupils demonstrating how completely she "thinks she is the God of Calvin" (Spark [1961] 1982: 120). Yet her penchant for forcing reality into accord with her vision – for fictions, art, and "making patterns with facts" generally (Spark [1961] 1982: 72) – also contributes to a role as an author-analogue, raising questions about the nature and ethics of writing familiar from the *nouveau roman* and postmodernist literature generally. Questions of this kind are considered throughout Spark's work: in *The Comforters* (1957), for example, or *The Driver's Seat* (1970), which concern themselves with the capacity of authors or author-surrogates to organise life into what the former novel calls "a convenient slick plot" (Spark [1957] 1978: 104). Similar questions interested a number of later Scottish writers – Giles Gordon, for example, who considered Robbe-Grillet "the most influential and intriguing twentieth-century fiction writer" (Gordon 1981: 26) and followed the manner of the *nouveau roman* closely in *Girl with Red Hair* (1974). Critics have pointed to a continuing influence from the *nouveau roman* in novels such as Ron Butlin's *The Sound of my Voice* (1987).[4]

Self-reflexive questions about the nature of writing are addressed still more directly in *Lanark*. Spark's heroine in *The Comforters* is only mildly disturbed, while working on her novel about "characters in a novel", by a persistent faint sound of typing, eventually attributed to "a writer on another plane of existence" somehow engaged in creating *her* life (Spark [1957] 1978: 202, 63). In *Lanark*, Gray's hero encounters such a figure directly, face-to-face, when he meets Nastler in the Epilogue – a figure who is mysteriously on the *same* plane of existence, yet apparently entirely responsible for creating and shaping his life. This life, Lanark learns, is apparently wholly controlled by print and the written word, unfolding in a "world" made only of "print" and "pages and pages and pages of white paper" (Gray [1981] 1984: 480, 485). Ensuing conversations in the Epilogue further extend some of the authorial self-portraiture evident in the earlier sections, highlighting and scrutinising the novel's own strategies in ways already familiar by the time *Lanark* was published, as Nastler admits, from the work of a range of postmodernist writers. In novels by B.S. Johnson, John Fowles, John Berger and others in the 1960s and 1970s, intrusions by authors or author-figures to explain their tactics, or discuss them with their characters, had become less an innovation than almost a postmodernist convention; a widely-familiar development of the embryonic self-consciousness of the modernists and of the "prophecies" of *Finnegans Wake*.

---

[4] Peter Zenzinger compares Butlin with Michel Butor (Zenzinger 1989: 231).

Gray's work also highlighted other levels, stylistic and structural, through which modernist legacies continued to shape later fiction. Ezra Pound's determination to "make it new", or Woolf's to write "Modern Fiction", shared a late nineteenth- and early twentieth-century enthusiasm for progress and innovation. Yet in other ways the modernists were highly sceptical of "progress": wary of threats to the integrity of the individual posed by a rationalised, materialist modern world. The industrial practices depicted by D.H. Lawrence in *Women in Love* (1922) – Taylorised, automated, and pre-Fordist – regimented working life more and more comprehensively, imposing ubiquitously the slogan "time is money". Time and history, especially after the nightmare experience of the First World War, seemed thoroughly compromised dimensions to the modernists. Preferring what Woolf called "time in the mind" to "time on the clock" (Woolf [1928] 1975: 69), they relied on memory to structure non-linear narrative forms which dominate modernist fiction from Marcel Proust's *À la recherche du temps perdu* (1913–27) to Lewis Grassic Gibbon's *A Scots Quair* (1932–34) and beyond. *Lanark* is in several ways part of that "beyond", envisaging later versions of the same problems, and offering comparable alternatives to them. "Life's easy when you're a robot", Coulter reflects in Book One: "You get up, dress, eat, go tae work, clock in etcetera etcetera automatically, and think about nothing but the pay packet on a Friday" (Gray [1981] 1984: 216). Repeating the kind of reified working life depicted in the "Industrial Magnate" chapter of *Women in Love*, Coulter's experience also anticipates the still more rationalised, commodified temporality which corporate industry has introduced to Unthank, expressed by the "decimal hour" and by the ubiquitous slogan, "**MONEY IS TIME. TIME IS LIFE.**" (Gray [1981] 1984: 416, 454).

Like many modernist characters, Lanark achieves almost nothing to alter the conditions of this hyper-industrialised, hyper-technologised world: Gray follows modernism in proposing an aesthetic, rather than a political or practical alternative to them. Significantly, Lanark escapes with Rima into an "Intercalendrical Zone" through a door marked "Exit 3124" – just the order, of course, of the books that make up the novel – and Nastler explains that *Lanark* should be "read in one order but eventually thought of in another"

(Gray [1981] 1984: 376, 483). Like much modernist fiction, *Lanark* suggests in this way that temporal systems constraining twentieth-century experience can still be escaped or reordered in narrative and imagination, if perhaps no longer in fact. This possibility offers Gray's readers a later version of opportunities Chris Guthrie often enjoys in *A Scots Quair*: to be "out of the winking flash of the days, to sit and look from the high places" (Gibbon [1933] 1995: 109). Though aware of the hot struggles of industrial life in Segget or Dundon, she is also partly immune to them: able to reconstrue in memory a temporality aloof from their quotidian pressures.[5]

Vestigial imaginative freedoms of this kind in *Lanark* may provide the best answer to Alison Lumsden's complaint – in her essay "Innovation and Reaction in the Fiction of Alasdair Gray" – that Gray's work offers "no imaginative escape route" from "systems which serve to entrap and enclose the individual" in Scottish life (Lumsden 1993: 120, 115). Lumsden argues persuasively that Gray's postmodernism is so derivative, "clumsily-handled", and formulaic as to annul most of the liberating unconventionality once promised by postmodernist techniques (Lumsden 1993: 119). For the present essay, her views are valuable less for their challenging re-evaluation of Gray's tactics than for stressing the extent to which *Lanark*, as well as some of Gray's later novels, share in a postmodernist idiom already well-established by the authors mentioned above. The extraordinary language and typographical layout of *1982 Janine* (1984), for example, extend the linguistic self-consciousness and experimentation of modernism in directions clearly shared by postmodernist authors such as B.S. Johnson, in *House Mother Normal* (1971), or Christine Brooke-Rose, in novels such as *Thru* (1975). *1982 Janine* also illustrates what may be the most widely influential legacy of modernism in later Scottish writing: its general shifting inward of narrative focalisation, and the development of a range of interior monologues, streams of consciousness and other registers for inner thought. This was a development strongly apparent in Scottish writing during the modernist period, in the inner voices sustained throughout *A Scots Quair* and in Grassic Gibbon's uniquely flexible transitions between them. As

---

[5] Evasive in a way, Chris's refuges nevertheless contribute to the utopian political vision asserted unusually clearly – for a modernist novel – throughout *A Scots Quair*.

Gavin Wallace has argued, subtlety and inwardness of "voice" remain distinguishing characteristics in recent Scottish fiction, which has often continued to incorporate techniques developed both by the modernists and their immediate successors (Wallace 1993). The disconsolate monologues of Beckett's trilogy echo throughout Jock McLeish's compulsive soliloquising in *1982 Janine*, and through the precarious imaginative worlds he constructs as distractions from unbearable immediate circumstance. They resound still more disturbingly in the intense attention to inner consciousness of novels such as James Kelman's *A Disaffection* (1989). Extending Beckett's bleakness into a more immediately politicised mode, Kelman's inner voices are probably the most compelling in recent Scottish fiction, though other writers such as Janice Galloway occasionally achieve a comparable intensity. Established modes of narrative inwardness were also developed distinctively by Robert Alan Jamieson, in his *Ulysses*-influenced *A Day at the Office* (1991), and by A.L. Kennedy, whose stream of consciousness style in *Everything You Need* (2000) communicates the thoughts not only of a wide range of human characters, but even of a canine one as well.

Like most analyses of postmodernist writing, the above discussion concentrates on fiction, the genre in which modernist legacies are probably easiest to trace. Drama in Britain is often thought to lack a distinctive modernist phase, and the tardy development of theatre until later in the century in any case made it asymmetric with the progress of other genres. A measure of self-referentiality and self-conscious artifice generally implicit in poetic language can make specifically postmodernist characteristics harder to distinguish in this area, too. Yet it would not be difficult to identify a postmodernist element at work in Scottish writing in both these genres later in the twentieth century. The huge diversity of Edwin Morgan's poetry reflects unusually wide-ranging influences and interests, but a postmodernist aspect clearly figures among them: in his sustained linguistic experimentation and ludic inventiveness, as well as the self-consciousness of poems such as "Cinquevalle", or sections of "In the Video Box". Self-conscious emphasis of the artificial, constructed nature of dramatic roles and representations in plays such as *Mary Queen of Scots Got her Head Chopped Off* (1987) show Liz Lochhead's work, too, sharing in some of the dominant characteristics of postmodernist literature.

But how might this literature – or any literature – relate to what Docherty identified as a second postmodern "trajectory", one evident primarily in philosophy? Most contributors to the postmodern debate envisage this trajectory as a movement away from the "happy match between the mind of man and the nature of things" which Theodor Adorno and Max Horkheimer attributed to the outlook of the late eighteenth century (Adorno and Horkeheimer [1944] 1986: 3). Consolidated by the Enlightenment thinkers of the time, this optimistic outlook shaped the grandest of all narratives – defined by Jürgen Habermas as a "project of modernity" which assumed that, universally, "the arts and the sciences would promote not only the control of natural forces, but [...] moral progress, the justice of institutions, and even the happiness of human beings" (Habermas [1981] 1993: 97, 98). By the early twentieth century, any match between mind and nature, happy or otherwise, had been severely challenged by the work of thinkers such as Nietzsche and Bergson. For Adorno and Horkheimer, the powers of reason, science, and technology emphasised by the Enlightenment and by the Industrial Revolution, had always been too narrowly bound by "the rule of computation and utility". In *Dialectic of Enlightenment*, written late in the Second World War, they concluded that "the fully enlightened earth radiates disaster triumphant" (Adorno and Horkeheimer [1944] 1986: 6) rather than justice and happiness. Enlightenment values had not only failed to prevent the war, but seemed to many commentators sinisterly complicit with its worst disasters. George Steiner, for example, considered the complex, efficient organisation of the concentration camps to have arisen from *within* "the dream of reason which animated western society" (Steiner 1967: 15) rather than in contradiction to it. As part of his influential definition of "the postmodern condition", Jean-François Lyotard likewise explained that he "used the name 'Auschwitz'" to sum up "grief in the *Zeitgeist*" and to emphasise the limitations of "the 'modern' project of the emancipation of humanity" (Lyotard [1985] 1993). In this view, the "project of modernity" and its faith in beneficent progress could not be confidently assumed to have outlasted the Second World War, and a period of "post-modernity" had succeeded instead.

In Alasdair Gray's helpful summary in *A History Maker* (1994), in the later twentieth century "critics called their period *postmodern* to separate it from the modern world begun [...] when most creative thinkers believed they could improve their community" (Gray [1994] 1995: 203).

These ideas, familiar enough within the postmodern debate, are worth revisiting just to confirm that another path really can be found through Harvey's "minefield" – and also to vindicate the commentators, mentioned earlier, who are highly critical of pervasive scepticism and pessimism in postmodern thinking. Yet, despite its negative qualities – or sometimes because of them – postmodern thought can help to identify trajectories in the evolution of literature, and of the historical and conceptual pressures shaping it, not only recently but over the past two hundred years. In this longer perspective, as well as extending characteristics of modernist writing, postmodernist literature can be seen to belong, following Romanticism and modernism, to a third phase of reaction against Enlightenment thought and against the capitalist industrialism it helped to foster. Romanticism broadly promoted the values of intuition, imagination and nature which Enlightenment emphases on "computation and utility" tended to exclude. As discussed earlier, modernism attempted to sustain comparable values in an increasingly industrialised world in the early twentieth century. Like much of Lawrence's writing, Chris Guthrie's refuges above the towns in *A Scots Quair* illustrate modernism's location of strong – though residual – values in the natural world. For the most part, though, modernist writers were more likely to seek in the inner reaches of consciousness, or the depths of memory, the kind of spaces, resistant to the pressures of modernity, which the Romantics had located in a redeeming vision of external nature. Towards the end of the century, with late capitalism now "penetrating and colonising Nature and the Unconscious", in Fredric Jameson's view (Jameson 1991: 49), such refuges or redeeming values became still harder to locate anywhere. Unable to find reliable alternatives to Enlightenment thought, or refuges from it, postmodern culture was prepared to deny its validity altogether – concluding, in Alan Wilde's estimation, that the project of modernity had established not "a world in need of mending" so much as "one beyond repair" (Wilde 1981: 131).

Such views might be considered less relevant in Scotland, and to its literature, than almost anywhere else. A country so centrally responsible for the birth of the Enlightenment – and for fostering the Industrial Revolution thereafter – might be supposed the least likely to accede to postmodern accounts of its demise, or to share in the resistive literary history outlined above. Yet a moment's thought – especially of the later consequences of the Industrial Revolution for Scottish life – suggests exactly the opposite case: that Scotland might have encountered particularly quickly, and painfully, the darker influences or disastrous "radiation" emphasised by recent views of the Enlightenment and its legacies. There is evidence of this throughout Scottish literature, and at an early stage in some of its classic pre-twentieth century texts. A descendant of heroically successful lighthouse engineers – presuming to order the waves with beacons they shone into the depths of the night – Robert Louis Stevenson might have had motives oedipal as well as historical for demonstrating darkness at the heart of enlightened reason and science. This demonstration at any rate duly appeared in 1886. *The Strange Case of Dr Jekyll and Mr Hyde* is of course generally interpreted in terms of religion – of Calvinist dualities of good and evil. But as Jekyll explains, it is "scientific studies" which lead him further towards the "mystic and transcendental": his reflections on the divided moral nature of humanity have not gone far, he records, before "a side light began to shine on the subject from the laboratory table" (Stevenson [1886] 1995: 278, 279). Hyde may be primarily a personification of evil, but he is also a kind of cousin to another monster embodying fears of the incipient powers of science, described by Mary Shelley in *Frankenstein* (1818): Jekyll is related equally clearly to its creator.

Both tales were originary points for a whole "trajectory" of technophobic imagination, expanding in influence throughout the next century and remaining a central element in postmodernist fiction written in Scotland towards its end. Significantly, Gray set his own version of the Frankenstein story, *Poor Things* (1992), in the 1880s, among characters still seduced by Enlightenment visions of "the radiant future of the human race a century hence, when science, trade and fraternal democracy will have abolished disease, war and poverty" (Gray 1992: 122). The irony of such visions, and of what followed

from them, is less a subject of *Poor Things* than of *Lanark*, in which
the Oracle represents a kind of nightmare consummation of the "rule
of computation and utility". An emotionless, disembodied figure, persuaded by Scottish education that "everything was untrustworthy
when compared with numbers" (Gray [1981] 1984: 108), the Oracle
has a key role in the structure of Gray's novel, connecting its fantastic
and realistic sections. Part of the fantasy apparatus of the Institute, he
– or it – nevertheless delivers the entire narrative, in Books One and
Two, of what may be Lanark's previous existence in the "real" world
of Glasgow. In earlier fiction – Huxley's *Brave New World* (1932), for
example – dystopian techno-hells like the Institute or Unthank were
usually imaginative projections of conditions in the contemporary
world, and used to comment on them. *Lanark* partly follows this strategy, but the novel's unusual structure ensures that the conventional
roles of fantasy and reality are largely reversed. Disasters extending
from enlightened thinking really have triumphed for Gray: what earlier fiction still treated as nightmare or fantasy is now fundamental to
the novel's vision of everyday experience in contemporary Glasgow,
and apparently provides the only medium through which late
twentieth-century realities can be understood.

    Lanark develops in this way a fluency of interchange between
fantasy and reality often considered definitive of the Scottish imagination. Along with Jekyll/Hyde or Thaw/Lanark dualities in character,
such interchanges are still regularly assessed in terms of the Caledonian antisyzygy identified by G. Gregory Smith in *Scottish Literature:
Character and Influence* in 1919. Further developed by Hugh
MacDiarmid in the 1920s, Smith's view of a "Scottish antithesis of the
real and fantastic", "union of opposites", and "mixture of contraries"
(Smith: 1919: 4, 19–20), established interpretative modes that are still
as influential as ever. Edward Cowan and Douglas Gifford's recent
adaptation of them in *The Polar Twins* has suggested they may even
be "grossly overused" (Cowan and Gifford 1991: 1). As in the inter-
pretations of *Jekyll and Hyde* and *Lanark* outlined above, the postmodern debate can further adapt and update antisyzygical exegesis,
shining at least a "side light" on areas it conventionally explores and
illuminating its connections with developments elsewhere. This is especially evident in relation to the genre of fantasy, which has,

according to Brian McHale, "close affinities" with postmodernist writing. Loss of confidence in a "match between the mind of man and the nature of things" and in the abilities of reason, science, or any "grand narrative" to explain the world – or even in the capacities of language to represent it at all – obviously makes "the postmodern condition" a highly problematic one (McHale 1987: 74). Yet it also contributes to a radical liberation from realism – to writers' opportunities to construct fantastic worlds of their own, freer than ever from the constraints of the everyday. As another commentator on the postmodern has confirmed, fantasy enjoyed a revival in the late twentieth century "on a scale unprecedented since the Middle Ages" (Alexander 1990: 13). This was strongly marked in Scottish writing, in the work of Emma Tennant or Iain Banks, as well as Alasdair Gray. Each also illustrated a direction widely followed by recent fantasy: towards forms of satire, and nightmare expansions of political or social problems which comment all the more clearly on the contemporary world even in the act of departing from it. Banks, in novels such as *The Bridge* (1986), or Gray, in *Lanark* particularly, share with writers such as J.G. Ballard a use of fantasy to enlarge and expose the deficiencies of a technologised, commercialised, late-twentieth century world. Emma Tennant uses fantasy comparably in novels such as *The Bad Sister* (1978) and *Two Women of London: the Strange Case of Ms Jekyll and Mrs Hyde* (1989) – though in ways that are also specific to contemporary women's writing and which are regularly developed in the work of Angela Carter and Jeanette Winterson. For each of these writers, the constraints of a male-oriented society offer especially good reasons for departing, in imagination, into dimensions beyond it: ones through which its problems, fantastically enlarged, could be conveniently exposed and satirised.

Tennant is indebted in *The Bad Sister* to James Hogg's *Confessions of a Justified Sinner* (1824), as well as obviously to Stevenson in *Two Women of London*. Her novels show a tradition of Scottish writing coinciding with postmodern influences not haphazardly, but through particular dispositions of Scottish imagination to share in them. The irony of critics' under-use of postmodern analysis of Scottish literature is that it may be *more* appropriate to that literature than to many others. While this is evident in splittings between reality and fantasy, it is still clearer in relation to another set of factors central to the antisyzygy – ones arising from Scotland's divided linguistic heritage. Divisions of the kind Chris Guthrie identifies in *Sunset Song* between "Scots words to tell to your heart" and English words "sharp and clean and true" – yet unable "to say anything that was worth the saying at all" (Gibbon [1932] 1995: 32) – have always seemed highly specific to Scottish experience. But they have never been altogether unique. Describing English in *Scottish Literature: Character and Influence* as "not exactly [...] a 'foreign' language, but at least [...] a half-familiar medium" (Smith 1919: 118), G. Gregory Smith followed almost word for word Stephen Dedalus's view of the English language in *A Portrait of the Artist as a Young Man* – published three years earlier – as "so familiar and so foreign" (Joyce [1916] 1973: 189). Feelings of "fretting" in the shadow of a language both familiar and foreign – and consequently of partial containment and partial exclusion by a culture – were widely shared in the twentieth century, and were a particular influence in disposing its literary imagination towards innovation and change. They are a fundamental part of the conditions Julia Kristeva describes in *Strangers to Ourselves*. Bulgarian by origin, but conducting her life's work in Paris, Kristeva was well placed to analyse a condition of freedom from "the reins of the maternal tongue" and the "extravagant ease to innovate" which results. Kristeva's "weightlessness in the infinity of cultures and legacies" (Kristeva 1991: 31–32) bears comparison with Salman Rushdie's definition of "the migrant sensibility" – of "new types of human being" resulting from movements of peoples and interactions of cultures which have grown steadily more influential in the later twentieth century. The experience of "strange fusions" and "unprecedented unions" between what they were and where they find themselves, inevitably disposes "migrants" towards "a new imaginative relation with the world [...] plural, hybrid, metropolitan" (Rushdie [1985] 1991: 124–25). No author made aware of two different cultures can remain unquestioningly content with either, in Rushdie's view. Contact with other languages, literatures and ways of seeing requires writers to identify the nature and limitations of their own, encouraging the pursuit of alternative possibilities and, in general, a disposition towards aesthetic experiment and innovation.

Locating the roots of literary experiment in this way suggests the wide relevance of the postmodern debate, yet also the limits to some of its habitual modes of interpretation. Commentators such as Stephen Slemon and Cornel West have extended the kind of reservations expressed by Terry Eagleton and Christopher Norris, suggesting that postmodern thinking habitually interprets in narrowly philosophic or aesthetic terms developments that are fundamentally social and geopolitical in their origins. For Slemon and West, such tactics illustrate a presumption – even a kind of imperialism – of just the sort postmodern challenges to universalising Enlightenment reason had originally sought to resist. "For all its decentering rhetoric", Slemon suggests, the postmodern has "paradoxically become a centralising institution, a Western problematic" (Slemon [1989] 1993: 435–46).[6] Whereas the postmodern debate presumes to *allow* the replacement of grand narratives by "*petits reçits*", in this view it was really these separate "stories" and the pressures from the margins they focussed which had in the first place *driven* supposedly "postmodern" questioning of established aesthetic conventions and of the universal claims of Enlightenment reason. Modern culture, in other words, is defined less by Stephen Dedalus's leisurely linguistic and aesthetic musing on his "day of dappled seaborne clouds" than by his later recognition of Ireland's troubled, subordinate relation to England, and of the complications that result in his use of the English language.

In this perspective, Scottish commentators, tardy in employing concepts of the postmodern, may simply have been waiting for something to arrive in a second "post": the postcolonial. In analysing tensions between centres and margins of power, the impact of cultures upon one another, and the "fretting" of overlapping languages, postcolonial criticism has come to offer at least as many key concepts for literary theorists as the postmodern over the last ten years or so. These have been taken up rather more often by Scottish critics, though a measure of reluctance evident in this area, too, may be more easily explained. Postcolonial criticism is itself often accused of ignoring – in favour of general theories and taxonomies – the local conditions or national particularities that are supposedly one of its principal

---

[6] See also West [1989] 1993 in the same volume.

interests. As a primary agent in the construction of the British Empire, and on the whole one of its beneficiaries, Scotland clearly cannot be assumed to share uncomplicatedly in the conditions of colonies or former colonies abroad. Nor, obviously, are Scottish writers "migrants" altogether in the way Rushdie outlines, nor are they as "weightless" in an infinity of cultural legacies as Kristeva proposes. On the contrary, they are thoroughly grounded in Scottish traditions and literary history. Yet, illuminating coincidences and homologies remain visible between Scotland's situation – within a waning but long-endured form of English empire – and the experiences postcolonial theory analyses. In belonging to a small country, of many internal divisions, still dominated by London-centred media and institutions, Scottish writers experience "strange fusions" and plural, hybridised forms of imagination without ever having to migrate from home. In *The Strange Case of Dr Jekyll and Mr Hyde*, Jekyll acknowledges that he views the individual as "not truly one, but truly two [...] because the state of [his] knowledge did not pass beyond that point". In Scotland at least as much as elsewhere, cultural and social conditions a century or so later have tended to fulfil his prediction that "others will outstrip me on the same lines [...] man will be ultimately known for a mere polity of multifarious, incongruous and independent denizens" (Stevenson [1886] 1995: 278).

All of which suggests that, with due care, Scotland might profitably take up posts- offered by recent critical movements. Firmer location within them could create a wider audience for Scottish writing, while also bringing a wider range of ideas to bear upon it, and placing recent developments within a wider history of literature and thought. At the turn of the millennium, and with a new parliament working in Edinburgh, there are especially strong historical reasons for critics to work in this way – to act on the wish MacDiarmid expressed, that "whatever Scotland is to me / Be it aye pairt o' a' men see" (MacDiarmid [1926] 1975: 97). History and literature, politics and culture in Scotland are not at "loggerheads" as complicated or paradoxical as Douglas Gifford suggests at the end of *The Polar Twins* (Cowan and Gifford eds 1999: 300), but related reciprocally, often with surprising directness. What history and politics refuse, literature and culture provide. The origin of the Scottish literary revival at the end of the twentieth century has often been seen in this way as compensating for the failure of the Referendum Bill in 1979, and for the imposition on a predominantly socialist country of nearly twenty years of unelected Tory government. Critical determinations to consolidate an independent Scottish literary tradition can be seen to derive from the same source, with Cairns Craig's four-volume *History of Scottish Literature*, published in 1987, early evidence of the results. The period between 1979 and 1999 may in this way come to be seen as a very particular one for the history and criticism of literature – as well as for writing itself – with independent, national vision necessarily a more exclusive influence than it was previously, or than it may need to be after 1999.[7] Craig's criticism once again reflects current potentials particularly clearly. His "Introduction" describes *The Modern Scottish Novel: Narrative and National Imagination* as "written in the context of Scotland's newly regained political status" and assesses the development of Scottish literature, comprehensively and convincingly, in terms of "underlying thematic or formal issues central to the Scottish tradition". But it also envisages national imagination and tradition shaped by Bakhtinian "heteroglossia" – by "dialogue between a variety of interacting discourses" and by a "continual series of interchanges with other nations" (Craig 1999: 36, 30–31). In this spirit – broadly postmodern and postcolonial – there is much scope for future studies with titles such as *Twentieth-Century Scottish Literature: Writing and Imagination, National and also International*. Or perhaps even snappier titles. In the meantime, the title *Beyond Scotland* provides exactly the right signpost for critics on the threshold of a new century.[8]

---

[7] This is equally evident outwith Scotland, in the forthcoming 12-volume *Oxford English Literary History*, for example, which is intended to be just that, a literary history of England. With Oxford University Press also committed to separate literary histories of Ireland, Scotland and Wales, there are signs that the independence of literary traditions within all the countries of the "United" Kingdom has recently been recognised more widely than ever – certainly more widely than it used to be in England.

[8] Many of the ideas in this paper derive from discussion at Strathclyde during the "Beyond Scotland" seminar in October 2000. I'm also very grateful for later help and advice from Professors Ian Campbell and Susan Manning in the University of Edinburgh.

Bibliography

Adorno, Theodor and Max Horkheimer. [1944] 1986. "The Concept of Enlighten-
    ment" in *Dialectic of Enlightenment* (tr. John Cumming). London: Verso, 1986.
Alexander, Marguerite. 1990. *Flights from Realism: Themes and Strategies in Post-
    modernist British and American Fiction*. London: Arnold.
Bell, Eleanor and Gavin Miller (eds). 2004. *Scotland in Theory: Reflections on Lit-
    erature and Culture*. Amsterdam: Rodopi.
Christianson, Aileen and Alison Lumsden (eds). 2000. *Contemporary Scottish Women
    Writers*. Edinburgh: Edinburgh University Press.
Connor, Stephen. 1989. *Postmodernist Culture: An Introduction to Theories of the
    Contemporary*. Oxford: Blackwell.
Cowan, Edward J. and Douglas Gifford (eds). 1999. *The Polar Twins*. Edinburgh:
    John Donald.
Craig, Cairns. 1999. *The Modern Scottish Novel: Narrative and National Imagination*.
    Edinburgh: Edinburgh University Press.
Docherty, Thomas. 1993. "Introduction" in Docherty, Thomas (ed.) *Postmodernism:
    A Reader*. Hemel Hempstead: Harvester Wheatsheaf.
Eagleton, Terry. 1996. *The Illusions of Postmodernism*. Oxford: Blackwell.
Gifford, Douglas and Dorothy McMillan (eds). 1997. *History of Scottish Women's
    Writing*. Edinburgh: Edinburgh University Press.
Gordon, Giles. 1981. "The Definite Article: The Novels of Robbe-Grillet" in *New
    Edinburgh Review* 53(February 1981): 26–27.
Gibbon, Lewis Grassic. [1932] 1995. *Sunset Song* in *A Scots Quair*. Edinburgh:
    Canongate, 1995.
—. [1933] 1995. *Cloud Howe* in *A Scots Quair*. Edinburgh: Canongate, 1995.
Gray, Alasdair. [1981] 1984. *Lanark: A Life in Four Books*. London: Granada.
—. 1992. *Poor Things*. London: Bloomsbury.
—. [1994] 1995. *A History Maker*. Harmondsworth: Penguin.
Habermas, Jürgen. [1981] 1993. "Modernity versus Postmodernity" in Natoli, Joseph
    and Linda Hutcheon (eds). *A Postmodern Reader*. Albany, N.Y.: State Univer-
    sity of New York Press.
Harvey, David. 1989. *The Condition of Postmodernity: An Enquiry into the Origins of
    Cultural Change*. Oxford: Blackwell.
Hassan, Ihab. 1987. *The Postmodern Turn: Essays in Postmodern Theory and Cul-
    ture*. Ohio: Ohio State University Press.
Jameson, Fredric. 1991. *Postmodernism, or, the Cultural Logic of Late Capitalism*.
    London: Verso.
Joyce, James. [1916] 1973. *A Portrait of the Artist as a Young Man*. Harmondsworth:
    Penguin.
Kristeva, Julia. 1991. *Strangers to Ourselves* (tr. Leon S. Roudiez). Hemel Hemp-
    stead: Harvester Wheatsheaf.
Lee, Alison. 1990. *Realism and Power: Postmodern British Fiction*. London:
    Routledge.

Lumsden, Alison. 1993. "Innovation and Reaction in the Fiction of Alasdair Gray" in Wallace, Gavin and Randall Stevenson (eds) *The Scottish Novel since the Seventies.* Edinburgh: Edinburgh University Press. 115–26.

Lyotard, Jean-François. [1979] 1984. *The Postmodern Condition: A Report on Knowledge* (tr. Geoffrey Bennington and Brian Massumi). Manchester: Manchester University Press.

—. [1985] 1993. "Note on the Meaning of "Post-" in Docherty, Thomas (ed.) *Postmodernism: A Reader.* Hemel Hempstead: Harvester Wheatsheaf.

MacDiarmid, Hugh. [1926] 1975. *A Drunk Man Looks at the Thistle* in Grieve, Michael and Alexander Scott (eds) *The Hugh MacDiarmid Anthology: Poems in Scots and English.* London: Routledge and Kegan Paul.

McHale, Brian. 1987. *Postmodernist Fiction.* London: Methuen.

—. 1992. *Constructing Postmodernism.* London: Routledge.

Maltby, Paul. 1991. *Dissident Postmodernists: Barthelme, Coover, Pynchon.* Philadelphia: University of Pennsylvania Press.

Norris, Christopher. 1990. *What's Wrong with Postmodernism: Critical Theory and the Ends of Philosophy.* New York and London: Harvester Wheatsheaf.

Robbe-Grillet, Alain. 1965. *Snapshots and Towards a New Novel* (tr. Barbara Wright). London: Calder and Boyars.

Rushdie, Salman. [1985] 1991. "The Location of *Brazil*" in *Imaginary Homelands: Essays and Criticism 1981–1991.* London: Granta Books.

Slemon, Stephen. [1989] 1993. "Modernism's Last Post" in Natoli, Joseph and Linda Hutcheon (eds) *A Postmodern Reader.* Albany, N.Y.: State University of New York Press. 426–39.

Smith, G. Gregory. 1919. *Scottish Literature: Character and Influence.* London: Macmillan.

Spark, Muriel. [1957] 1978. *The Comforters.* Harmondsworth: Penguin.

—. [1961] 1982. *The Prime of Miss Jean Brodie.* Harmondsworth: Penguin.

Steiner, George. 1967. *Language and Silence: Essays 1958–1966.* London: Faber & Faber.

Stevenson, Randall. 1991. "Alasdair Gray and the Postmodern" in Crawford, Robert and Thom Nairn (eds) *The Arts of Alasdair Gray.* Edinburgh: Edinburgh University Press. 48–63.

Stevenson, Robert Louis. [1886] 1995. *The Strange Case of Dr Jekyll and Mr Hyde* in *Shorter Scottish Fiction* (ed. Roderick Watson). Edinburgh: Canongate.

Walker, Marshall. 1996. *Scottish Literature since 1707.* London: Longman.

Wallace, Gavin. 1993. "Voices in Empty Houses: the Novel of Damaged Identity" in Wallace, Gavin and Randall Stevenson (eds). 1993. *The Scottish Novel since the Seventies.* Edinburgh: Edinburgh University Press. 217–31.

Waugh, Patricia. 1992. *Practising Postmodernism/Reading Modernism.* London: Arnold.

Waugh, Patricia (ed.). 1992. *Postmodernism: A Reader.* London: Arnold.

West, Cornel. [1989] 1993. "Black Culture and Postmodernism" in Natoli, Joseph and Linda Hutcheon (eds) *A Postmodern Reader.* Albany, N.Y.: State University of New York Press. 390–97.

Whyte, Christopher (ed.). 1995. *Gendering the Nation*. Edinburgh: Edinburgh University Press.

Wilde, Alan. 1981. *Horizons of Assent: Modernism, Postmodernism and the Ironic Imagination*. Baltimore and London: The Johns Hopkins University Press.

Woolf, Virginia. [1927] 1973. *To the Lighthouse*. Harmondsworth: Penguin.

—. [1928] 1975. *Orlando*. Harmondsworth: Penguin.

Zenzinger, Peter. 1989. "Contemporary Scottish Fiction" in *Scotland: Literature, Culture, Politics*. Heidelberg: Carl Winter Universitätsverlag. 215–42.

Scotland and Hybridity

Cairns Craig

Whether in "racial" or cultural terms, hybridity has frequently been regarded as a
constitutional weakness within Scottish identity. However, the work of Bhabha and
Bakhtin on hybridity has lead to a revaluation of Scotland's divided literary heritage.
Although this is welcome, such theories ignore dialogic philosophies developed
within Scotland. Further, theories of hybridity insist on the myth of national unity and
purity which they aim to oppose: nations, however, are always and already dialogic.
Keywords: Mikhail Bakhtin, Homi Bhabha, Robert Crawford, John Macmurray, dia-
logism, hybridity, nationalism.

1.

In Robert Young's *Colonial Desire: Hybridity in Theory, Culture and
Race*, Robert Louis Stevenson's *The Strange Case of Dr Jekyll and
Mr Hyde* is used as an index of the fear and longing of the West for its
repressed, colonised "Other":

Many novels of the past have also projected such uncertainty and difference outwards,
and concerned with meeting and incorporating the culture of the other, whether of
class, ethnicity or sexuality, they often fantasize crossing into it, though rarely so
completely as when Dr Jekyll transforms himself into Mr Hyde. (Young 1995: 3)

Jekyll and Hyde is the fictional transposition of the fear of degeneration that will result from miscegenation between the superior human
specimens of white, western culture and any of the lesser races with
which it comes into contact in the process of colonisation – of the terror of what Kipling called "the monstrous hybridism of East and
West" (cited in Young 1995: 3). Such fear may have been given
mythic expression in the work of an Edinburgh author in the 1880s,
but it had its roots in the Edinburgh of the 1820s and 1830s, where
Robert Knox – famous as a pioneer anatomist and the surgical entre-
preneur who engaged the services of Burke and Hare – developed
theories of racial evolution that were deeply to influence Victorian

culture. The different races of humanity were, for Knox, different species, the products of whose cross-breeding – like the product of the mating of a horse and a donkey after which the *mulatos* of the Caribbean were named – would produce a sterile outcome; as Knox puts it, "by that physiological law which extinguishes mixed races [...] and causes the originally more numerous one to predominate, unless supplies be continually drawn from the primitive pure breeds" (Knox 1862: 48–49).[1] In Stevenson's *Jekyll and Hyde*, Young implies, there is reflected the final outcome of mutual self-destruction which flows from sexual contamination between the "higher" and "lower" species of humanity.

The importance of a Scottish thinker like Knox to the development of nineteenth-century theories of race and hybridity suggests a concern somehow embedded in the very nature of Scottish culture. One might see in Knox's genetics of racial purity a response to what Colin Kidd has identified as the problematic nature of Scottish culture's construction of its origins from the early medieval period onwards – the deliberate assertion, despite the many ethnic and cultural elements that went into the making of Scotland, of a single cultural and racial origin, which remained the unique source of Scotland's continuing independent identity:

The various peoples who composed the emerging kingdom, including the Dalriadic Scots, Picts, Strathclyde and Galwegian Britons, and Northumbrians, as well as Anglo-Norman and Flemish immigrants, were gradually amalgamated under a Scotic umbrella identity as the *regnum Scottorum*. Although the Scottish regnal line included some Pictish as well as Dalriadic-Scottish kings, the monarchy which was to form the core of Scottish identity was clearly linked to the early history of Dalriada. The Scottish War of Independence firmly established the Scotic identity of the nation. In particular, the Anglo-Scottish propaganda warfare of the late thirteenth and early fourteenth centuries linked Scottish independence to the ancient autonomy of the Dalriadic Scots as a means of rebutting the claim derived from the Brutus legend that the Plantagenet monarchy enjoyed suzerainty over the whole island of Britain. The history of the Gaelic Scots had become the national history of all-Scotland; indeed, this particular ethnic past justified the sovereignty of the whole. (Kidd 1999: 123–24)

---

[1] See Knox 1862: 503 for a summary of his theory of race difference and its relation to hybridity.

Hybridity represents an underlying threat to Scottish culture because any compromise of the purity of its "Celtic" origins in the *regnum Scottorum* undermines its refusal to accept English suzerainty. At the same time, Scottish development since the Wars of Independence, focused on the Lowlands and on the *Inglis* language, increasingly marginalised and devalued the very culture – Gaelic – on which the nation's independence was based. The nation was forced to assert the purity of its original Gaelic roots at the same time as distancing itself from the actual Gaelic culture which derived from those roots. According to Kidd, Scotland's Lowlanders

inherited distinctively non-Gaelic manners and speech together with a history whose content was Gaelic. This unusual combination of inherited cultural characteristics formed the identity of Scottish Lowlanders, a people untroubled by an ethnic schizophrenia in large part because political discourse was not driven by an ethnic imperative. (Kidd 1999: 140)

By the nineteenth century, however, such a hybrid identity seems, to Knox at least, to have become profoundly uncomfortable. Kidd's account of the traditional conception of the Scottish past is overthrown by Knox to produce a history in which Celt and Saxon are entirely incompatible races maintaining an unmixed genealogy and separate historical trajectories:

To me the Caledonian Celt of *Scotland* appears a race as distinct from the Lowland Saxon of the same country, as any two races can possibly be: as negro from American; Hottentot from Caffre; Esquimaux from Saxon. [...] The Caledonian Celtic race, not Scotland, fell at Culloden, never more to rise; the Boyne was the Waterloo of Celtic Ireland. If the French Celt recovers from the terrible disaster of 1815 it will cause my surprise. (Knox 1862: 14–15)

The saxonising of Lowland Scotland, its absolute separation from the *national* inheritance of a Celtic past, required not only that the races of Scotland had never become hybrid, however mixed its culture might sometimes have been, but that the nation itself was redundant. The impure nation had to be dissolved back into the constituents of its racial types, allowing history to be rewritten *not* as the story of the nation, but rather as the story of the pure types who were either genetically predisposed to political liberty (the Saxons), or submission to tyranny (the Celts).

It is ironic, therefore, that when Kidd, in an earlier book, undertook to explain the failure of Scottish national culture in the eighteenth century, he proposed that its weakness lay precisely in the fact that it was a *hybrid* culture. Failing to generate its own authentic national identity, Scotland had adopted an English model of history and imposed it on Scottish circumstances, producing a hyphenated, hybrid "Anglo-British" identity:

> Anglo-Britishness is almost as pervasive in Scotland as in the English heartland of the United Kingdom. This ready acceptance of English ideals in Scottish political culture is almost certainly connected to an ideological non-occurrence in Scotland's modern history whose causes pose a second historical problem for this study. During the nineteenth century, the Scots, unlike the Irish, Italians, Hungarians, Poles and most of the other historic nations of Europe, who, at that stage, lacked full political autonomy, missed out on the development of a full-blown "romantic" nationalism. (Kidd 1993: 1)

Scotland's failed *national* identity, in Kidd's analysis, may be based on legal and cultural assimilation to Englishness, but his separation of *Anglo*-Scotland from the leftover remnant of the rest of Scotland has precisely the same effect as Knox's saxonising of the Lowlander in opposition to Celtic Highlanders: Scotland's *national* integrity is destroyed and its future lies in its assimilation to the stronger and purer tradition of its southern neighbour. The hybrid nature of Kidd's conception of Scottishness after the mid-eighteenth century is emphasised by his adoption of a nomenclature used by no Scot of that or any other period:

> It might be objected that this chapter has ignored the rise of North British identity among eighteenth-century Scots. Rather that is exactly what has been described, though termed Anglo-British on the basis of its historical content. North Britishness was a Scottish version of English whig identity, based on a commitment to English constitutional history. North Britishness involved the appropriation of English whig materials in an attempt to construct a more inclusive and properly British whig culture. North Britishness was an aspiration towards full British participation in English liberties; a set of intellectual approaches to the history of English liberty; and a celebration of the growing contribution made by post-Union Scots to the domestic security and imperial expansion of the new British state. (Kidd 1993: 214)

Scotland's Anglo-British identity is incapable of maintaining its own historical vigour, and hybridity, as with Jekyll and Hyde, becomes both Scotland's characteristic feature and its inherent failure, its claim to special significance and the negation of its cultural efficacy in the world.

Kidd's analyses are only one strand of the long effort by Scottish cultural theorists since the 1960s to make sense of Scotland's "mongrel" identity. For some, like Kidd, the hyphenated Anglo-Scottish tradition of the Enlightenment is both the great achievement of Scottish culture and the inevitable destroyer of any conceptions of an autonomous and authentic Scottish culture; for others, like Tom Nairn in *The Break-up of Britain*, the deformed offspring of a Scoto-Celtic coupling has generated the "tartan monster" of Scottish popular culture (Nairn 1981).[2] In all such theories the fundamental weakness of Scotland's cultural history is its hybrid formation, a hybridity that undermines its capacity for reproduction and prophesies its eventual extinction as, in Knoxian terms, it enters terminal degeneration or is assimilated back into one of the pure forms from which it originally derived.

2.

In an inversion of conventional oppositions typical of post-Derridean literary criticism, the relationship of the hybrid to its pure origins has been reversed in postcolonial theory, overturning its subsidiary status to make it the defining value of modern writing. "Hybridity", particularly in the work of Homi Bhabha, has been used to characterise contemporary cultures of immigration and diaspora, which are represented not as a degeneration from cultural health, but as the index of true cultural vitality (see Bhabha 1994). Challenging critical traditions that identify cultures with national territories, Bhabha applauds that "range of contemporary critical theories" which "suggest that it is from those who have suffered the sentence of history – subjugation,

---

[2] Hyphenated hybridities proliferate in Nairn's account of the Scottish past, which is home to a "cultural sub-nationalism", an "Id-culture" with "an extraordinary blatant super-patriotism – in effect, a kind of dream-nationalism" (Nairn 1981: 162–63).

domination, diaspora, displacement – that we learn our most enduring
lessons for living and thinking" (Bhabha 1994: 172). Those who live
in the interstices *between* cultures are the models for the modern
culture-critic, since "it is from this hybrid location of cultural value –
the transnational as the translational – that the postcolonial intellectual
attempts to elaborate a historical and literary project" (Bhabha 1994:
173). The hybrid, in defiance of Knox's biological theory, is for
Bhabha the truly creative and procreative condition of the modern
world.

A key component of Bhabha's conception of the hybrid are the
theories of Mikhail Bakhtin, for whom hybridity is a defining feature
of the language of the novel. In answer to the question, "What is a hy-
bridization?", Bakhtin replies,

It is a mixture of two social languages within the limits of a single utterance, an encounter, within the arena of an utterance, between two different linguistic consciousnesses, separated from one another by an epoch, by social differentiation or by some
other factor. (Bakhtin 1981: 358)

In a Scottish context, Bakhtin provided the theoretical basis for challenging the long-standing criticism that Scotland's literatures have
been undermined by their lack of a single and unitary linguistic context. Instead of being a weakness, the division of Scotland's literary
heritage between a variety of languages and cultural traditions becomes a strength, and interaction between Scotland's languages and
dialects produces the kind of creative speech that, in Bakhtin's terms,

belongs, by its grammatical (syntactic) and compositional markers, to a single
speaker, but that actually contains mixed within it two utterances, two speech manners, two styles, two "languages", two semantic and axiological belief systems. (Bakhtin 1981: 304)

The celebration of Scotland's hybridity, of Scotland's *Bakhtinianism*,
became, in the 1980s and 1990s, Scottish criticism's version of
Bhabha's reversal of the valuation of the hybrid. The 1993 conference
on "Bakhtin and Scottish Literature" at St Andrews University was
perhaps the high point of this conjunction, celebrated in Robert
Crawford's article "Bakhtin and Scotlands" (Crawford 1994).

Crawford suggests that "a nation whose culture is under pressure often clings to traditional notions of itself, since change seems to threaten a dissolution of identity", and that Bakhtin provides a conception of "identity not as fixed, closed, and unchanging, but as formed and reformed through dialogue" (Crawford 1994: 57). Bakhtinian dialogic identity challenges what Crawford describes as "notions of an essentialist Scotland", opening up the possibility that "various Scotlands may enter into dialogue", characterised by awareness of "other tongues", of "one speaker using and reaccenting elements from another's speech, and of the fructifying impurity" that comes from being aware that "one's own language is never a single language" (Crawford 1994: 60).

The literary context of this Bakhtinianism was the rediscovery of Scottish vernacular speech. In Tom Leonard's poetry, in the exploitation of historical and contemporary Scots on stage, in the demotic of James Kelman's or Irvine Welsh's novels, the speech of lowland and working-class Scotland had come to play an increasingly decisive role in modern Scottish writing.[3] There is, Crawford argues, a "mutual awareness of cultural differences (primarily between various native tongues)" that "is quite different in Scotland or in Wales from the overall awareness in Britain". Bakhtin's theories, in other words, are not simply a culturally neutral account of the workings of literary language, but an account particularly appropriate to the context of "linguistic and cultural pluralism" that results "in Scotland [being] significantly removed from that of England or of Britain as a whole" (Crawford 1994: 60). Bakhtin's emphasis on the possibility of there being "two social languages within the limits of a single utterance" justifies Scottish writing that exploits the interplay between the traditions of written English and the orality of working-class Scots speech. Bakhtinian hybridism thus provided a means of *accepting* rather than *regretting* the nation's mixed linguistic and cultural history, while at the same time shaping a strategy that aligned Scottish writing with those "postcolonial" cultures which were producing some of the most theoretically inspiring contemporary writing. If literature in English was now underpinned by the need for the Empire to *write back* to the

---

[3] See Craig 1999: ch.5 for a discussion of this issue.

colonising centre, resisting the homogenising force of the old colonial culture and accepting its own hybrid nature; if, as Wilson Harris argued, "hybridity in the present is constantly struggling to free itself from a past which stressed ancestry, and which valued the 'pure' over its threatening opposite, the 'composite'" (Ashcroft et al. eds 1989: 35–36), then the assumption that Scotland was actually a hybrid allowed critics not only to distance Scottish writing from the "purity" of English cultural traditions, but to make it a major contributor to postcolonial resistance to English cultural imperialism. The "belatedness" of Scotland's nationalist resistance to English culture, its failure to produce a romantic nationalism in the nineteenth century, could thus be represented as Scotland's prophetic anticipation of the terms of the postcolonial.

It was a parallel that James Kelman asserted in the published version of his acceptance speech for the Booker Prize in 1994, in which he situated his own writing as part of the movement "towards decolonisation and self-determination" based on "the validity of indigenous culture" and "the right to defend it in the face of attack" ("The speech" 1994). And it is a parallel emphasised by Michael Gardiner, in one of the few theoretically informed discussions of Scotland and the postcolonial, where he argues that while Scotland was not "in any sense postcolonial", the reading strategies of postcolonial criticism were, nonetheless, particularly appropriate to Scotland, because those reading strategies "foreground questions of race and nation" and "questions of race and nation are already foregrounded in situations where they have been uncleanly and indecisively split between national centres" (Gardiner 1996: 36, 39). For critics such as Gardiner, Scotland, as a place characterised by exactly the kinds of "ambivalent postcolonial agencies" (Gardiner 1996: 36) defined by Bhabha, may not itself be *post-colonial* (in the sense of having been directly colonised), but it is so profoundly responsive to *postcolonial* modes of interpretation that it "is *already* implicated in postcolonial theory" (Gardiner 1996: 39). From this perspective, whatever the sources of Scotland's particular condition, it is one which, like truly *post*-colonial cultures, can be redeemed by those strategies that postcolonial theory has developed in order to "give back to the postcolonial subject the tools needed to develop a politics of the subject" and so allow the culture to escape its otherwise "truly marginal condition" (Gardiner 1996: 40).

The fact that Gardiner focuses on a specifically *textual* notion of the postcolonial, just as Crawford focuses on a narrowly *linguistic* notion of hybridity, emphasises how problematic is Scotland's adoption into the language of the postcolonial hybrid. Both are concerned with those elements of Scotland's *internal* cultural situation that conform to the requirements of hybridity theory: neither is concerned with the fact that Scotland is indeed only too truly *post*-colonial – in the historical sense of having come (almost) to the end of being a *colonising* nation. Concentration on the nation's *internal* hybridity emphasises what Scotland is assumed to have in common with the colonised of the English-speaking world – the interaction of local language or dialect with standard English, the interplay of local mythology and literary tradition with the "standard" literature of the English cultural imperium – and represses the fact that it was Scottish writers such as Walter Scott from whom the colonised had to learn in order to acquire the imperial language and culture.

The compromises and silences involved in this view of Scottish culture are evident if one compares it to what has been happening in Irish criticism during the same period. Much more easily able to identify their history as the history of the *colonised*, and to refuse any direct complicity in the process of colonisation, Irish critics have, in the 1990s, evolved a breathtaking redefinition of Irish literature as both the original postcolonial culture and as the fulfilment of Bakhtinian hybridity. In *Inventing Ireland*, for instance, Declan Kiberd describes Oscar Wilde as a writer whose "identity was dialogic" because

the other was also the truest friend, since it was from that other that a sense of self was derived. [...] Wearing the mask of an English Oxonian, Wilde was paradoxically freed to become more "Irish" than he could ever have been back in Ireland. (Kiberd 1995: 48)

As a result, Wilde "loved England as genuinely as Goethe loved the French" (Kiberd 1995: 48). In their relation with English culture, the Irish are engaged in a truly Bakhtinian dialogic. In Kiberd's construction of the history of Irish literature, Irish precedence in – indeed, Irish prescience of – the terms of postcolonial literature is what gives it its fundamental significance. The culture that has lived in the margins of English literature becomes, ironically, the centre from which all later marginal literatures derive the structure of their identity:

> Davis's description of the Irish as "a composite race" had been borne out yet again. What had been billed as the Battle of the Two Civilizations was really, and more subtly, the interpenetration of each by the other: and this led to the generation of the new species of man and woman, who felt exalted by rather than ashamed of such hybridity. (Kiberd 1995: 162)

This "mixed" nature of the Irish, as both the earliest victims of colonisation and the "first modern people to decolonize in the twentieth century", is what makes them "so representative" (Kiberd 1995: 5). By being the archetypally *hybrid* culture, resisting national purity, Ireland is the model from which all the postcolonialisms since the Second World War are copied:

> Were the Irish a hybrid people, as the artists generally claimed, exponents of multiple selfhood and modern authenticity? Or were they a pure, unitary race, dedicated to defending a romantic notion of integrity? These discussions anticipated many others which would be heard across the "Third World": in Ireland, as elsewhere, artists celebrated the hybridity of the national experience, even as they lamented the underdevelopment which seemed to be found alongside such cultural richness. (Kiberd 1995: 7)

With the Irish experience of colonisation, of course, Scotland cannot compete. By a further reversal of the role of margin and centre, however, Robert Crawford has challenged the Irish pre-eminence in the role of postcolonial mentor by presenting Scotland as not only the site of resistance to English cultural hegemony, but as the very source of the cultural hegemony that postcoloniality has to resist (Crawford ed. 1998). If Ireland is the first nation of postcoloniality in its resistance to linguistic and cultural imperialism, then Scotland had already, in the eighteenth century, made a more radical move by seeking to define from the margin what the centre itself ought to represent, by seeking to shape the very nature of English Literature in advance of its imposition on the rest of the imperial territory. If English Literature in the modern world is best represented by postcolonial writers and critics, English Literature in its historical origins is no less a product of the margins, since it was invented and defined by the Scots, who not only invented the university discipline, but were also the first, in the words of William Barron, to insist that "there is nothing, therefore, in the nature of the thing that should hinder the language of England from being written well in India or America" (Crawford ed. 1998: 15).

Crawford's *The Scottish Invention of English Literature* thus proposes an even more ambitious – and ambiguous – claim than Kiberd's *Inventing Ireland*, making Scotland the source of both canonical English literature *and* of postcolonial opposition to it. If, as much postcolonial theory insists, postcoloniality is a condition which begins contemporaneously with colonialism, Scotland has lived the deconstructive relationship between the two since their inception, performing the roles both of creator of canonical "English" and of guerrilla fighter dedicated to its subversion. If Ireland is the product of the miscegenation of English Literature and the Celtic imagination, then English *Literature* itself is a product of the marriage of Scottish criticism and English writing. English Literature, as originally evolved in Scotland, is a hybrid construction, generating "heteroglot and multicultural kinds of writing which form not a peripheral exception to but a model for international writing in the English-speaking world in the nineteenth and twentieth centuries" (Crawford ed. 1998: 6–7).

Crawford's revisionist account of the history of Scoto-English literature leads to an equally deconstructive account of modern Scotland, in which Bakhtinian hybridity encourages us to resist "an essentialist position which assumes some sort of unaltering Scotland or Wales or Canada" (Crawford 1998: 13), and to celebrate the emergence of multiple "Scotlands" to replace the Scotland of old:

So we have Catholic Scotland, which means not only those constituent individuals and areas of Scotland which might be identified as Catholic, but also the views of Scotland which the Catholic community holds, and which are likely, in some ways at least, to differ from those of Islamic Scotland or Protestant Scotland. So we have Gaelic Scotland, whose vision is constructed through and by the Gaelic language, we have Scots Scotland, Urdu-speaking Scotland, English-speaking Scotland. And there are Scotlands beyond our national boundaries, yet which construct their own Scotland that in turn influences our state. (Crawford 1998: 56–57)

Hybridity allows us to get away "from the pressure for pure Scottish canons and for one essentialist Scotland that have tended to plague us" (Crawford 1998: 57). The historical irony of such Bakhtinianism, however, is that it is precisely Scotland's divided and plural past which has "tended to plague us", rather than any one notion of an "essentialist" Scotland. Scotland is the exemplar of the *failed* unity of the nation, its whole literary history back to the eighteenth century fraught with doubles, fratricides and outcasts representing the fractured, uncompletable project of national unity. Crawford's litany of modern, multiple Scotlands could be repeated of the Scotland of any period of its history, so that hybridity can scarcely represent a *new* configuration in our understanding of Scottish culture: indeed, Robert Knox may have been inspired in his theories of hybridity precisely because Scotland has always been a prime example of a mixed culture.

More importantly, however, Crawford's use of Scotland's modern linguistic "hybridity" to celebrate anti-essentialist notions of the "self" ignores the canons of Scottish culture itself, since the dialogic conception of the self has been a fundamental aspect of Scottish thought from Andrew Seth's *Hegelianism and Personality* in the 1880s to John Macmurray's *The Form of the Personal* in the 1950s (Seth 1887; Macmurray 1957, 1961). Had those who proposed Bakhtin as a means of understanding Scottish culture grasped the evolution of Scottish philosophy, they would have known that the notion of the dialogic self was itself fundamental to the whole tradition of Scottish thought: not the *accidental* parallel to the theories of Adam Smith that Crawford suggests, but integral to the very nature of Scottish philosophy's conception of the self. In Macmurray's philosophy, the most important Scottish contribution to twentieth-century thought, the Self is not – as traditionally conceived – the self as thinker ("I think therefore I am") but the self as agent, a self which "exists only in dynamic relation with the other" (Macmurray 1961: 17); and if language, for Bakhtin, is characterised by "heteroglossia" – a mode of writing that set in interaction the "the social diversity of speech types" in a society, including "social dialects, characteristic group behaviour, professional jargons, generic languages, languages of generations and age groups" (Bakhtin 1981: 262–63) – then the self, as defined by Macmurray, is equally polyglot, or as he describes it, "heterocentric", since

the centre of interest and attention is in the other, not in himself. The other is the centre of value. For himself he has no value in himself, but only for the other. But this is
mutual: the other cares for him disinterestedly in return. Each, that is to say, acts, and
therefore thinks and feels for the other, and not for himself. But because the positive
motive contains and subordinates its negative, their unity is no fusion of selves, neither is it a functional unity of differences – neither an organic nor a mechanical unity
– it is a unity of persons. Each remains a distinct individual; the other remains really
other. Each realizes himself in and through the other. (Macmurray 1961: 158)

The attribution of notions of "essentialism" to a national tradition
which had been engaged, for at least a hundred years, in deconstruct-
ing conceptions of the self or of the nation as unified and autonomous,
can only reveal how impoverished contemporary conceptions of
Scotland's cultural past have become. To ignore – or to be unaware of
– the ways in which Scottish culture had already developed theoretical
foundations for understanding a self that is the product of multiple
cultural traditions must inevitably lead to misconceptions about the
history of the culture that one is trying to comprehend, effectively devaluing its past in order to inflate its current – and supposedly superior
– self-consciousness. To suggest, as Crawford does, that Charles
Taylor's *Sources of the Self: the Making of Modern Identity*, offers us
a potential breakthrough in understanding Scottish identity, because it
incorporates elements of Bakhtin's theories, is a revelation only of the
benightedness in which the achievements of modern Scottish thought
remain unacknowledged by those who are its inheritors. Equally, to
imply that it is only through the ideas of Russian or American intellectuals that one can grasp the real nature of the Scottish condition is
to continue Scotland's submission to cultural imperialism rather than
fulfil its "post-colonial" identity, reproducing the inferiorism by which
Scotland is always the *object* of an understanding that can only come
from outside Scotland itself, never a *subject* capable of understanding
itself. If we, in Scotland, are not simply to be the consumers of the
cultural paradigms promulgated in the globalised economy of the
modern intellectual arena, we have to take account of what the traditions of Scottish thought provide, both towards the interpretation of
Scottish culture and as contributions to our current international environment. Becoming properly "post-colonial" in a Scottish context
would involve a re-grounding of our intellectual life in the traditions
of Scottish culture, so that, at the very least, we recognise when con-

temporary concepts – such as hybridity – have already been engaged with by those traditions.

3.

Homi Bhabha's deployment of "hybridity" (as argued in Easthope 1998) is fundamentally negative – it is much clearer what hybridity is being mobilised *against* than what it means in itself. Hybridity is for Bhabha what *différance* is for Derrida, that which destabilises the structured hierarchies of traditional Eurocentric thought. And the most important element of the Eurocentric tradition is, for Bhabha, the nation, which is seen as the source and justification of "culture". The hybrid "destroys this mirror of representation in which cultural knowledge" is usually couched, and "challenges our sense of the historical identity of culture as a homogenizing, unifying force, authenticated by the originary Past, kept alive in the national tradition of the People" (Bhabha 1994: 37). It is towards the destabilisation of the unitary nation that hybridity is directed, a nation whose

political unity [...] consists in a continual displacement of its irredeemably plural modern space, bounded by different, even hostile nations, into a signifying space that is archaic and mythical, paradoxically representing the nation's modern territoriality, in the patriotic, atavistic temporality of Traditionalism. (Bhabha 1994: 149)

Hybridity undoes the process by which the nation turns "Territory into Tradition, [...] the People into One", and thereby reveals that "cultural difference is no longer a problem of 'other' people", but a "question of the otherness of the people-as-one" (Bhabha 1994: 150). The national subject is, by this means, split and fragmented in order to undo "any supremacist, or nationalist claims to cultural mastery", making it impossible to "hark back to any 'true' national past" (Bhabha 1994: 150, 152). In the backward glance of the hybrid, the national cultures of the European world are simply aspects of that "invention of tradition" by which ancient authenticity and authority are invoked to justify what are entirely modern and pragmatic constructions of political power:

The transmission of *cultures of survival* does not occur in the ordered *musée imaginaire* of national cultures with their claims to the continuity of an authentic "past" and a living "present" – whether this scale of value is preserved in the organicist "national" traditions of romanticism or within the more universal proportions of classicism [...]. The natural(ized), unifying discourse of "nation", "peoples", or authentic "folk" tradition, those embedded myths of culture's particularity, cannot readily be referenced. The great, though unsettling, advantage of this position is that it makes you increasingly aware of the construction of culture and the invention of tradition. (Bhabha 1994: 172)

Bhabha's "hybridity", in other words, is developed in the context of the most prominent contemporary theory of nations and of nationalism, derived from the work of Ernest Gellner, in which nationalism is presented not as "the awakening of nations to self-consciousness" but as the force which "invents nations where they do not exist" (Gellner 1964: 168). For Gellner and those who follow his lead, nationalism is an entirely modern phenomenon, a product of the political, technological and industrial revolutions of the late-eighteenth and early-nineteenth centuries, which yet seeks to authenticate its claims to modern power by claiming ancient origins and a primordial place in the fabric of the political world. Those origins, however, are fictional, mythic, invented, so that nationalism is the false consciousness of the modern world, blinding populations into believing that they participate in some transhistorical identity when in fact that identity is a modern and manufactured construction: nations are, in Benedict Anderson's terms, "imagined communities" which live in the delusion of the modern nation's imaginary past (Anderson 1991). Bhabha himself acknowledges his filiation to this tradition by quoting Gellner to the effect that "nationalism is not what it seems, and above all not what it seems to itself [...]. The cultural shreds and patches used by nationalism are often arbitrary historical inventions" (Gellner 1983: 56). In this construction, the nation is not only necessarily fictional, it is also necessarily totalising, not to say totalitarian, since it can only maintain itself by a constant reassertion of the originary purity and unity of its founding myth.

The value of hybridity, to Bhabha, is that it undermines the false unities of the national subject, providing

counter-narratives of the nation that continually evoke and erase its totalizing boundaries – both actual and conceptual – and disturb those ideological manoeuvres through
which "imagined communities" are given essentialist identities. (Bhabha 1994: 149)

Even in the most well-established nation, Bhabha sees a conflict between the "pedagogic" nation – the nation as it is taught to us on the
basis of the nation's past – and the "performative" nation – the nation
that discovers itself through its contemporary actions, actions which
always escape the unifying totality of the pedagogic narrative. As a
consequence, "the liminal figure of the nation-space would ensure that
no political ideologies could claim transcendent or metaphysical authority for themselves", since any claim to transcendent or metaphysical authority would inevitably run foul of that "discursive ambivalence that emerges in the contestation of narrative authority between
the pedagogical and the performative" (Bhabha 1994: 148). Nationalism, in other words, is always doomed to failure because its political
claim rests on a conception of the nation that invokes an imaginary
unity of the past that the nation, in its contemporary actions, will always fracture. In defiance of the nation as imagined by nationalisms,
the inhabitants of the nation always live in an "in-between" condition,
in a "beyond" that represents an "interstitial passage between fixed
identifications" and "opens up the possibility of a cultural hybridity
that entertains difference without an assumed or imposed hierarchy"
(Bhabha 1994: 4).

That nationalism should thus be posed as the antithesis of hybridity is deeply ironic, both in fact and in theory. Hybridity is presented as the alternative to nationalist theories of the unity of the nation, to that notion, as Ernest Renan put it, that the nation is "a soul, a
spiritual principle" (Renan 1990: 19). But, as is clear from Robert
Young's *Colonial Desire*, conceptions of national and racial purity are
themselves a *response* to the perceived problem of mixed cultures: it
is the issue of cultural hybridity that leads to the search for cultural
purity, rather than the reverse. Thus, for Renan, the importance of
Irish Celtic culture is – in direct contradiction of recent constructions
of Irish culture as fundamentally hybrid – that it represents one of the
few cases in the world of cultural purity, where a race remains unmixed with foreign blood. Renan's Celticism, like that of Matthew
Arnold (who drew heavily on Renan's views), is a nostalgic escape

from a world of the hybrid – the world of the modern British and French nations – to the possibility of the revival of pure cultural and racial forms. Knox's "scientific" explanation of how any human hybrid will always revert to one or other of its contributory racial forms is equally characteristic of this process: hybridity is the apparently overwhelming condition of the modern world against which a continuing purity has to be defended. National histories, Knox argued, ignored the fact that most nations were constituted of several races and that, as a consequence, nations themselves were fundamentally unstable. The modern nations of the world were mixed entities that would, in time, revert to their pure racial forms and the boundaries of those purified racial territories. Equally, Knox believed that colonialism would always fail, since the colonisers could never sustain their dominion, where their racial type would steadily decay through miscegenation with the local population and under the effects of an environment hostile to their racial characteristics. In the great experiment in both colonialism and hybridity that was the United States, Knox expected Anglo-Saxon domination to wane as the strength of the race was sapped by climate and by cross-breeding, just as he expected the Anglo-Saxon domination of South Africa to fail for the same reasons (Knox 1862: 532ff.).

The nation, for Knox, is the antithesis of the racially and culturally pure just as much as, for Bhabha, the nation is the antithesis of the culturally and sociologically hybrid. Bhabha, in other words, attributes to the nation precisely the characteristics of an originary purity that Knox attributed to race, while Knox attributed to the nation precisely the characteristics of plurality and hybridity that Bhabha denies to it. The contradiction underlines the problem of the nature of the nation as we have inherited it, both from the traditions of nineteenth-century nationalism and from contemporary nation-theory. The notion of the nation as a "pure" cultural form, each race having its own organic process of development that is ensconced in its national being, is usually attributed the first stirrings of German nationalism and, in particular, to Johann Gottfried Herder. As Anthony Smith states it – following the arguments of John Breuilly – Herder's account of the nature of the nation rested on the fact that

Thought, therefore, like language, was group-specific and unique; so was every other cultural code – dress, architecture, music – in tandem with the society in which it developed. In its original state of nature, as created by God, each nation is both unique and "authentic". The task of the nationalist is clear: to restore his or her community to its natural, authentic state [which] […] can only be done by realising the cultural nation as a political nation, thereby reintegrating what modernity had sundered. (Smith 1998: 87)

This interpretation ignores, however, the fact that Herder asserted the importance of cultural purity only in the context of resistance to imperialism, and a rejection of the enforced combination of "native" and "alien" forms of culture of the kind that would impose French "liberty" on Germany. For Herder, however, natural culture – which was also national culture – developed precisely by a process of "grafting" and cross-breeding, by the same kind of cultivation that produces new forms of organic life in the world of nature (Young 1995: 41). What Herder pitched against each other were not the pure and the hybrid but the organic and the artificial, the chosen and the enforced. To attribute to the nation and to nationalisms a fundamental belief in the purity of the nation – whether racial or cultural – may therefore reflect on some of the ideological assertions of particular nationalist movements, but it does not characterise either the founding statements of romantic nationalism or the nature of the nation *per se*. Indeed, for Herder, it is not race nor even language that *defines* the nation; in the words of F.M. Barnard, it is

(i) the land of the *Volk's* common heritage;
(ii) the law of the constitution, as a covenant freely entered upon;
(iii) the family or clan origin, fostered and perpetuated by;
(iv) reverence for the forefathers. (Barnard 1965: 62)

The nation is first and foremost an *institutional* environment, one which subsequently finds its unique expression in the language of the people, but which begins in the institutions that are the carriers of a sense of national community. Neither, for Herder, was nationalism the isolationism of the purified: it was the development of the maximum diversity and inter-relationship of human cultures:

A world of "organic" nation-States, in which political government in the orthodox sense was replaced by centrally uncoordinated autonomous *ad hoc* institutions, presupposed, therefore, not only a highly developed sense of social co-operation within individual States, but also an unusual degree of international harmony in the relations between States. Herder visualized the attainment of such national and international conditions as the outcome of the tendency which he held to be inherent in human society no less than in nature: the tendency of diversity towards unity. (Barnard 1965: 86)

The problem with the language of hybridity is that it refuses such "diversity-in-unity" as the nature of the nation: there can be no hybrid forms unless there are pure forms, unadulterated species, whose cross-breeding will produce a mixed and impure outcome. But if all cultures are grafted, crossed, mixed, then there is *nothing but* hybridity and the term itself becomes redundant. It is only possible to characterise *any* human culture as hybrid if it is possible to characterise *some* human culture as *not* hybrid and the fundamental problem of all modern theories of hybridity is that they require the maintenance of the very purity against which, in social and political terms, they are in revolt.

Definitions of the nation and of nationalisms which, like Gellner's and Bhabha's, assume that nationalism is the desire for cultural purity have profoundly mistaken both the ideology of nationalism and the history of the nation. That nationalist movements make a virtue of unity tells us no more than that, like all political movements, nationalists believe that the solidarity of their own supporters and the integration of the state they aspire to control are presuppositions of their immediate political effectiveness and their long-term political survival. Gellnerite theories of nationalism are obsessively concerned with the issue of the unity of the nation and submission of the individual to the national community. In Anderson's words, the ultimate expression of "imagined community" is

a special kind of contemporaneous community which language alone suggests – above all in the form of poetry and song. Take national anthems, for example, sung on national holidays. No matter how banal the words and mediocre the tunes, there is in this singing an experience of simultaneity. At precisely such moments, people wholly unknown to each other utter the same verse to the same melody. The image: unisonance [...]. How selfless this unisonance feels! If we are aware that others are singing these songs precisely when and as we are, we have no idea who they may be, or even where, out of earshot, they are singing. Nothing connects us but imagined sound. (Anderson 1991: 145)

It is such epiphanies of the nation by which the "modernist" theorists of the nation are appalled: "nothing connects" people in reality but the fictions encoded in "imagined sound", and yet it is to these fictions that people give their ultimate commitments. It may be, however, that the very "Romantic" conceptions of the nation that Gellner and Anderson wish to oppose have blinded them to the reality of nations and nationalism, since, far from being the projections of an ultimate unity, nations are the necessary negotiations of profound internal conflicts. Almost every nation is born out of civil war and continues as the unended but suspended confrontation of the parties to that war. The temporary unity of any actually existing nation, the projected unity of any desired nation, has to be balanced by the reality of its civil conflicts, conflicts that project alternative bases for the unity of the nation. As anyone who has been involved in them knows only too well, nationalist movements are characterised not by their unity but by the constant threat of secession. It is only in the imaginations of those who are appalled by the power of the nation in the modern world that nationalisms, or the nations they create, can be defined by "unisonance" rather than by dissonance. The nation, to apply an idea of Alasdair MacIntyre's, is an "embodied argument", a body that retains the shape of the conflict in which it was founded and which grows as the continuing dialectic of the positions that argument makes possible. It is not, as Robert Crawford implies, that we have somehow to discover a dialogic nation of hyphenated hybrids to oppose to the "essential" nation; nor is it, as Bhabha argues, that we need an alternative – hybridity – which negates all the positive affirmations of the totalising nation: the nation is and always was a dialogic entity, constituted by the ongoing argument – the suspended civil war – of its internal differences.

The crucial fact which Gellnerite theory ignores is that there is never only one nationalism in a nation. As Martin Thom's "Tribes within nations" reveals all too clearly about France in the nineteenth century, the nationalism with which the nation is to be infused is deeply contested – even in the country held out as the exemplar of a modern nation state. Renan, for instance, bases his conception of France on a notion of "liberty, which derived from the Germanic invasions" of the fifth century, while an equally committed seeker after "a perfect, founding myth for conservative French nationalism", Fustel de Coulanges, in the second volume of his *The Ancient City*, written after the Prussian invasion of 1870, "simply demolished the Germanist interpretation of French history" (Thom 1990: 32, 33). The "essentialist" nation never has been a singular unity in reality nor even in imagination: it is the focus of a series of competing claims about what will count as the central value of the nation. Actually-existing nations are compromises in which the parties to civil war have agreed to maintain their argument within existing boundaries rather than commit themselves to an alternative territory and an alternative set of arguments. In whatever terms we define that internal dialogue of alternative nationalisms, there is no sense in which they can be opposed to "hybridity" as a condition somehow outside and beyond the embodied argument of the nation. The nation is always the host to multiple nationalisms, to marginal and antagonistic communities: neither the nation nor nationalism is singular, unified and "unisonant".

Why then should hybridity have become so significant in contemporary postcolonial theory? The answer, as Ajiz Ahmad has pointed out, lies not in the nature of the formerly colonised cultures; nor in the nature of the colonising cultures; nor even in the globalisation process that has both deepened and intensified nationalisms around the world, while at the same time planting American "international" culture into the soil of national and regional cultures (Ahmad 1996). The prominence of hybridity derives instead from the tradition of a certain kind of literary criticism that locates the significance of the critical act in the ability of the critic to stand outside the boundary of values which are entirely culturally conditioned. Those who are "purely" inside a culture cannot know that culture properly because they are "totally" shaped by it: those who would aspire to the status of a critic, therefore, those who aspire to degree of independence in their critical judgments, must be people who are able to look back at their culture from a point "beyond" its borders. Having reached that "beyond" is a marker of the critic's freedom from the merely conditioned response to cultural products and cultural environments. To see the

world from *within* a culture, and through the lens of that culture, is to
see the world falsely: to see truly is to find a position outside of one's
originating culture without involving submission to the interiority of
another culture. In the collapse of the critical positions from which
modern societies could be interrogated in terms of a "truth" which
transcended all cultural determinations (such as Marxism), the only
position left is that in which the critic is released from the determination of one culture without being submitted to the determination of
another. The complementary titles of the key works in this tradition –
Raymond Williams's *Culture and Society* (Williams 1958), Edward
Said's *Culture and Imperialism* (Said 1993) and Homi Bhabha's *The
Location of Culture* (Bhabha 1994) – reveal the continuity of a critical
tradition in which the existential situation of the author, as a person
redeemed from the determinations of a merely singular culture, is the
very basis of the act of criticism. The critic is a "hybrid" person, inheritor of two different cultural traditions, living at the centre of the
dominant culture and yet not trapped by it, belonging to some other
cultural location and yet not defined by it. The autobiographical
ground of such criticism – Williams's position as a man born "on the
border" between England and Wales; Said's assertion that his book "is
an exile's book"; Bhabha's sense of "living on the borderlines" – is
asserted precisely in order to insist that the critic is not grounded *in* a
culture, but lives "between" cultures; as though those who lived *within*
a culture were somehow, therefore, limited to a single angle of vision,
while the migrant, the exile and the international academic had access
to a double vision that was not disabling, but could reveal what neither
culture was capable of seeing by itself. The paradox of the hybrid
critics is that they need always to assert the "purity" of the cultures
they stand outside of, since only by everyone else's circumscription
within such purity can the superiority of their critical positions – being
beyond the restrictions of any one culture – be maintained.

Scotland, a country whose doubleness has never been in doubt,
might stand as exemplar of the fact that nations have never been pure
and that identity is precisely the dialogue between alternative possibilities of the self rather than the submersion of the self in "unisonance"; Scotland might stand as exemplar of the fact that nationalisms and national cultures are always multiple, not because they are

"hybrids", but because they are bounded accidentally and within those boundaries there are always alternative versions of the national culture. Scotland might stand as exemplar of the fact that multiplicity and pluralism is not a denial of national "identity" precisely because identity is, as John Macmurray insisted, constituted not by one's uniqueness, but by one's *relations* to others. Macmurray noted that "a relation of agents can never be mere matter of fact" because "it must be matter of intention" (Macmurray 1961: 148); intentions, of course, are always projections "beyond" – retrospective explanations of past action or prospective preparations for future action. For Macmurray, the *cogito* was the wrong starting point for thinking about the self because it made the self a disembodied thinker rather than an active person; equally, conceptions of the nation which start from the notion of an "imagined community" mistake the nature of their object, for the nation, as much as the person, is an agent. To begin from the agency of the nation, rather than its imagination or its self-perception, would be to bring us back to a world in which nations are the media of our practical and ethical endeavours; a world in which nations, as constituted by the relations of agents, would be neither totalitarian "imagined communities" nor our open-ended pluralistic habitats; they would be, like all intentions, a constant redefinition of the "beyond" from which they emerge and to which they are directed. Scotland, like any other nation, exists not as an expression of our essence, nor as the by-product of our hybrid graftings, but as the object of our intentions. Scotland is already "beyond", was always "beyond", because as long as we wish it to be so, it is the medium for translating into action our communal intentions. Scotland is our intended nation.

Bibliography

Ahmad, Ajiz. 1996. "The Politics of Literary Postcoloniality" in Mongia, Padmini (ed.) *Contemporary Postcolonial Theory: A Reader*. London: Arnold. 276–93.

Anderson, Benedict. 1991. *Imagined Communities: Reflections on the Origin and Spread of Nationalism*. London: Verso.

Ashcroft, Bill, Careth Griffiths and Helen Tiffin (eds). 1989. *The Empire Writes Back: Theory and Practice in Post-colonial Literature*. London and New York: Routledge.

Bakhtin, Mikhail. 1981. *The Dialogic Imagination* (ed. Michael Holquist). Austin, Texas: University of Texas Press.

Barnard, F.M. 1965. *Herder's Social and Political Thought: From Enlightenment to Nationalism*. Oxford: Clarendon Press.

Bhabha, Homi K. 1994. *The Location of Culture*. London and New York: Routledge.

Craig, Cairns. 1999. *The Modern Scottish Novel: Narrative and National Imagination*. Edinburgh: Edinburgh University Press.

Crawford, Robert. 1994. "Bakhtin and Scotlands" in *Scotlands* 1: 55–65.

Crawford, Robert (ed.). 1998. *The Scottish Invention of English Literature*. Cambridge: Cambridge University Press.

Easthope, Antony. 1998. "Bhabha, hybridity and identity" in *Textual Practice* 12(2): 341–48.

Gardiner, Michael. 1996. "Democracy and Scottish Postcoloniality" in *Scotlands* 3(2): 24–41.

Gellner, Ernest. 1964. *Thought and Change*. London: Weidenfeld and Nicholson.

—. 1983. *Nations and Nationalism*. Oxford: Basil Blackwell.

Kiberd, Declan. 1995. *Inventing Ireland*. London: Jonathan Cape.

Kidd, Colin. 1993. *Subverting Scotland's Past: Scottish Whig Historians and the Creation of an Anglo-British Identity, 1689–c.1830*. Cambridge: Cambridge University Press.

—. 1999. *British Identities before Nationalism: Ethnicity and Nationhood in the Atlantic World, 1600–1800*. Cambridge: Cambridge University Press.

Knox, Robert. 1862. *The Races of Men: A Philosophical Enquiry into the Influence of Race over the Destinies of Nations* and *An Inquiry into the Laws of Human Hybridité*. London: Henry Renshaw.

Macmurray, John. 1957. *The Self as Agent*. London: Faber and Faber.

—. 1961. *Persons in Relation*. London: Faber and Faber.

Nairn, Tom. 1981. *The Break-up of Britain: Crisis and Neo-Nationalism*. London: Verso.

Renan, Ernest. 1990. "What is a Nation?" in Bhabha, Homi K. (ed.) *Nation and Narration*. London: Routledge.

Said, Edward. 1993. *Culture and Imperialism*. London: Chatto & Windus.

Seth, Andrew [later A.S. Pringle-Pattison]. 1887. *Hegelianism and Personality*. Edinburgh: William Blackwood and Sons.

Smith, Anthony D. 1998. *Nationalism and Modernism: A Critical Survey of Recent Theories of Nations and Nationalism*. London: Routledge.

Thom, Martin. 1990. "Tribes Within Nations: the ancient Germans and the history of Modern France" in Bhabha, Homi K. (ed.) *Nation and Narration*. London: Routledge. 23–43.

Williams, Raymond. 1958. *Culture and Society 1780–1950*. London: Chatto & Windus.

Young, Robert J.C. 1995. *Colonial Desire: Hybridity in Theory, Culture and Race*. London and New York: Routledge.

"The speech he had no time to make at the Booker ceremony" in *The Sunday Times* (16 October 1994). 21.

Index

Visions of Alterity
Representation in the Works of John Banville

Elke D'hoker

Amsterdam/New York, NY 2004. VII, 243 pp. (Costerus NS 151)
ISBN: 90-420-1671-X   € 50,-/US$ 63.-

Visions of Alterity: Representation in the Works of John Banville offers detailed and original readings of the work of the Irish author John Banville, one of the foremost figures in contemporary European literature. It investigates one of the fundamental concerns of Banville's novels: mediating the gap between subject and object or self and world in representation. By drawing on the rich history of the problem of representation in literature, philosophy and literary theory, this study provides a thorough insight into the rich philosophical and intertextual dimension of Banville's fiction. In close textual analyses of Banville's most important novels, it maps out a thematic development that moves from an interest in the epistemological and aesthetic representation of the world in scientific theories, over a concern with the ethical dimension of representations, to an exploration of self-representation and identity. What remains constant throughout these different perspectives is the disruption of representations by brief but haunting glimpses of otherness. In tracing these different visions of alterity in Banville's solipsistic literary world, this study offers a better understanding of his insistent and thought-provoking exploration of what it means to be human.

USA/Canada: One Rockefeller Plaza, Ste. 1420, New York, NY 10020,
Tel. (212) 265-6360, Call toll-free (U.S. only) 1-800-225-3998,
Fax (212) 265-6402
All other countries: Tijnmuiden 7, 1046 AK Amsterdam, The Netherlands.
Tel. ++ 31 (0)20 611 48 21, Fax ++ 31 (0)20 447 29 79
Orders-queries@rodopi.nl   www.rodopi.nl
Please note that the exchange rate is subject to fluctuations

Resisting Alterities
Wilson Harris and Other Avatars of Otherness

Edited by Marco Fazzini

Amsterdam/New York, NY 2004. XIV, 255 pp. (Cross/Cultures 71)
ISBN: 90-420-1601-9   Bound € 56,-/US$ 70.-
ISBN: 90-420-1200-5   Paper € 27,-/US$ 34.-

This volume – of essays, poetry, and prose fiction – records various attempts to read the fracture zones created by the discursive strategy of a democratic imagination, where space and ideas are opened to new linguistic and literary insights. Pride of place is taken by essays on the Caribbean writer Wilson Harris which explore the implications of his awareness of a polyphony of coexistent voices that dislodges the hegemony of Cartesian dualism. This group of studies is rounded off with an interview with, and searching testimony by, Harris himself.

The further contributions take up the implications of the encounter with 'alterity' (strangers, natives, barbarians) in order to underline not only wonder in the face of an unknown presence, or the 'shame' through which the subject discovers itself, but also the *ressentiment* involved in the creation of demonized Others.

As the poet Charles Tomlinson states, "what we take to be otherness, alterity, can be readmitted into our literary consciousness and seen as part of the whole, causing us to readjust our awareness of the possibilities of English." These essays confirm that resistance is an interface of ambivalence between discursive worlds, encouraging us to read the "living network" of a text contrapuntally.

Specific topics include Billy Bragg and New Labour, Schopenhauer in Britain, Objectivist poetry, gender and sexual identity (in Nancy Cunard; in Scottish fiction), multivocal discourse in South Africa, specific forms of alterity (in Jamaica Kincaid; in the poetry of Edwin Morgan; in allosemitism) and the deculturalizing perils of globalization.

USA/Canada: One Rockefeller Plaza, Ste. 1420, New York, NY 10020,
Tel. (212) 265-6360, Call toll-free (U.S. only) 1-800-225-3998,
Fax (212) 265-6402
All other countries: Tijnmuiden 7, 1046 AK Amsterdam, The Netherlands.
Tel. ++ 31 (0)20 611 48 21, Fax ++ 31 (0)20 447 29 79
Orders-queries@rodopi.nl   www.rodopi.nl
Please note that the exchange rate is subject to fluctuations

Rodopi

Gothic Motifs in the Fiction of William Gibson

Tatiani G. Rapatzikou

Amsterdam/New York, NY 2004. XXIV, 253 pp. + 15 pp. ill.
(Postmodern Studies 36)
ISBN: 90-420-1761-9   € 60,-/US$ 75.-

Gibson's startlingly new form of science fiction opens inner vistas through his sense of how technological development increasingly removes the boundaries between the realms of the imagined and the real. This important new study focuses on the visual elements in Gibson's work, suggesting how his extraordinary mindscapes are locatable in terms of both gothic and the graphic novel traditions in a subtle interweaving of physical and virtual space that creates new forms of spatial being.

Gibson describes the space of the Walled City as "Doorways flipping past, each one hinting at its own secret world": Tatiani G. Rapatzikou's thoughtful analyses of those secret worlds will fascinate all those who have wondered where these fictions have come from – and where they may be headed.

USA/Canada: One Rockefeller Plaza, Ste. 1420, New York, NY 10020,
Tel. (212) 265-6360, Call toll-free (U.S. only) 1-800-225-3998,
Fax (212) 265-6402
All other countries: Tijnmuiden 7, 1046 AK Amsterdam, The Netherlands.
Tel. ++ 31 (0)20 611 48 21, Fax ++ 31 (0)20 447 29 79
Orders-queries@rodopi.nl   www.rodopi.nl
Please note that the exchange rate is subject to fluctuations

The Singer and the Scribe
European Ballad Traditions and European Ballad Cultures

Edited by Philip E. Bennett and Richard Firth Green

Amsterdam/New York, NY 2004. IV, 223 pp.
(Internationale Forschungen zur Allgemeinen und Vergleichenden Literaturwissenschaft 75)
ISBN: 90-420-1851-8   € 48,-/US$ 60.-

The Singer and the Scribe brings together studies of the European ballad from the Middle Ages to the twentieth century by major authorities in the field and is of interest to students of European literature, popular traditions and folksong. It offers an original view of the development of the ballad by focusing on the interplay and interdependence of written and oral transmission, including studies of modern singers and their repertoires and of the role of the audience in generating a literary product which continues to live in performance. While using specific case studies the contributors systematically extend their reflections on the ballad as song and as poetry to draw broader conclusions. Covering the Hispanic world, including the Sephardic tradition, Scandinavia, The Netherlands, Greece, Russia, England and Scotland the essays also demonstrate the interconnections of a European tradition beyond national boundaries.

USA/Canada: One Rockefeller Plaza, Ste. 1420, New York, NY 10020,
Tel. (212) 265-6360, Call toll-free (U.S. only) 1-800-225-3998,
Fax (212) 265-6402
All other countries: Tijnmuiden 7, 1046 AK Amsterdam, The Netherlands.
Tel. ++ 31 (0)20 611 48 21, Fax ++ 31 (0)20 447 29 79
Orders-queries@rodopi.nl   www.rodopi.nl
Please note that the exchange rate is subject to fluctuations